RELIGION, EDUCATION AND THE STATE

In the context of education, church and state issues are of growing importance and appear to be increasingly divisive. This volume critically examines the developing jurisprudence relating to religion in the schools beginning with *Everson v. Board of Education*, where the US Supreme Court discussed the wall of separation between church and state. The study traces both how the Court's views have evolved during this period and how, through recharacterizations of past opinions and the facts underlying them, the Court has appeared to interpret Establishment Clause guarantees in light of the past jurisprudence when in reality that jurisprudence has been turned on its head. The Court not only offers an unstable jurisprudence that is more likely to promote than avoid the problems that the Establishment Clause was designed to prevent, but approaches Establishment Clause issues in a way that decreases the likelihood that an acceptable compromise on these important issues can be reached.

The study focuses on the situation in the US but the important issue of religion, education and the state has great relevance in many jurisdictions.

To George, Emma, and Nathan

Religion, Education and the State

An Unprincipled Doctrine in Search of Moorings

MARK STRASSER
Capital University Law School, USA

ASHGATE

© Mark Strasser 2011

EDUC

KF
4162
.S77
2011

Published by
Ashgate Publishing Limited
Wey Court East
Union Road
Farnham
Surrey, GU9 7PT
England

Ashgate Publishing Company
Suite 420
101 Cherry Street
Burlington
VT 05401-4405
USA

www.ashgate.com

British Library Cataloguing in Publication Data
Strasser, Mark Philip, 1955–
    Religion, education and the state : an unprincipled doctrine in search of moorings.– (Law, justice and power series)
    1. Church and state–United States. 2. Religion in the public schools–Law and legislation–United States. 3. Universities and colleges–United States–Religion. 4. Government aid to education–United States.
    I. Title II. Series
    344.7'30796–dc23

Library of Congress Cataloging-in-Publication Data
Strasser, Mark Philip, 1955–
    Religion, education and the state : an unprincipled doctrine in search of moorings / by Mark Strasser.
        p. cm. – (Law, justice and power)
    Includes bibliographical references and index.
    ISBN 978-1-4094-3644-7 (hardback : alk. paper) – ISBN 978-1-4094-3645-4 (ebook)
    1. Religion in the public schools–Law and legislation–United States. 2. Church and education–United States. 3. Church schools–Finance–Law and legislation–United States. 4. Universities and colleges–United States–Religion. 5. Religion in the public schools–Law and legislation–United States–History. I. Title.
    KF4162.S77 2011
    344.73'0796–dc23

2011018599

ISBN 9781409436447 (hbk)
ISBN 9781409436454 (ebk)

Printed and bound in Great Britain by the
MPG Books Group, UK

Contents

Acknowledgments

I have discussed these subjects in various law reviews:

Thou Shalt Not?, 6 *University of Maryland Law Journal of Race, Religion, Gender and Class* 439 (2006).

Establishing the Pledge: On Coercion, Endorsement and the Marsh Wild Card, 40 *Indiana. Law Review* 529 (2007).

The Protection and Alienation of Religious Minorities: On the Evolution of the Endorsement Test, 2008 *Michigan State Law Review* 667 (2008).

Death by a Thousand Cuts: The Illusory Safeguards against Funding Pervasively Sectarian Institutions of Higher Learning, 56 *Buffalo Law Review* 353 (2008).

State Funding of Devotional Studies: A Failed Jurisprudence that Has Lost its Moorings, 11 *Journal of Law and Family Studies* 1 (2008).

The Coercion Test: On Prayer, Offense, and Doctrinal Inculcation, 53 *Saint Louis University Law Journal* 417 (2009).

Religion in the Schools: On Prayer, Neutrality, and Sectarian Perspectives, 42 *Akron Law Review* 185 (2009).

Repudiating Everson: On Buses, Books, and Teaching Articles of Faith, 78 *Mississippi Law Journal* 567 (2009).

Passive Observers, Passive Displays, and the Establishment Clause, 14 *Lewis and Clark Law Review* 1123 (2010).

I thank each of the law reviews without whose cooperation this book would not have been possible.

Introduction

The First Amendment to the United States Constitution specifies that "Congress shall make no law respecting an establishment of religion." At the time the Constitution was adopted, several states had their own established churches, for example, Congregationalist, and one of the concerns motivating the amendment's adoption was that the federal government might establish an official religion and force that choice upon the states. Thus, one purpose behind the First Amendment's Establishment Clause guarantee was to protect state churches from the federal government.

Yet, it would be inaccurate to suggest that the only concern of the Framers was to prevent the federal government from infringing upon the power of the states to establish a particular religion. As Frank Ravitch suggests, a number of the Framers were concerned about religious divisiveness and about the possibility that the federal government would financially support religion.[1] Indeed, the Framers also questioned some of the state practices involving support of religion. For example, Thomas Jefferson and James Madison opposed the renewal of a Virginia tax on the citizenry to support an established church. Such taxes were imposed on believers and nonbelievers alike, which meant that some of the taxpayers would be paying to have their own religious views criticized from the pulpit or in the classroom.

There had been and continued to be a practice of religious intolerance in many of the states and, for example, Catholics, Baptists, Quakers and Jews were all subjected to adverse treatment. While almost all states had a constitutional provision protecting religious freedom by 1789, those rights were sometimes confined to Christians,[2] and in any event those rights did not guarantee that there would be no religious discrimination.

Thomas Jefferson discussed a wall of separation between church and state, a phrase that has been interpreted in a variety of ways in the case law. Both Jefferson and Madison worried about the possible abuses that might take place were religious institutions given too much power.[3]

The First Amendment expressly refers to "Congress," and that amendment was long interpreted to impose no limitations on the states. However, First Amendment

---

1   See Frank S. Ravitch, *Masters of Illusion: The Supreme Court and the Religion Clauses* 3 (2007).

2   See Joseph P. Viteritti, *The Last Freedom: Religion from the Public School to the Public Square* 151 (2007).

3   See Marci A. Hamilton, *God vs. the Gavel: Religion and the Rule of Law* 261–2 (2005).

protections were eventually held to be incorporated against the states via the Fourteenth Amendment to the Constitution.

By the time that the Fourteenth Amendment was ratified, no state had an established church. But this means that some of the concerns motivating the adoption of the First Amendment did not play a similar role in the adoption of the Fourteenth Amendment. Thus, while it is plausible to suggest that the First Amendment Framers intended to provide protection for existing state religious establishments, it is not plausible to impute a similar intent to the Fourteenth Amendment Framers, because at that time there were no state religious establishments in need of protection. As Kent Greenawalt points out, the lack of established state churches at the time of the adoption of the Fourteenth Amendment makes it more plausible to believe that the Framers of that amendment intended that some of the Establishment protections against the federal government should be applicable to the state governments as well.[4]

In 1947, the United States Supreme Court decided the seminal case in modern Establishment Clause jurisprudence, *Everson v. Board of Education.* In this decision, the Court suggested that the Clause's protections applied not only to actions by the federal government but also to actions taken by the states, which had important implications for the kinds of religious activities that could permissibly occur in public schools and for the ways that public funding could be used by parochial schools.

The jurisprudence in this area has been evolving ever since it began. There have been and continue to be great disagreements about the conditions under which religious activities can occur in public schools and about the kinds of educational activities in parochial schools that can be supported by public funds. Supreme Court members cannot agree about what the First Amendment and Fourteenth Amendment Framers intended the Establishment Clause to do or what role in the analysis the Framers' intentions should play. It is thus not surprising that one of the most contentious areas of law involves the degree to which the United States Constitution requires that church and state be separate in the field of education, whether public or private, elementary or post-graduate.

A lot is at stake here. Parents and society more generally have conflicting and deeply held convictions about what their children should be taught in public school and about whether or how state funds should be spent in support of parochial education. It is simply unclear how or whether these issues can be resolved. Several tests have been offered to determine when Establishment Clause guarantees have been violated, but the Court has failed to articulate when one test rather than another should be used. This is unfortunate, because the tests do not yield the same results with respect to what the Establishment Clause requires, permits, and prohibits.

Various factors are thought to play an important role in the analysis; for example, the degree to which targeted individuals are being coerced or are

---

4   See Kent Greenawalt, *Does God Belong in Public Schools?* 39 (2005).

susceptible to indoctrination. An additional factor involves whether state funds are being used to promote secular rather than sectarian activities. The first four chapters are structured to explore these considerations.

Chapter 1 discusses the developing jurisprudence with respect to public funding of religious primary and secondary schools. Beginning with *Everson*, the chapter discusses how the Court initially justified state funding of transportation to religious schools and then modified the relevant criteria to permit state funding of secular education at such schools. Then, the jurisprudence was gradually modified in a series of cases, ultimately resulting in the Court's upholding a program in which public funds support sectarian education of elementary school children, a result that is simply irreconcilable with either the language or spirit of *Everson*.

Chapter 2 discusses religion in public elementary and secondary schools. Many of the cases involve the conditions under which prayers can be said in school. Here, too, the jurisprudence has been evolving in unusual and unpredictable ways, sometimes involving surprising interpretations of the holdings or facts of past cases.

Chapter 3 discusses public funding of sectarian institutions of higher education. The Court has articulated fairly clear criteria by which to determine whether Establishment Clause guarantees are violated by challenged funding, although the Court's applications of these criteria cast some doubt on whether these factors should be taken at face value. Ironically, the Court has upheld public funding of sectarian education when doing so would seem to have been precluded by the Establishment Clause and has permitted the state denial of public funding of sectarian education when the Court's more recent jurisprudence would seem to have required such funding.

Chapter 4 discusses whether public universities must recognize religious students groups. While the Court's ultimate conclusion that universities must recognize a broad range of student groups might seem quite sensible as a policy matter, the Court mangled the existing jurisprudence to reach that result, thereby obscuring not only Establishment Clause doctrine in particular but First Amendment doctrine more generally.

Chapter 5 addresses an issue that has been litigated in various circuits recently, namely, the conditions under which school policy can require that elementary school students begin the day with the Pledge of Allegiance. Surprisingly, the Court's announced criteria to determine whether a particular practice violates Establishment Clause guarantees suggest that such a practice is impermissible, although various Justices have announced in dicta that they do not consider current Pledge practices constitutionally problematic.

Chapter 6 discusses the conditions under which the Ten Commandments might be posted in public schools. Regrettably, the most recent Ten Commandments cases decided by the Court help illustrate the utter incoherence of current Establishment Clause jurisprudence, because the Court can neither agree about what test to use nor even which factors are relevant when attempting to determine the appropriate test. While it is clear that the Constitution does not bar the introduction of the

Ten Commandments into public schools under all circumstances, the Court's jurisprudence provides school officials shockingly little guidance about where the constitutional line would be drawn between permissible and impermissible displays.

Both the Justices and members of society have radically differing views about the degree to which religion and the state must be kept separate in the context of education. That is unsurprising, given the importance of the issue. What seems more surprising is that the Establishment Clause case law has been rife with mischaracterizations of past cases and ad hominem attacks on Justices in opposing camps. Not only is the current jurisprudence in utter disarray with respect to religion and the schools in particular or with respect to the permissible relationship between religion and the state more generally, but an examination of the underlying development of the law undercuts the belief that members of the Court are approaching this area in good faith.

In our religiously diverse society, it will become more and more important to develop a consistent and reasonable approach with respect to the circumstances under which the state can support religious activities in public and private schools. Regrettably, the current Court has rejected the longstanding jurisprudence, not only in its attempt to strike a balance so that religion and the state would remain separate in some respects but not in others, but also in its implicit attempt to prevent divisiveness on the basis of religion. Unless the Court changes course, we can only look forward to increasing divisiveness and dissension in an area of great importance — the respects in which religion and the state must or need not be separate in the education of our children.

Chapter 1
Everson and Aid to Private Schools

Ever since deciding *Everson v. Board of Education*,[1] the Court has wrestled with the proper way to characterize the Establishment Clause limitations on the states. Many of the cases have involved the extent to which a state can provide aid to parents of children attending primary and secondary sectarian schools. While the Court's understanding of the constitutional limits imposed on such aid has changed markedly over the past several decades, accurately characterizing that evolution is difficult for two distinct reasons. First, the Court usually does not fully and clearly articulate its position when issuing opinions, so the Court's rationale is often somewhat opaque. Second, perhaps even more in this area than in others, the Court often recasts past opinions as a way of retroactively modifying their legal import. For these reasons, it is often unclear exactly where and when particular changes in the jurisprudence occurred. Nonetheless, what is clear is that the jurisprudence has undergone a radical transformation over the relevant period.

At first, the Court suggested that the constitutionality of state aid to sectarian schools depended upon whether that aid was being used to promote health and safety rather than education. Then, the Court modified the criterion, instead saying that the Constitution permitted states to provide funding to private schools as long as the aid was supporting secular rather than religious education. That position was modified yet again so that the focus was on whether the state was offering nonsectarian benefits to the religious and nonreligious alike, even if those nonsectarian benefits in fact promoted religious education. Finally, the Court adopted yet another approach in which the constitutionality of state aid to sectarian schools would depend upon whether what was admittedly support of religious teaching could reasonably be imputed to the state. While the changes in the jurisprudence were often not dramatic, they have cumulatively resulted in a position that is hard to reconcile with either the spirit or the holding of *Everson*, even when *Everson* is understood to be much more accommodationist than is commonly supposed.

Support for Safety and Health

Contemporary Establishment Clause jurisprudence can hardly be called transparent if only because it has changed markedly over the past several decades. That said, the jurisprudence with respect to the conditions under which the state is permitted to provide aid benefiting primary and secondary sectarian institutions has not

---

1   330 U.S. 1 (1947).

always been as difficult to fathom as is sometimes claimed. While the Court has never articulated a principle clearly demarcating the line between permissible and impermissible kinds of aid, a rough rule emerged permitting aid as long as certain conditions had been met. This understanding governed the Court's holdings in this area at least through the 1970s, although the dicta in some of the Court's decisions during this period provided the basis for the stark changes that subsequently occurred.

Everson v. Board of Education is the seminal case in contemporary Establishment Clause jurisprudence. It is important both because of its holding that Establishment Clause guarantees constrain not only the federal government but state and local governments as well, and because it attempts to set out some of the parameters regarding the conditions under which state aid can be offered to sectarian schools without offending constitutional guarantees. The decision itself sent rather mixed messages, however, because its very robust language regarding the required degree of separation between church and state seemed incompatible with the Court's decision to uphold the statute at issue.

The disparity between the tone and the holding of the opinion has led some commentators to suggest that the Court was simply being inconsistent. Other commentators suggest that the decision is unproblematic in reasoning and result, although perhaps incorporating some overly exuberant rhetorical flourishes. In any event, *Everson* demands close attention, both because it was the first case in modern Establishment Clause jurisprudence and because it foreshadows many of the competing considerations that continue to play a role when the Court seeks to draw a line between permissible and impermissible state aid to sectarian schools.

At issue in *Everson* was the following statute:

> Whenever in any district there are children living remote from any schoolhouse, the board of education of the district may make rules and contracts for the transportation of such children to and from school, including the transportation of school children to and from school other than a public school, except such school as is operated for profit in whole or in part.
>
> When any school district provides any transportation for public school children to and from school, transportation from any point in such established school route to any other point in such established school route shall be supplied to school children residing in such school district in going to and from school other than a public school, except such school as is operated for profit in whole or in part.[2]

The statute performed two functions: (1) it authorized school boards to provide transportation for children attending public and private nonprofit schools, and (2) it required school districts providing transportation to public school students to provide transportation to children attending private, nonprofit schools, as long as

---

2   *Id.* at 3 n.1.

the private school was along the established school route. Arguably, (2) would require no extra expenditure of funds beyond the de minimis expenditure involved in stopping along the route to pick up and drop off the children at the bus stops near their homes. In contrast, (1) permitted but did not require additional expenditures, since the local boards were authorized to provide transportation for children who were going to a private school that was not located along an established school route.

A New Jersey taxpayer challenged the right of the school board to authorize reimbursement of transportation expenses incurred by children using public buses to go to and from parochial school, arguing that the authorizing statute violated state and federal constitutional guarantees. The New Jersey Supreme Court upheld the constitutionality of the statute, and the case was appealed to the United States Supreme Court.

After making clear that the constraints imposed by the Establishment Clause on the federal government also apply to the states, the *Everson* Court tried to explain the limitations imposed by that clause. States are precluded from "set[ting] up a church" or from passing "laws which aid one religion, aid all religions, or prefer one religion over another."[3] Indeed, the Court suggested that "the clause against establishment of religion by law was intended to erect a wall of separation between church and State,"[4] thereby implying that the Constitution requires church and state to be in completely non-overlapping spheres.

While speaking in rather absolute terms, the *Everson* Court nonetheless found that the reimbursement at issue did not violate constitutional guarantees. The Court explained that the Constitution's prohibiting the use of public funds for the support of religion was not meant to preclude every use of public funds that might in some way benefit religion. Such a broad interpretation of the rule would prohibit states from extending any kind of aid, including police and fire services, which would make states hostile to religion. An interpretation making each state an adversary of religion misrepresents the constitutional guarantee, since state power "is no more to be used so as to handicap religions, than it is to favor them."[5] Instead, the prohibition on state aid is narrower in scope, so that some kinds of aid, but not others, are permissible.

When upholding the state reimbursement of parents for transportation costs, the Court emphasized that this aid was "so separate and so indisputably marked off from the religious function"[6] that the state could not plausibly be thought to be directly supporting religious activities or teaching. By focusing on the function that the aid was to perform, the Court implied that sectarian aid could not be offered to support religious functions, but could be offered to support nonreligious functions.

---

3 *Id.* at 15.
4 *Id.* at 16.
5 *Id.*
6 *Id.*

One complicating factor in *Everson* not emphasized by the Court was that the township resolution at issue only authorized reimbursement for parents of children attending public and Catholic schools. While there was no evidence that any child attending a private, nonprofit, non-Catholic school had been denied travel reimbursement or even that there was a child who would have attended such a school if only transportation reimbursement had been provided, the resolution nonetheless facially discriminated among religions. Had the resolution's constitutionality been analyzed in light of its expressly distinguishing among religions, the statute would likely have been struck down. As Justice Robert Jackson pointed out in his dissent, if the Court were examining the permissibility of reimbursing children attending Catholic, but not other private, nonprofit schools, then the police/fire services analogy would have cut the other way—the question would have been whether it would be permissible for the state to afford fire services to Catholic establishments but permit other religious establishments to burn.[7]

Yet, it could be that the Court did not focus on the benefit accorded to Catholic schools for a different reason. As Marci Hamilton notes, the curriculum in the public schools historically favored a Protestant perspective, which was one of the reasons that Catholics started parochial schools.[8] It may be that the Court viewed the provision at issue not as a way of favoring Catholics but as a way of reducing the burden placed on them.

The *Everson* Court did not analyze the constitutionality of state reimbursement for transportation costs to and from Catholic schools in particular but, instead, whether the state's paying for the transportation costs of children attending religious schools violated the Establishment Clause. The Court offered a quick history of the Establishment Clause, observing that "dissenters were compelled to pay tithes and taxes to support government-sponsored churches whose ministers preached inflammatory sermons designed to strengthen and consolidate the established faith by generating a burning hatred against dissenters."[9] After noting that practices burdening dissenters "became so commonplace as to shock the freedom-loving colonials into a feeling of abhorrence," the Court explained that the people of Virginia, "as elsewhere, reached the conviction that individual religious liberty could be achieved best under a government which was stripped of all power to tax, to support, or otherwise to assist any or all religions, or to interfere with the beliefs of any religious individual or group."[10] Here, too, a broad reading of the Court's language in *Everson* suggests strict separation between church and state.

Yet, the Court's language regarding the taxing power might be given a much narrower interpretation. Just as the Court denied that a state was precluded from offering fire protection services to a religious school, the Court would also deny

---

7 *Id.* at 25–6 (Jackson, J., dissenting).

8 See Marci A Hamilton, *God vs. the Gavel: Religion and the Rule of Law* 111–12 (2005).

9 *Everson*, 330 U.S. at 10.

10 *Id.* at 11.

that a state was precluded from spending public funds to extinguish a fire in a chapel, even though that would mean that public support (in the use of public equipment, the payment of fire personnel salaries, et cetera) was being expended to aid religion. Thus, when suggesting that "New Jersey cannot consistently with the 'establishment of religion' clause of the First Amendment contribute tax-raised funds to the support of an institution which teaches the tenets and faith of any church,"[11] the Court did not mean that the state was prohibited from spending monies in any way that might provide some benefit to a religious institution.

It is underappreciated that even Justice Wiley Rutledge rejected the robust claim that no tax monies could be expended in a way that would benefit religion—in his *Everson* dissent, he recognized that "the fire department must not stand idly by while the church burns."[12] Basically, he suggested that the "First Amendment does not exclude religious property or activities from protection against disorder or the ordinary accidental incidents of community life,"[13] arguing that the proper way to characterize the difference between the permissible and impermissible use of tax dollars to aid religion is that the First Amendment "forbids support, not protection from interference or destruction."[14]

Yet, Justice Rutledge seemed not to appreciate the potential difficulties in applying the distinction between support and protection. For example, the *Everson* Court implied that the bus transportation was being provided as a kind of safety measure, noting:

> [S]tate-paid policemen, detailed to protect children going to and from church schools from the very real hazards of traffic, would serve much the same purpose and accomplish much the same result as state provisions intended to guarantee free transportation of a kind which the state deems to be best for the school children's welfare.[15]

Thus, the Court suggested, the provision of free transportation to schools should be viewed in the same light as the provision of policemen at a crosswalk. Yet, if indeed the transportation reimbursement should be characterized as providing protection rather than support, that would make the program constitutionally permissible even according to Justice Rutledge's criterion.

At least one of the issues dividing the members of the *Everson* Court was whether the Court's characterization of the reimbursement as a safety measure was plausible. Justice Jackson pointed out that the school children rode as ordinary passengers on public buses.[16] It was not as if the town was taking measures to

---

11 *Id.* at 16.
12 *Id.* at 61 (Rutledge, J., dissenting).
13 *Id.* at 61 n.56 (Rutledge, J., dissenting).
14 *Id.* at 61 (Rutledge, J., dissenting).
15 *Id.* at 20.
16 *Id.* at 20 (Jackson, J., dissenting).

increase safety, for example, by providing buses that had much better safety records than the buses that the children would otherwise have used. Instead, the township would reimburse parents for the fares paid by children attending public or Catholic schools. But such an expenditure had "no possible effect on the child's safety or expedition in transit. As passengers on the public busses they travel as fast and no faster, and are as safe and no safer."[17] Justice Jackson reasoned that the reimbursement at issue could not accurately be characterized as promoting safety if those monies could not plausibly be said to be contributing to the safety of the buses carrying the children.

Justice Jackson assumed that either (1) the children would ride the buses whether or not their parents were reimbursed, or (2) those who could not afford the cost of transportation in addition to the cost of tuition, books, et cetera, simply would not attend the parochial school. The *Everson* majority seemed to be operating under a different assumption, namely, that at least some of the children who could not afford the cost of transportation in addition to the other expenses would hitchhike or walk to school if their parents were not reimbursed for transportation expenses. If offering the travel reimbursement would induce a significant number of children to ride buses rather than hitchhike or walk, and if hitchhiking or walking to school was much more dangerous than riding buses, then the majority's characterization of the reimbursement as a safety measure was reasonable.

Regrettably, the *Everson* Court failed to cite any evidence that there was or would be much hitchhiking or walking along busy streets to be averted, and failed to appreciate that offering the reimbursement might not have deterred the use of those modes of transport anyway. Because the reimbursement was not based on receipts or any other proof of the students having used public transport but instead was based on attendance records at school, it may be that those students who were hitchhiking or walking to school would still do so and the monies paid in "reimbursement" would be used to defray other costs.

The *Everson* Court concluded that the Establishment Clause did not prohibit "New Jersey from spending tax-raised funds to pay the bus fares of parochial school pupils as a part of a general program under which it pays the fares of pupils attending public and other schools."[18] Of course, to reach that conclusion, the Court had to characterize the statute before it in a somewhat misleading way. For example, the Court wrote that the state "does no more than provide a general program to help parents get their children, regardless of their religion, safely and expeditiously to and from accredited schools."[19] Yet, the program was general only in that it covered both public and Catholic schools. Facially, it did not provide reimbursement for students attending non-Catholic religious schools, and thus *Everson* upheld a statute that facially distinguished among religions.

---

17 *Id.*
18 *Id.* at 17.
19 *Id.* at 18.

In his dissent, Justice Rutledge seemed to read the Establishment Clause prohibition quite broadly, suggesting that it "broadly forbids state support, financial or other, of religion in any guise, form or degree. It outlaws all use of public funds for religious purposes."[20] He characterized the tax at issue as furnishing support for religion in that it helped children "in a substantial way to get the very thing which they are sent to the particular school to secure, namely, religious training and teaching."[21] Indeed, he argued that "transportation, where it is needed, is as essential to education as any other element,"[22] and is no less essential to the educational process than is "the very teaching in the classroom or payment of the teacher's sustenance."[23] Because he viewed the provision of transportation as an essential factor in the religious education of these children, he believed that its provision could not pass constitutional muster.

Yet, Justice Rutledge's argument proved too much. The Court admitted the "possibility that some of the children might not be sent to the church schools if the parents were compelled to pay their children's bus fares out of their own pockets when transportation to a public school would have been paid for by the State,"[24] that is, that the state's providing the transportation might be a necessary condition for the children's attending the schools. But section (2) of the state ordinance would also have permitted some children to attend parochial school who otherwise would not have been able to do so. Thus, children living along a bus route who attended a parochial school along that bus route might not have attended the school if they had been forced to pay the transportation costs, even if the additional expenses incurred by the state by transporting these students for free was minimal. Presumably, Justice Rutledge did not think that the Constitution precluded a state from offering free transportation to children who lived along an existing bus route and who were going to a religious school along that route. The same point might be made about state funds that were provided so that parochial school children could receive lunch at school at a reduced price. State subsidization of such meals might free up monies to be used for other expenses and, further, the students being well-nourished might help them learn better, which might be thought to be aiding church schools in their mission. Yet, presumably, Justice Rutledge would not have thought that providing lunches to needy children whether in public or private school (including religious schools) offends the Establishment Clause. Indeed, although the provision of food to hungry children attending parochial schools might be characterized as support of religion, it might also be characterized as protecting the children from harm, which was the sort of state aid to religion that Justice Rutledge did not think precluded by the Establishment Clause.

---

20 *Id.* at 33 (Rutledge, J., dissenting).

21 *Id.* at 45 (Rutledge J., dissenting).

22 *Id.* at 47 (Rutledge J., dissenting).

23 *Id.* at 48 (Rutledge J., dissenting).

24 *Id.* at 17.

While sympathetic to the plight of parents wishing to send their children to religious schools, Justice Rutledge believed that permitting a state to finance transportation would open the door to state financing of tuition or teachers' salaries. "No more unjust or discriminatory in fact is it to deny attendants at religious schools the cost of their transportation than it is to deny them tuitions, sustenance for their teachers, or any other educational expense which others receive at public cost."[25] Yet, Justice Rutledge's argument that a state cannot justify refusing to pay parochial school tuition if paying for school transportation assumes that there is no principled way to distinguish between these expenses. If the reimbursement at issue is justifiable as a safety measure, and the Constitution permits a state to promote safety but not instruction in religious institutions, then Justice Rutledge's slippery slope claim is untenable. Indeed, he believed that a principled distinction could be made between the different types of expenses; he just believed that the transportation expenses at issue were more accurately characterized as promoting education than safety. But this understanding of Rutledge's view puts the dissent in a much different light. For example, Frank Ravitch suggests that the *Everson* "dissenting opinions argued that neutrality mandated a separationist outcome and thus the funding was unconstitutional."[26] But it may instead be that the dissents believed that the Constitution permits funding of parochial schools as long as those monies are used to promote health rather than religious teaching.

Justice Jackson also dissented in *Everson*, suggesting that as a constitutional matter it makes no difference whether "the beneficiary of this expenditure of tax-raised funds is primarily the parochial school and incidentally the pupil, or whether the aid is directly bestowed on the pupil with indirect benefits to the school."[27] Under Justice Jackson's view, states cannot directly or indirectly support religious teaching. Yet, merely because a state is barred from supporting religious teaching does not mean that the state must also be barred from making religious schools safer for children. Further, because Justice Jackson believed that the statute on its face benefited one religion in particular, he was not forced to confront a statute that offered benefits, perhaps indirectly, on a facially nondiscriminatory basis.

The issues dividing the *Everson* Court continue to divide the Court today. For example, the members of the Court were divided about whether the use to which the monies had been allocated was itself constitutionally significant. Justice Rutledge believed that this was irrelevant—the program was unconstitutional because tax dollars were being used to support religion in that they were being used to help students receive religious instruction. It did not matter to him that the dollars themselves were not used to pay the teachers giving the instruction or to buy the books that would be used in class. The *Everson* majority emphasized that the monies were not being directly used for religious instruction. That was true in

---

25 *Id.* at 58 (Rutledge, J., dissenting).

26 See Frank S. Ravitch, *Masters of Illusion: The Supreme Court and the Religion Clauses* 20 (2007).

27 *Everson*, 330 U.S. at 24 (Jackson, J., dissenting).

that (a) the monies were going to the parents rather than the schools, and (b) the reimbursement was for transportation costs rather than religious instruction.

A point that seems underappreciated is that the majority and dissent in *Everson* did not seem so far apart after all. Most if not all members of the Court believed that public expenditures to promote the safety of children in or on the way to/ from religious settings are permissible, and the disagreement was really about whether the expenditure at issue could accurately be characterized as promoting safety. Yet, if the reading of *Everson* offered here is correct, then the opinion is not as separationist as some commentators imply. For example, Kent Greenawalt describes the *Everson* Court as having adopted a "highly separationist account of nonestablishment"[28] and Joseph Viteritti describes the "separationist posture" of the opinion.[29] However, it is argued here that *Everson* is merely preventing state support of teaching in religious schools.

There is another advantage of the reading offered here. The *Everson* Court did uphold the funding at issue, which might lead commentators to follow Viteritti's lead in characterizing the result as "accommodationist."[30] But that might lead one to misunderstand the *Everson* result and believe that the opinion opens the door to all kinds of support for parochial schools. While *Everson* does stand for the proposition that public funds can be used to protect children or to prevent destruction of religious facilities, the decision does not stand for the proposition that public funds can also be used to pay religious school tuition or parochial school teachers' salaries.

No Support for the Teaching of Religion

The *Everson* Court upheld the statute before it because the funding was "so separate and so indisputably marked off from the religious function,"[31] that it could not plausibly be thought to be supporting religious teaching. At issue in *Board of Education v. Allen*[32] was a statute requiring local public school authorities to lend textbooks to all children in grades 7 through 12, whether those students were in public or private school. While recognizing that the line between neutrality towards and support of religion is not easy to draw, the *Allen* Court employed a previously announced test that "to withstand the strictures of the Establishment Clause there must be a secular legislative purpose and a primary effect that neither advances nor inhibits religion."[33] The Court suggested that the statute at issue had

---

28 Kent Greenawalt, *Does God Belong in Public Schools?* 18 (2005).

29 See Joseph P. Viteritti, *The Last Freedom: Religion from the Public School to the Public Square* 121 (2007).

30 See *id.*

31 *Everson*, 330 U.S. at 18.

32 392 U.S. 236 (1968).

33 *Id.* at 243.

a secular purpose and a primary effect neither advancing nor inhibiting religion, just as the law permitting the provision of bus transportation in *Everson* had a secular purpose and a primary effect that neither advanced nor inhibited religion. Yet, there were important differences between bus transportation on the one hand and the provision of books to students on the other. As the *Allen* Court recognized, "books are different from buses," and most "bus rides have no inherent religious significance."[34]

By discussing whether bus rides performed a religious function, the *Allen* Court shifted the focus away from whether the aid was promoting safety rather than education to whether the aid had religious significance. This shift was important, because it allowed the Court to distinguish the aid in *Allen* from other kinds of impermissible support by noting that the books at issue in this case had no religious significance. These books had to be approved by public school authorities and only secular books would receive the necessary approval. Now the focus of discussion was not on whether books were more aptly characterized as promoting education rather than health and safety but, instead, on whether the public officials in charge of making the selection would surreptitiously approve religious books as texts or, perhaps, would be unable to distinguish between religious and nonreligious books.

The appellants had claimed that textbooks, unlike buses, are central to the teaching process, and that the state could not offer support for something central in providing a religious education. The Court rejected that argument, suggesting that parochial schools provide religious instruction and secular education. Given these different functions performed by parochial schools and the Court's unwillingness to accept "that the processes of secular and religious training are so intertwined that secular textbooks furnished to students by the public are in fact instrumental in the teaching of religion,"[35] the Court held that provision of these textbooks did not violate the Establishment Clause.

The *Allen* Court did not state which of two possible positions it was maintaining: (1) state aid to parochial schools as a general matter is permissible unless it can be shown that the aid in fact will support religious teaching, or (2) because it is implausible that secular texts in particular will be used to promote religion, the use of public monies to buy such textbooks will be struck down only if it can be shown that the books in fact are being used to support religion. The first position imposes a heavy burden as a general matter on those challenging state support of religious institutions, whereas the second imposes a heavy burden on those challenging state support of religion only where the support is being used for something quite secular in nature.

There were three dissents in *Allen*, two questioning whether the approved texts would in fact be secular and one questioning the Court's reading of *Everson*. Justice William Douglas worried in his dissent that a "parochial school textbook

---

34 *Id.* at 244.
35 *Id.* at 248.

may contain many, many more seeds of creed and dogma than a prayer,"[36] pointing out as an example a general science text that distinguished among animal and human embryos by noting that the latter "has a human soul infused into the body by God."[37] Because the textbook plays such a central role in religious education and can be so central in teaching aspects of a religious creed, Justice Douglas suggested that the Constitution could not possibly permit the aid in question. Justice Abe Fortas had related concerns, pointing out that the program at issue did not simply involve the approval of textbooks that would be used in both public and private schools. Rather, the books were chosen by sectarian authorities specifically for the children attending their parochial schools. Thus, he suggested, because the books used by the students were selected by religious authorities, the statute had to be struck down as a violation of Establishment Clause guarantees. However, the Court was not convinced that sectarian texts would in fact be approved, and so was not persuaded by the points of Justices Douglas and Fortas.

Justices Douglas and Fortas worried that (1) the actual choice of the textbooks might be affected by virtue of the books being used in parochial schools, and (2) texts incorporating subtle or not-so-subtle religious views might be chosen. Justice Hugo Black made a different but related point when suggesting that even if the texts were secular, they would be used to promote particular religious views. The Court disagreed that it was inevitable that the secular texts would be so used, however, and rejected that the statute should be struck down without more of a showing that the state aid was actually promoting religion.

Justice Black made another point in his *Allen* dissent, disagreeing with the majority's implicit reading of *Everson* and suggesting that the law at issue in *Everson*

> was treated in the same way as a general law paying the streetcar fare of all school children, or a law providing midday lunches for all children or all school children, or a law to provide police protection for children going to and from school, or general laws to provide police and fire protection for buildings, including, of course, churches and church school buildings as well as others.[38]

Thus, Justice Black explained that the bus service upheld in *Everson* was analogous to the provision of police protection for children going to and from school, which is distinguishable in kind from providing money for books, tuition, or teacher salaries.

Viteritti suggests that Justice Black was probably correct when implying that religion would pervade most aspects of the parochial school curriculum.[39] But Justice Black was not merely suggesting that, but also was suggesting that the

---

36 *Id.* at 257 (Douglas, J., dissenting).
37 *Id.* at 258 (Douglas, J., dissenting).
38 *Id.* at 252 (Black, J., dissenting).
39 See Viteritti, *supra* note 29, at 123.

principle upon which *Everson* had been decided was that the state could fund health and safety but not education in parochial schools. That way, it would not be necessary for the Court or state to decide the relative likelihood that particular subjects would be taught from a religious perspective.

A few points might be made about Justice Black's *Everson* analysis. First, given that he authored the opinion, his interpretation of it is due some deference, at least with respect to the distinction that the opinion was trying to draw. Second, his interpretation of *Everson* as approving a safety measure both underscores that members of the Court may have been less far apart in their view of what the Establishment Clause permits than is commonly supposed and suggests that the result in *Allen* should have come out the other way if *Everson* was controlling—it could not plausibly be argued that the provision of textbooks promoted safety rather than instruction.

Allen modified the relevant criterion from "Is the program receiving state support promoting health/safety rather than instruction?" to "If the program receiving state support involves instruction, is the instruction secular?" To answer whether the instruction was secular, the Court considered among other matters the nature of the materials.

That the texts were secular in nature was helpful, although not dispositive, in establishing that the texts would not be used to promote religious instruction. Presumably, had the Court accepted Justice Black's claim that the secular materials inevitably would have been used to promote religion, the Court would have struck down the use of the public funds to buy such secular materials—else, there would have been no need for the Court to have discussed the dual functions of parochial education. Nonetheless, one infers, because of the secular nature of the textbooks at issue, the Court believed it reasonable to assume that the books would be used to promote secular learning and was unworried by the bare possibility that such texts could be used to promote religious views.

Echoing Justice Rutledge's warning in his *Everson* dissent that the majority opinion was opening the door to a variety of kinds of support for religious institutions, Justice Black warned in his *Allen* dissent that the majority opinion could be used to justify state support of religious schools in other ways. "It requires no prophet to foresee that on the argument used to support this law others could be upheld providing ... to pay the salaries of the religious school teachers."[40] That very issue was addressed in *Lemon v. Kurtsman*.[41]

State Augmentation of Religious Teachers' Salaries

Lemon involved a challenge to Pennsylvania and Rhode Island statutes providing support to sectarian elementary and secondary schoolteachers. The Rhode Island

---

40 *Allen*, 392 U.S. at 253 (Black, J., dissenting).
41 403 U.S. 602 (1971).

Act supplemented teacher salaries by 15 percent based on a legislative finding that the quality of education available in nonpublic elementary schools had been jeopardized by rising salaries in the teaching market—private schools were having some difficulty in attracting and retaining good teachers. The only instructors eligible for the salary supplements were those who (a) only taught subjects offered in the public schools, (b) only used teaching materials available in the public schools, and (c) agreed in writing not to teach religion while receiving any salary supplement under the Act.

The Pennsylvania statute authorized private school reimbursement for teacher salaries and instructional materials expenditures. Reimbursement was limited to those teaching certain courses, and the textbooks and instructional materials had to be approved by the State Superintendent of Public Instruction. There would be no reimbursement for any course containing "any subject matter expressing religious teaching, or the morals or forms of worship of any sect."[42] Thus, just as the only textbooks that could receive state funding in *Allen* were books that were secular in content, the only teachers whose salaries would be supplemented in *Lemon* were those teaching secular subjects.

The *Lemon* Court began its analysis by offering the relevant criteria for determining whether legislation passed constitutional muster:

1. The statute must have a secular legislative purpose.
2. The statute's principal or primary effect must neither advance nor inhibit religion.
3. The statute must not cause excessive government entanglement with religion.[43]

The Court then applied the criteria to the statutes before it. While accepting that there was a secular legislative purpose in attempting to enhance the quality of secular education in all schools, the Court did not decide whether the principal and primary effect of the statute was to advance or inhibit religion. Instead, the Court suggested that the requirement that *only* secular education receive support violated the excessive entanglement prong, because continuing supervision of the teachers would be required to assure that they would not be engaging in sectarian teaching while receiving state support.

While states are permitted to provide aid to religious schools with respect to neutral materials, facilities, or services, the aid at issue in *Lemon* was allegedly of a different sort. Teachers are quite different from books—it is much easier to tell whether a particular book's content includes religious matters than it is to predict whether a teacher's handling of a particular subject will include religious matters.

The *Lemon* Court was not assuming that parochial school teachers would act in bad faith or attempt to circumvent constitutional limitations, but merely noted that

---

42 *Id*. at 610.
43 See *id*. at 612–13.

a teacher might have some difficulty in completely separating secular and religious teaching. This was in part a function of the different perspectives that individuals might have with respect to particular course contents, since what might "appear to some to be essential to good citizenship might well for others border on or constitute instruction in religion."[44]

To avoid even inadvertent state support of sectarian teaching, the state would have to monitor the classrooms. After all, unlike a book, "a teacher cannot be inspected once so as to determine the extent and intent of his or her personal beliefs and subjective acceptance of the limitations imposed by the First Amendment."[45] Yet, the *Lemon* Court did not explore whether its observations about teachers would have any implications for its prior approval of secular texts, which would be used by the very teachers whom the Court believed had to be under continuing surveillance. Even a close and careful inspection of a book could not reveal how it would be used in class. The *Lemon* rationale for striking down salary augmentation of parochial school teachers for fear that a state would thereby be unwittingly supporting the inculcation of religious doctrine would also suggest that a state should not provide even secular books for fear of how they would be used.

An additional defect in the Pennsylvania statute was that the monies were given directly to the schools. This was a concern because the "government's post-audit power to inspect and evaluate a church-related school's financial records and to determine which expenditures are religious and which are secular creates an intimate and continuing relationship between church and State."[46] Continuing contact creates an opportunity for constitutional mischief because, for example, the government might pressure a school to modify its curriculum to achieve more secular aims.

Yet, by noting some of the additional difficulties associated with a direct grant to sectarian institutions, the *Lemon* Court was not implying that indirectly funneling funds to religious schools somehow should or would immunize the grant from constitutional review. Both *Everson* and *Allen* were predicated on the secular nature of that which was funded. Had the fact that the monies were not directly going to the schools immunized the funding from further constitutional review, there would have been no need for an analysis of whether the funds were supporting something secular rather than sectarian.

That aid is not immunized merely because it goes indirectly to religious schools is illustrated in *Committee for Public Education and Religious Liberty v. Nyquist.*[47] The *Nyquist* Court examined a New York program that would partially reimburse low-income parents if they sent their children to private schools, and that would also pay monies directly to private schools for facilities maintenance and repair based on the number of students in attendance. Few if any restrictions were placed

---

44 *Id.* at 619.
45 *Id.*
46 *Id.* at 621–2.
47 413 U.S. 756 (1973).

on which facilities would be maintained or repaired with these monies. The state justified these expenditures by noting that the public schools would be massively overburdened were all those children currently attending private schools to start attending public schools instead. The Court struck down both types of aid because "neither form of aid is sufficiently restricted to assure that it will not have the impermissible effect of advancing the sectarian activities of religious schools."[48] Thus, the fact that the reimbursement was going to low-income families rather than the schools themselves did not immunize the funding from further constitutional review.

An additional difficulty posed by the New York system was that the reduced taxes associated with the program flowed primarily to parents of children attending private, sectarian schools, although the Court did not indicate that this factor alone was dispositive to establish the unconstitutionality of the program. The *Nyquist* Court made clear that had the benefit to religious institutions only been indirect and incidental, the statute would have been upheld. While Viteritti describes *Nyquist* as based on "reasoning that was ridiculously flawed,"[49] it is difficult to see why that is so. The Court has been trying to strike a balance among a variety of competing factors. The Establishment Clause had been interpreted to preclude state funding of religious education, and the *Nyquist* Court recognized that the fact that the families rather than the schools were the direct recipients of the funding should not be thought to immunize the practice from further constitutional review.

In *Everson, Allen, Lemon* and *Nyquist,* the Court offered guidelines with respect to the kinds of state aid to religious institutions that will pass constitutional muster. The Court in *Everson* and *Allen* suggested that secular aid is permissible, although indicated in *Nyquist* and *Lemon* that aid that is too readily divertible to promote sectarian instruction is impermissible. These guidelines left a large gray area, as was illustrated in *Meek v. Pittenger*.[50]

At issue in *Meek* was a Pennsylvania statute authorizing the provision to students in nonpublic primary and secondary schools of:

1. auxiliary services,
2. textbooks, and
3. instructional materials and equipment.[51]

The Court examined the provision of each of these in light of the *Lemon* test.

The Court upheld the loaning of the textbooks, citing *Allen*, and noted that the textbooks were secular and would be used for purely secular purposes. The Court emphasized that the textbooks were loaned directly to the student, reasoning that

---

48 *Id*. at 794.

49 Viteritti, *supra* note 29, at 125.

50 421 U.S. 349 (1975), overruled by *Mitchell v. Helms*, 530 U.S. 793 (2000).

51 See *id*. at 353–5.

the financial benefits were therefore to the parents and children, and not to the private schools.

Yet, there was reason to question whether the books were really loaned to the students in more than a merely formal sense. As Justice William Brennan pointed out in his concurrence and dissent, it was "pure fantasy to treat the textbook program as a loan to students,"[52] because "virtually the entire loan transaction [was] … conducted between officials of the nonpublic school, on the one hand, and officers of the State, on the other."[53] Further, the loaned textbooks were stored on campus. Finally, while the books were sometimes described as being loaned to the students, at other times they were described as being loaned to the schools themselves, for example, when discussing when the books were to be presumed lost, obsolete, or worn out. That said, however, the arrangement at issue in *Meek* was similar to the arrangement whose constitutionality was upheld in *Allen*, and it would have been difficult to justify striking down the loan program at issue in *Meek* without overruling *Allen*.

One of the surprising aspects of *Meek* was the degree to which the Court emphasized the importance of the identity of the individuals receiving the loans. Consider the *Meek* Court's analysis of the constitutionality of the program whereby instructional equipment and materials were loaned directly to the schools rather than to the pupils. Doing so, the Court reasoned, had the "unconstitutional primary effect of advancing religion because of the predominantly religious character of the schools benefiting from the Act."[54] Yet, it is not clear how the loan of the instructional materials and equipment significantly advanced religion in a way that the loan of the books did not.

It might be argued that the instructional materials and equipment might be diverted to religious uses in a way that the secular books could not, and that this is why the loan of the latter was constitutional but the former was not. But that was not the reasoning of the Court. The *Meek* Court accepted the district court's conclusion that "the material and equipment that are the subjects of the loan— maps, charts, and laboratory equipment, for example—are self-polic[ing], in that starting as secular, nonideological and neutral, they will not change in use."[55] Nonetheless, the Court reasoned that "it would simply ignore reality to attempt to separate secular educational functions from the predominantly religious role performed by many of Pennsylvania's church-related elementary and secondary schools and to then characterize Act 195 as channeling aid to the secular without providing direct aid to the sectarian."[56] However, this analysis has implications that the Court failed to take into account. Basically, the Court suggested that even secular materials will promote sectarian ends if used within pervasively sectarian

---

52   *Id.* at 379 (Brennan, J., concurring in part and dissenting in part).
53   *Id.* at 380 (Brennan, J., concurring in part and dissenting in part).
54   *Id.* at 363.
55   *Id.* at 365.
56   *Id.*

institutions. But the same point might be made about texts, namely, even secular texts might be used to promote sectarian ends if used within pervasively sectarian institutions.

A separate issue addressed by the Court involved how to characterize the loan. Rather than suggest that ownership of the loaned materials remained with the state, the Court instead discussed the substantial amount of direct support involved, as if the loans of the equipment were instead cash that had been given directly to the religious institutions. While accepting that the aid could only be used for secular purposes, the Court nonetheless concluded that "when it flows to an institution in which religion is so pervasive that a substantial portion of its functions are subsumed in the religious mission, state aid has the impermissible primary effect of advancing religion."[57] Yet, money was not flowing to these institutions. While the institutions were receiving the benefits involved in having instructional materials and equipment loaned to them so that, for example, these goods would not have to be purchased and the saved monies might be used for other purposes, an analogous claim might have been made about the loaned books.

Had the equipment not been loaned, the schools presumably would have been forced to buy that equipment and at least some of those costs would have been passed on to the students and their families. Had the books not been loaned, the students would have been forced to buy them. But the schools might then have been forced to bear some of those costs, for example, by being forced to lower tuition or reduce other fees. Or, in the alternative, if the textbooks were loaned, the schools might have been able to charge more in tuition or fees, and the families who did not have to spend money on the books might now be able to afford to pay additional fees to the schools. There is no reason to think that the loan of the equipment benefited only the schools and not in addition the families of those attending the schools, just as there is no reason to think that the loan of the textbooks was only a financial boon for the students' families and not the schools.

Suppose that the instructional equipment and materials had been loaned to the student body with the understanding that the equipment and materials would be stored and used at the school. The equipment would be used for the students' benefit, and some of the materials such as maps might even be permitted to leave the school under appropriate circumstances. The *Meek* Court's analysis suggests that this formal maneuver might well have made the difference with respect to the program's constitutionality, even though the schools would have received the same functional benefits whether the equipment was loaned in name to the students or instead to the schools.

The *Meek* Court is more appropriately subject to criticism for its apparent willingness to uphold or not uphold the loan of school materials based on the formal identity of the loan recipient than for its striking down the loaning of maps while at the same time upholding the loaning of books containing maps. The Court's reluctance to overrule *Allen* precluded it from striking down the loaning

---

57 *Id.* at 360.

of books. Nonetheless, the Court emphasizing the formal identity of the recipient was likely to and did yield absurd results and, further, was open to a variety of kinds of abuse.

The *Meek* Court also examined whether auxiliary services could be provided without offending the Constitution. The Court explained that the district court had "emphasized that auxiliary services are provided directly to the children involved and are expressly limited to those services which are secular, neutral, and nonideological,"[58] thus making these services seem analogous to the loaned texts whose constitutionality had been upheld. However, the *Meek* Court chided the district court for "relying entirely on the good faith and professionalism of the secular teachers and counselors functioning in church-related schools to ensure that a strictly nonideological posture is maintained."[59] Like the *Lemon* Court, the *Meek* Court worried that teachers in religious schools might inadvertently include religious teaching within their secular instruction, and also worried that those providing auxiliary services at pervasively sectarian schools might feel pressured to promote religion, which would necessitate states maintaining continual surveillance to make sure that this perceived pressure did not result in religious instruction. In short, the *Meek* Court upheld the practice that had already been upheld in *Allen*, but struck down the remaining provisions, notwithstanding the Court's professed confidence that the materials, equipment, and services at issue were secular and would not be put to sectarian uses.

Meek left open a variety of questions whose answers were clarified in *Wolman v. Walter*.[60] At issue in *Wolman* were appropriations by the Ohio Legislature whereby various books, materials, and services could be provided to both public and private school students. The *Wolman* Court followed *Allen* and *Meek* and upheld Ohio's textbook loan program, and also upheld appropriations for various kinds of services involving speech, hearing, and psychological diagnosis and treatment. Those of the services that would be performed on site were unlikely to provide an opportunity for the promotion of sectarian views, and other services involving a greater risk of the communication of sectarian views would be provided off site. Given that the personnel providing these off-site services were either under contract with the state health department or were employed by the local board of education, the Court did not believe that there was a great risk that these individuals would engage in sectarian instruction.

The *Wolman* Court explained that the Ohio program did not have the constitutionally worrisome features of the auxiliary services program at issue in *Meek*, which had been struck down because of the danger that arose from services being provided in the pervasively sectarian atmosphere of the private school. The important consideration involved the environment in which the services would be offered, and as long as the services were offered at religiously neutral locations,

---

58 *Id.* at 368.

59 *Id.* at 369.

60 433 U.S. 229 (1977), overruled by *Mitchell v. Helms*, 530 U.S. 793 (2000).

the danger perceived in *Meek* would not arise. Because in *Wolman* those services that had the potential to involve sectarian instruction were offered off site and those provided on site did not have that potential, the Court held that there was insufficient likelihood that the state would be promoting sectarian education through its funding of any of the services at issue and thus found no violation of the Establishment Clause.

Wolman made clear that the Court was willing to look past the formal identity of the loan recipients when considering whether aid to sectarian schools violated Establishment Clause guarantees, striking down the Ohio materials/equipment loan program as an attempt to do an end-run around the constitutional requirements. The Court noted, "Before *Meek* was decided by this Court, Ohio authorized the loan of material and equipment directly to the nonpublic schools. Then, in light of *Meek*, the state legislature decided to channel the goods through the parents and pupils."[61] Rejecting the legislature's move attempting to save the program, the Court explained that while there had been a "technical change in legal bailee, the program in substance is the same as before: The equipment is substantially the same; it will receive the same use by the students; and it may still be stored and distributed on the nonpublic school premises."[62]

By emphasizing the history of the program, the Court made clear that it would not permit states to do an end-run around their constitutional obligations. Yet, the *Wolman* Court did not thereby resolve all relevant issues. For example, it is not clear what the Court would have said if Ohio had initially loaned these materials directly to the students or if a period of years had elapsed between the ending of the program involving loans to the schools and the beginning of the new program involving loans directly to the students.

When striking down the material/equipment loan program, the *Wolman* Court analogized these loans to the grants at issue in *Nyquist* and suggested that the Ohio loans were more clearly unconstitutional than the New York grants. The Court reasoned that the New York grants could be used by the parents in any way they wanted and thus might not go to religious schools, whereas the loaned materials and equipment in *Wolman* could only be used in conjunction with courses. The Court thus suggested that the fact that the benefit was restricted in that it had to be used in a way connected to a sectarian institution was itself constitutionally significant.

By arguing that the required tie between the courses and the loaned materials/equipment militated in favor of the program's unconstitutionality, the *Wolman* Court was implicitly undercutting the constitutionality of the textbook loan program, because the use of the textbooks was also tied to courses. The Court appreciated this implication, but upheld the textbook loan provision as a matter of stare decisis. The Court then explained that it was refusing to extend *Allen*, and

---

61 *Id.* at 250.
62 *Id.*

struck down both the equipment loan provision and a provision which funded field trips.

In the series of cases discussed above, the Court at least seemed to have adopted a relatively consistent approach. The Court would approve programs permitting the provision of secular services if those services did not pose a risk of sectarian instruction or, where there was such a risk, if those services were not provided on site. The Court would approve provision of secular texts in sectarian schools, but would likely not approve the provision of other kinds of materials, even if secular. This approach was continued in the 1980s, with at least one important modification that, when coupled with some developments in other areas of the law, had important implications in the 1990s. Those changes culminated in the current jurisprudence regarding aid to sectarian primary and secondary schools. Regrettably, the new jurisprudence simply is not reconcilable with either the letter or the spirit of *Everson*.

Reimbursing Families for Parochial School Expenses

As discussed above, the *Nyquist* Court struck down a New York plan to offer grants to low-income families whose children attended private schools. Ten years after that opinion was issued, the Court in *Mueller v. Allen*[63] considered a Minnesota statute permitting individuals to take a tax deduction for the tuition, textbooks, and transportation expenses of dependents attending elementary or secondary schools. The *Mueller* Court noted that the Court had upheld reimbursement systems in the past for bus transportation, and that states could loan secular textbooks to parochial schoolchildren without running afoul of constitutional guarantees. The Court further noted that the Minnesota program promoted legitimate secular purposes of the state such as helping to produce an educated citizenry and preventing an already heavily burdened public school system from being forced to shoulder an even greater burden.

The *Mueller* Court suggested that the universality of the deduction militated in favor of its constitutionality. That was accurate, at least in the sense that Minnesota's having limited the deduction to families with children attending private school would have militated in favor of the program's unconstitutionality. As the *Nyquist* Court had noted, a flaw of the New York program was that it only offered the grant at issue to parents of children in private schools. Indeed, the *Mueller* Court emphasized that the case before it was "vitally different from the scheme struck down in *Nyquist* ... [where] public assistance amounting to tuition grants was provided only to parents of children in nonpublic schools."[64] However, while the Minnesota and New York programs were distinguishable in that respect,

---

63 463 U.S. 388 (1983).
64 *Id.* at 398.

there were at least two important ways in which the *Mueller* Court misrepresented *Nyquist*.

First, while it is true that the *Nyquist* Court had worried that a program that primarily benefited parents of children attending sectarian schools would be politically divisive, the *Mueller* Court failed to note that such a program might primarily benefit a group in one of two ways: (1) most of the individuals receiving the benefit belong to one particular group, or (2) while individuals belonging to many different groups receive some benefit from the program, most of the individuals receiving a substantial benefit from the program belonged to one particular group. As Justice Thurgood Marshall noted in his *Mueller* dissent, the benefits afforded by the Minnesota program to parents of children attending public and private schools were not comparable. Children attending public schools would have no tuition to pay. Although parents of children in the public schools could deduct the cost of gym clothes, pencils, and notebooks, the amount that those items cost pales in comparison to the cost of tuition.[65] A program affording thousands of dollars to individuals in one group and tens of dollars to individuals in other groups might be quite divisive, although it would be false to claim that only members of the first group received any benefit from the program.

Second, the *Mueller* Court was somewhat misleading when suggesting that "by channeling whatever assistance it may provide to parochial schools through individual parents, Minnesota has reduced the Establishment Clause objections to which its action is subject,"[66] as if most, if not all, constitutional difficulties could be avoided by doing such channeling. Although the *Mueller* Court was correct to imply that there can be additional difficulties posed by direct funding because of the possible need for continuing audits to assure that the monies are not misspent, no Court had previously held or even implied that funneling the monies through individuals would immunize the use of those monies from further scrutiny. Indeed, the *Wolman* Court expressly repudiated Ohio's (alleged) attempt to avoid its constitutional obligations by channeling aid though parents and students.

The *Mueller* Court recognized that the "financial assistance provided to parents ultimately has an economic effect comparable to that of aid given directly to the schools attended by their children."[67] However, the Court reasoned that public funds became available to the private schools "only as a result of numerous private choices of individual parents of school-age children,"[68] as if the fact that parents had made intervening choices would somehow permit the state to promote sectarian education. If that were correct, the *Everson* Court would hardly have based its decision on the aid being "so separate and so indisputably marked off from the religious function."[69] As Justice Marshall pointed out in dissent, *Nyquist*

---

65 See *id*. at 408 (Marshall, J., dissenting).
66 *Id*. at 399.
67 *Id*.
68 *Id*.
69 *Everson*, 330 U.S. at 18.

"established that a State may not support religious education either through direct grants to parochial schools or through financial aid to parents of parochial school students."[70] While claiming to follow the opinion, the *Mueller* Court ignored *Nyquist's* reasoning.

Someone reading *Mueller's* interpretation of *Nyquist* would think that: (1) the *Nyquist* Court had struck down the program at issue because the benefit was reserved for parents of children attending private schools, and (2) the *Nyquist* Court would have upheld the program, notwithstanding its indirectly promoting sectarian education, if only the New York program had also benefited parents of children attending public schools. But that reading turns *Nyquist* on its head.

The *Nyquist* Court struck down the program benefiting parents because it was not "sufficiently restricted to assure that it will not have the impermissible effect of advancing the sectarian activities of religious schools."[71] The Court noted in dictum that the "tax reductions authorized by this law flow primarily to the parents of children attending sectarian, nonpublic schools," but nonetheless refused to intimate "whether this factor alone might have controlling significance in another context in some future case."[72] Thus, the *Nyquist* Court struck down the program at issue because it did not include adequate restrictions to prevent its advancing sectarian objectives, but the Court also implied that a program with adequate restrictions still might not pass muster if the benefits of the program were reserved for members of a particular group. Without overruling *Nyquist*, the *Mueller* Court held that the program at issue was permissible because parents of children in both public and private schools received some benefit, even though the Minnesota program lacked restrictions to assure that the sectarian activities of religious schools would not be advanced. Indeed, the Court in both *Nyquist* and *Everson* had emphasized the importance of the state not advancing sectarian instruction even indirectly, but that essential element was somehow considered irrelevant in *Mueller*.

Certainly, it would be unsurprising for some to prefer the position articulated in *Mueller* to the one that had previously been articulated. Yet, it is an entirely different matter to suggest that *Mueller* somehow accounts for the then-existing Establishment Clause jurisprudence.

Viteritti writes, "So long as citizen interaction with religion is a voluntary choice, and the state acts in a neutral fashion as to not favor any one religion or religion in general, a program does not present an Establishment Clause problem."[73] However, it is important to understand what counts as religious neutrality. As Viteritti himself notes,[74] 96 percent of the private school beneficiaries in *Mueller* attended Catholic schools. While *Mueller* is distinguishable from *Nyquist* in that

---

70 See *Mueller*, 463 U.S. at 404 (Marshall, J., dissenting).

71 *Nyquist*, 413 U.S. at 794.

72 *Id.*

73 Viteritti, *supra* note 29, at 134–5.

74 See *id.* at 135.

public school children could receive some benefit in the former program but not in the latter, that difference cannot plausibly support the claim that the *Mueller* Court had been following the existing jurisprudence. Rather, the Court had rejected the existing jurisprudence while pretending to follow it.

The Prohibition on Advancing Sectarian Objectives

Mueller had the potential to effect an important change in sectarian aid jurisprudence. However, two subsequent decisions concerning aid to sectarian primary and secondary schools seemed to ignore *Mueller* and follow the example set in *Meek* and *Wolman*.

In *School District of Grand Rapids v. Ball*, the Court considered two enrichment and remedial programs in which classes for private school students were financed by tax dollars, taught by teachers hired by the public school system, and conducted in leased classrooms in the private schools.[75] Because almost all of the schools in the case were pervasively sectarian, the Court worried that the program at issue might advance religion in three different ways:

1. Teachers might intentionally or inadvertently teach particular religious tenets or beliefs.
2. The program might create a symbolic link between religion and the state.
3. The program might directly promote religion by subsidizing the religious mission of the schools.[76]

Some of the instructors in the after-school program who taught in the religious schools during the day would be expected to inculcate religious beliefs during school hours but offer strictly secular education once the school day was over. The Court was not confident that the teachers would be able to reverse gears so completely when the bell signaling the end of the school day had rung. After all, as the *Lemon* Court pointed out years before, it may not always be so easy to determine which teaching is sectarian and which is secular. Justice Sandra Day O'Connor noted in her concurrence and dissent that the program at issue would advance the religious aims of the pervasively sectarian schools, especially because the teachers would bring religion into all aspects of the curriculum.[77] Because of the great likelihood that state funds would be used to promote religion, the Court struck down the program as a violation of Establishment Clause guarantees.

The Court reached a similar result in *Aguilar v. Felton*,[78] in which the Court considered the constitutionality of instructional services provided to parochial

---

75 473 U.S. 373, 375 (1985), overruled by *Agostini v. Felton*, 521 U.S. 203 (1997).
76 *Id.* at 385.
77 *Id.* at 400 (O'Connor, J., concurring in part and dissenting in part).
78 473 U.S. 402 (1985), overruled by *Agostini v. Felton*, 521 U.S. 203 (1997).

students on parochial school premises. The programs included remedial reading and mathematics, as well as English as a second language and some counseling services. These programs were carried out by public school employees who volunteered to work in the private schools. The volunteers were directed to avoid religious activities and not to have religious materials in the classroom. The classrooms were to be cleared of all religious symbols.

Appellants sought to distinguish this program from the one at issue in *Ball* by the oversight system that had been devised to assure that there would be no religious content in these classes. However, the Court suggested that this monitoring system itself violated the Establishment Clause's prohibition against excessive entanglement. Justice Lewis Powell in his concurrence noted that the "government surveillance required to ensure that public funds are used for secular purposes inevitably present[s] a serious risk of excessive entanglement."[79] That risk was present whether the state was subsidizing religious school teachers or, instead, was paying public school teachers to teach secular subjects at a parochial school. Whenever the risk of government entanglement was too great, the program would be held to violate Establishment Clause guarantees.

One might have inferred from *Ball* and *Aguilar* that the Court was limiting the force of *Mueller* to cases involving tax deduction programs. However, such an inference would have been inaccurate, as was made clear in the 1990s.

The Laundering Effect of Parental Choices

In part because of some of the seeds planted in previous cases and in part because of some unusual readings of previous cases, Establishment Clause jurisprudence regarding aid to primary and secondary sectarian institutions had changed radically by the year 2000. While members of the Court disagreed about which case represented a major break with the past jurisprudence, it was nonetheless clear that an important change had taken place.

The Court's new understanding of the limits on state support of sectarian education in the primary and secondary setting was suggested in *Zobrest v. Catalina Foothills School District*[80] in which the Court examined whether it was permissible for the state to provide a sign-language interpreter for a deaf student attending a parochial high school. Foreshadowing that the limitations imposed by the Constitution on sectarian aid would thereafter be less robust, the *Zobrest* Court offered a misleading summation of the past jurisprudence by stating that "government programs that neutrally provide benefits to a broad class of citizens defined without reference to religion are not readily subject to an Establishment Clause challenge just because sectarian institutions may also receive an attenuated

---

79 *Id.* at 415 (Powell, J., concurring).
80 509 U.S. 1 (1993).

financial benefit,"[81] and implying that a contrary rule would require that churches not receive police or fire protection.

Yet, the correctness of the claim that general benefit programs to sectarian primary and secondary schools had been upheld against Establishment Clause challenges depended in large part on the type of benefits at issue. For example, *Everson* established that bus transportation can be provided, even if doing so would provide an attenuated benefit to sectarian institutions, and a series of cases including *Allen*, *Meek*, and *Wolman* established that textbooks can be loaned to students even if doing so would provide an attenuated sectarian benefit. Yet, in all of these cases the state was funding something secular. The important point was not merely that the aid itself, for example, money, was secular, but that the services or products purchased by the money were secular.

Consider what the Court deciding *Allen*, *Meek*, and *Wolman* would have said if a legislature had decided that it would provide the money to purchase textbooks for both public and private school students. If there were no reference to religion and if there were no requirement that the texts be secular, the Court would have struck down the program as a violation of the Establishment Clause. The "neutral" provision of textbooks could not have withstood scrutiny unless the state had explicitly referred to religion by requiring that the purchased books be secular—it was precisely because of the *Allen* Court's confidence that only secular textbooks would be approved that the Court upheld the textbook loan program in the first place.

The *Zobrest* Court implied that any potential Establishment Clause difficulties resulting from a state facilitating religious school education were cured if they occurred as a result of an individual parent's private decision-making. After all, because there was "no financial incentive for parents to choose a sectarian school, an interpreter's presence there cannot be attributed to state decision-making."[82] But up until this point, the constitutionality of state support of sectarian primary and secondary education had never been based on whether the presence in the school of that which had been funded could be attributed to state decision-making.

Suppose, for example, that the choice of a sectarian textbook could in no way be attributed to the state because that textbook had already been chosen and would be used in certain grades whether or not the state offered to reimburse the purchase price of that text. Prior to *Zobrest*, a state having no role in the choice of a religious textbook would not have been thought a reason that a state could help purchase such books without offending Establishment Clause guarantees.

The *Zobrest* Court suggested that disabled children rather than the parochial schools were the direct beneficiaries of the federal funds. But the same rationale would permit a state to buy sectarian texts for students, since it would be the students rather than the schools who would be the direct beneficiaries of the state's largesse. So, too, that rationale would permit a state to fund sectarian auxiliary

---

81 *Id.* at 8.
82 *Id.* at 10.

services like counseling, since the students in need rather than the schools would be the direct beneficiaries of that aid. Yet, both *Meek* and *Wolman* stood for the proposition that a state could not fund sectarian counseling services, and *Allen*, *Meek*, and *Wolman* all emphasized the secular nature of the textbooks that were being provided by the state when upholding that aid.

Finally, the *Zobrest* Court suggested that the interpreter should not be viewed as the analog of a teacher but, instead, more like a machine that would translate oral language into sign language. Because the parents chose to place their child in a pervasively sectarian environment and because the sign-language interpreter would "neither add to nor subtract from that environment,"[83] the Court held that the Establishment Clause did not bar the provision of that assistance.

Certainly, there was precedent for the suggestion that services could be funded by states where there was no danger that the individuals providing the relevant service would intentionally or inadvertently alter that service by including sectarian instruction—the provision of diagnostic services within sectarian institutions was upheld in *Wolman* precisely because the Court believed that these services would not be used to impart sectarian instruction. But in *Wolman* the Court was approving the provision of services where there was no risk of adulteration because of the secular nature of the unadulterated service. The point was not simply that the funded service would not add to or subtract from the environment; on the contrary, the point was that whatever was added to the environment via the expenditure of state funds would be secular. As Justice Harry Blackmun suggested in his dissent, the Court had never before suggested that the Establishment Clause permits a state to participate in religious indoctrination in a primary or secondary school setting. He noted that the sign-language interpreter employed by the state would communicate the sectarian views in religion class or, perhaps, would provide assistance during religious services, and concluded that while there are relatively few absolute prohibitions in the Court's Establishment Clause jurisprudence, "the Clause does absolutely prohibit government-financed or government-sponsored indoctrination into the beliefs of a particular religious faith."[84]

Of course, it is not as if the government was telling the school or the sign language interpreter what to say. Justice Blackmun's criticism might be viewed as missing the mark because the sign-language interpreter would do no "more than accurately interpret whatever material is presented to the class as a whole,"[85] and so might be thought analogous to a machine facilitating communication in some way. Suppose, for example, that James Zobrest had not been deaf but instead hard of hearing, and the state had merely provided a hearing aid. That would not offend constitutional guarantees, notwithstanding that the state was providing the means by which the individual might be indoctrinated into the beliefs of a particular

---

83 *Id.* at 13.

84 *Id.* at 21 (Blackmun, J., dissenting).

85 *Id.* at 13.

faith. Indeed, the provision of a hearing aid would presumably be characterized as promoting health and safety, and thus compatible with *Everson*.

Yet, the hearing aid analogy is misleading because the hearing aid would presumably be used at all times and thus might more plausibly be argued to be related to health and safety, whereas the interpreter would only be used in class and thus would seem more closely associated with the instruction. That difference is important. If the function of the sign language interpreter is to assist in instruction rather than promote safety and health, the constitutionality of the program would be in doubt—*Meek* had suggested that even secular materials and equipment could not be provided to facilitate education in sectarian schools. Indeed, the respondent argued that just as *Meek* had made clear that the Constitution precluded a state from loaning equipment like a tape recorder to sectarian schools, the Constitution also precluded a state from supplying an interpreter to a sectarian school. However, the Court rejected the analogy to *Meek* because *Meek* involved aid given directly to the school.

The *Zobrest* Court's point that *Meek* was distinguishable because precluding direct aid was accurate, although not dispositive, because *Wolman* had precluded even indirect aid. Yet, arguably, *Wolman's* invalidation of the indirect aid was based on the Court's view that Ohio was trying to do an end run around *Meek*, and there was no history of an end run around constitutional requirements in *Zobrest*. If the sign language interpreter was viewed as more analogous to a mechanical aid than to a teacher or counselor, and the benefit was viewed as being given directly to the student, then the *Zobrest* decision might seem compatible with the existing jurisprudence.

Yet, there was at least one additional difficulty that the *Zobrest* Court did not adequately address. The interpreter was a person rather than a machine. An interpreter performing her duties would seem more likely to be viewed as an agent of the state engaging in religious instruction than would a machine amplifying sound. Nonetheless, had the *Zobrest* Court somehow undermined the assertion that the provision of a sign language interpreter created a symbolic link between government and religion, its contention that the decision was compatible with the existing jurisprudence would have been more plausible.

Regrettably, the *Zobrest* Court simply chose not to address this possible symbolic link, even after mentioning that the Court of Appeals had relied in part on this symbolic union of government and religion to strike down the provision of this aid. Perhaps the Court could have undermined this claim about symbolism by emphasizing that other state-paid professionals could work on site in a sectarian institution without creating a symbolic link, although Justice Blackmun argued to the contrary in his dissent.

Rather than offer a careful analysis of the entire line of cases and explain how the provision of sign language interpreters fit within the existing jurisprudence, the *Zobrest* Court chose to rely heavily on two cases in particular that involved government programs aiding education, *Mueller* and *Witters v. Washington*

Department of Services for the Blind.[86] While *Witters* might seem on point because it also involved aid to the handicapped, the Court seemed to forget that the case was distinguishable because that aid went to a sectarian institution of higher education and not to a sectarian primary and secondary institution. Further, both *Ball* and *Aguilar* had been decided after *Mueller*, so it was somewhat difficult for the *Zobrest* Court to suggest with any plausibility that *Mueller* had relaxed the limitations on a state promoting sectarian education.

Without providing a plausible explanation of why it might be thought that *Mueller* had this effect, the *Zobrest* Court nonetheless suggested that its decision was compatible with the existing jurisprudence, implying that *Meek* and *Ball* were distinguishable. Justice Blackmun disagreed, suggesting in his dissent that the Court was straying "from the course set by nearly five decades of Establishment Clause jurisprudence."[87]

Of course, even were Justice Blackmun correct that the Court was changing course, a separate question would involve how much or what kind of a change. For example, it might have been thought that *Zobrest* was merely permitting the state to fund neutral services analogous to the provision of hearing aids or glasses. Admittedly, the provision of such services would facilitate religious indoctrination, although perhaps no more so than the provision of free bus transportation. Subsequent cases suggest, however, that some members of the Court viewed *Zobrest* as marking a sea change in the relevant jurisprudence.

Recognition of the Allegedly Implicit Overruling

The Court's sectarian aid jurisprudence from *Mueller* to *Zobrest* might be read in several ways. For example, *Mueller* might be read as modifying *Nyquist* but not as having significant implications for the kinds of issues raised in *Ball* and *Aguilar*. *Zobrest* might be read as either compatible with or as signaling an important break from *Ball*. In *Agostini v. Felton*,[88] the Court made clear that its understanding of the relevant jurisprudence had undergone a radical transformation.

In *Agostini*, the Court was asked to reconsider its holding in *Aguilar* in light of the intervening jurisprudence. The Court summed up its reasoning in *Ball* and *Aguilar* as follows:

1. Any public employee who works on the premises of a religious school is presumed to inculcate religion in her work.
2. The presence of public employees on private school premises creates a symbolic union between church and state.

---

86 474 U.S. 481 (1986). For further discussion of *Witters*, see Chapter 3, third section.
87 *Zobrest*, 509 U.S. at 24 (Blackmun, J., dissenting).
88 521 U.S. 203 (1997).

3. Any and all public aid that directly aids the educational function of religious schools impermissibly finances religious indoctrination, even if the aid reaches such schools as a consequence of private decision-making.[89]

The Court noted that *Aguilar* had assumed that public employees who teach on the premises of religious schools must be closely monitored, but observed that it had "abandoned the presumption erected in *Meek* and *Ball* that the placement of public employees on parochial school grounds inevitably results in the impermissible effect of state-sponsored indoctrination or constitutes a symbolic union between government and religion."[90] Yet, the Court had already rejected the idea that the placement of public employees on parochial school grounds inevitably has impermissible effects even before *Ball* had been decided, having decided in *Wolman* that services that were not amenable to being used for sectarian indoctrination could be performed on site. Further, it was accurate but misleading for the *Agostini* Court to note that the *Zobrest* Court had "refused to presume that a publicly employed interpreter would be pressured by the pervasively sectarian surroundings to inculcate religion by add[ing] to [or] subtract[ing] from the lectures translated."[91] Part of the reason that the publicly employed interpreter in *Zobrest* was unlikely to modify the message by inculcating religion was that she was working within a pervasively sectarian setting and thus would be translating material that already had a religious message. Another part of the reason involved the very function performed by the interpreter—the Court had suggested that interpreters are qualitatively different from teachers and can be presumed to do no more than accurately translate the material.

The *Agostini* Court implied that just as it had assumed in *Zobrest* that an interpreter would act in good faith and translate accurately, the Court should assume that the instructors and counselors in the program at issue in *Agostini* also would act in good faith. But this analysis rejected both the reasoning of *Zobrest* and what the Court had been suggesting since *Lemon*. *Zobrest* was predicated at least in part on the difference between interpreters and teachers—"the task of a sign-language interpreter seems to us quite different from that of a teacher or guidance counselor."[92] Further, the Court had never suggested that teachers would act in bad faith and try to incorporate religious messages whenever they could. Rather, the fear had been that sectarian indoctrination might occur inadvertently. But if the fear is that this indoctrination would occur inadvertently, then even individuals attempting to teach the appropriate subject matter and act professionally might nonetheless perform (what at least some would call) religious instruction. The *Agostini* Court was doing exactly what the *Meek* Court chided the district court below for having done, namely, "relying entirely on the good faith

---

89 *Id*. at 222.
90 *Id*. at 223.
91 *Id*.
92 *Zobrest*, 509 U.S. at 13.

and professionalism of the secular teachers and counselors functioning in church-related schools to ensure that a strictly nonideological posture is maintained."[93]

In what might most charitably be described as a cursory discussion in great need of further analysis and explanation, the *Agostini* Court reasoned, "Because the only government aid in *Zobrest* was the interpreter, who was herself not inculcating any religious messages, no government indoctrination took place and we were able to conclude that the provision of such assistance [was] not barred by the Establishment Clause."[94] Yet, the question was why the Court believed that the interpreter herself was not inculcating any religious message. Certainly, she was the individual who was communicating the message and, further, there would have been no inculcation of any religious message if she had not performed her job. To the extent that she was viewed as a mere mouthpiece and thus could not be understood to be inculcating any message, she would be distinguishable in kind from a teacher who could not be viewed as behaving so mechanically. If there were some other way to understand why the interpreter would not accurately be thought to be inculcating any religious message, the Court regrettably failed to provide that explanation.

Justice David Souter in his *Agostini* dissent emphasized the difference between the functions performed by the interpreter and the teacher, suggesting that the interpreter was more analogous to a hearing aid than a teacher. On this understanding of sign-language interpretation, the service provided by the interpreter "could not be understood as an opportunity to inject religious content in what was supposed to be secular instruction,"[95] and *Zobrest* was compatible with *Meek* and *Ball*. However, the Court suggested in response that if there were no opportunity to inject religious content, there would have been no reason for the Court to have consulted the record for reported instances of inaccurate translation.

Yet, the exchange between the majority and dissent in *Agostini* did little to clarify the relevant issues. Suppose, for example, that a hearing aid had been provided by the state. One might still want to make sure that the hearing aid was performing properly and see if there had been complaints about the aid's operation and performance. That one had checked to see if the aid was working properly would not establish that there had been an *opportunity* for inaccurate translation, although it would suggest that there had been a *possibility* of inaccurate translation.

We would not describe the hearing aid as having had an opportunity to perform incorrectly because we do not think of hearing aids as deciding to act improperly. However, human beings might choose to inject religious content at inappropriate times and, in this sense, the Court was correct to suggest that interpreters, like teachers and counselors, might have similar opportunities to violate their duty. Further, the *Agostini* Court was correct that there was no reason to assume that only sign language interpreters would be responsible or that only interpreters

---

93 See *Meek*, 421 U.S. at 369.

94 *Agostini*, 521 U.S. at 224.

95 *Id.* at 248–9 (Souter, J., dissenting).

would not consciously try to undermine their official role by injecting religion into secular instruction. Thus, the *Agostini* Court was correct to suggest that there was no reason to think that only interpreters would refrain from surreptitiously smuggling in sectarian content. The only difficulty with the Court having made these points is that they misrepresented the danger that had been discussed since *Lemon*, and thus involved arguments that were beside the point.

The *Agostini* Court was addressing a danger that had never been taken seriously with respect to either signers or teachers—namely, that they would consciously try to take advantage of opportunities to smuggle in religious content. That this was not the worry is illustrated by *Wolman*, where the Court distinguished between the functions performed by diagnosticians and counselors, suggesting that the diagnostics could be performed on site because there was relatively little chance that they would result in attempts at religious indoctrination, whereas the counseling could only be performed off site because of a greater chance of indoctrination. If the concern had been that public personnel might seize any and all opportunities to promote sectarian objectives, then the Court would presumably have worried that those providing health services to children might use those opportunities to inculcate religious doctrine. But the *Wolman* Court made clear that it was not worried that those providing health services would use their time interacting with students to give religious instruction, instead worrying about programs which were "susceptible to the intrusion of sectarian overtones."[96] Thus, the *Wolman* Court was not worried about individuals intentionally giving sectarian instruction when they should not but, instead, that such instruction might occur as a result of more subtle influences.

The focus of the *Ball* Court had been on teachers in particular, who might inadvertently inculcate religious beliefs or tenets. Regrettably, the *Agostini* Court described *Ball* as having a much broader focus and as standing for the proposition that "*any* public employee who works on the premises of a religious school is presumed to inculcate religion in her work."[97] But the Court in cases prior to *Agostini* had tried not to paint with such a broad brush, instead distinguishing among the types of public employees working within sectarian institutions and suggesting that certain occupations, such as teaching and counseling, involve a much greater risk of inadvertent promotion of sectarian objectives than do others. The *Agostini* Court simply ran roughshod over the Court's previous attempts to offer a more nuanced discussion in what is admittedly a difficult area requiring great care.

In what might be viewed as a surprising admission, the Court noted that "even the *Zobrest* dissenters acknowledged the shift *Zobrest* effected in our Establishment Clause law when they criticized the majority for stray[ing] ... from the course set by nearly five decades of Establishment Clause jurisprudence."[98]

---

96 *Wolman*, 433 U.S. at 243 n.11.
97 *Agostini*, 521 U.S. at 222 (emphasis added).
98 *Id.* at 225.

Here, the Court implied that everyone on the Court understood that *Zobrest* was radically transforming the jurisprudence—the *Agostini* Court suggested that "it was *Zobrest*—and not this litigation—that created "fresh law" ... Our refusal to limit *Zobrest* to its facts despite its rationale does not, in our view, amount to a "misreading" of precedent."[99] Yet, this is simply breathtaking. The *Agostini* Court looked at what the *Zobrest* Court had suggested was compatible with the existing jurisprudence and turned it into a watershed, allegedly understood to be so by all members of the Court at the time *Zobrest* was decided.

The *Agostini* Court modified the existing jurisprudence in yet another respect, undercutting the degree to which the state would have to entangle itself to assure that funds would not be used to promote sectarian indoctrination. The Court noted that "the factors we use to assess whether an entanglement is 'excessive' are similar to the factors we use to examine 'effect,'"[100] and thereby made the three-part *Lemon* test into a two-part test, at least for purposes of determining whether aid to sectarian schools violated the Establishment Clause. The Court further noted that because it no longer presumed that state employees working in a sectarian environment would be at risk of inculcating religion, believing instead that "properly instructed public employees [will not] fail to discharge their duties faithfully,"[101] a state would not be required to engage in pervasive monitoring of publicly funded teachers to assure that Establishment Clause guarantees were being observed. Given these changes in the jurisprudence, the Court could no longer say that the program at issue violated Establishment Clause guarantees, even though that very program had been held unconstitutional in *Aguilar*.

By modifying when state funds might be presumed to be at risk of being used to promote sectarian objectives and modifying how the entanglement prong of *Lemon* would be analyzed, the *Agostini* Court created a much more forgiving Establishment Clause. That said, however, members of the *Agostini* Court did not cast doubt on the impermissibility of the state promoting sectarian education. Regrettably, members of the Court did just that in *Mitchell v. Helms*.[102]

Further Assaults on the Jurisprudence

In *Mitchell*, the Court examined a federal program channeling monies to public and private elementary and secondary schools to help provide services, materials, and equipment that were secular, neutral, and nonideological. The plurality interpreted *Agostini* to stand for the proposition that the Establishment Clause prohibits the state from extending aid to sectarian schools only if the religious indoctrination that occurs could reasonably be attributed to that state. To distinguish between

---

99   *Id.*
100   *Id.* at 232.
101   *Id.* at 234.
102   530 U.S. 793 (2000).

indoctrination that might reasonably be attributed to a state and indoctrination that could not, the plurality suggested that neutrality was the key consideration, claiming that the Court had consistently upheld aid that was offered to a broad range of people without regard to religion. The *Mitchell* plurality reasoned that "[i]f the religious, irreligious, and areligious are all alike eligible for governmental aid, no one would conclude that any indoctrination that any particular recipient conducts has been done at the behest of the government."[103] This reasoning suggests that a state could offer to pay the costs of textbooks in public and private schools, without regard to content, since no one would conclude that the sectarian texts chosen by the authorities in the sectarian schools were selected at the behest of the government.

The *Mitchell* plurality's Establishment Clause interpretation is incredibly permissive, suggesting that as long as (1) the government is providing something that itself is secular, such as money, rather than something that has sectarian content, such as a religious book, and (2) eligibility for the state aid violates no constitutional guarantees, use of that aid to promote sectarian objectives will not involve government indoctrination and thus will not be of constitutional concern. Lest the implications of this position be missed, the plurality made clear that the use of state aid to promote sectarian objectives could not be equated with religious indoctrination by the state.

According to the *Mitchell* plurality, the relevant Establishment Clause question is not about whether state funds are being used to promote sectarian objectives, but only about whether the aid itself has sectarian content. Needless to say, this is a huge change from what even *Agostini* would allow. Justice O'Connor noted in her concurrence in the judgment that the plurality's "approval of actual diversion of government aid to religious indoctrination is in tension with ... [the Court's] precedents,"[104] whereas Justice Souter put the matter more forcefully in his dissent—"The plurality position breaks fundamentally with Establishment Clause principle, and with the methodology painstakingly worked out in support of it."[105]

Even where state aid would qualify as neutral according to the *Mitchell* plurality and, for example, went directly to both secular and sectarian institutions, Justice O'Connor suggested that the religious indoctrination resulting from the aid might nonetheless be attributed to the government. She wrote, "Because the religious indoctrination is supported by government assistance, the reasonable observer would naturally perceive the aid program as government support for the advancement of religion."[106] She contrasted this with what an observer would think if the government monies were going to the institution as a result of the private choice of the individual, suggesting that no reasonable observer would infer that a

---

103   *Id.* at 809.
104   *Id.* at 837–8 (O'Connor, J., concurring).
105   *Id.* at 869 (Souter, J., dissenting).
106   *Id.* at 843 (O'Connor, J., concurring).

state was endorsing a religious practice if the state aid went to a sectarian school as a result of independent decisions by private individuals.

Several points might be made about the exchange between the *Mitchell* plurality and concurrence. First, the *Mitchell* plurality suggested that no reasonable person would infer state endorsement of religion under the facts of the case, notwithstanding that two members of the Court inferred endorsement under those very facts. Either at least two members of the Court are not reasonable or the proposed standard is simply unworkable. Add to this that the plurality's position "would break with the law" and "would be the end of the principle of no aid to the schools' religious mission,"[107] and it should be clear that the test proposed by the *Mitchell* plurality cannot be thought to capture the previous Establishment Clause jurisprudence with respect to state aid to sectarian primary and secondary schools.

Second, Justice O'Connor is no longer on the Court. It is simply unclear whether Justice Alito will agree with the plurality about what no reasonable person would think, views to the contrary expressed by members of that very Court notwithstanding.

Third, the facts of *Mitchell* can be read in very different ways. Both the plurality and the dissent believed that there had been a significant diversion of funds to promote sectarian education, while the concurrence believed the diversion de minimis. In future cases, it is quite likely that at least some on the Court will cite *Mitchell* as upholding direct state aid to sectarian schools that a majority on the Court had recognized was being used to promote sectarian education, although it is of course unclear whether this account of *Mitchell* will be offered in a majority, concurring, or dissenting opinion.

Viteritti asserts that the *Mitchell* plurality attempted to introduce "neutrality as the primary standard for reviewing aid."[108] But that is a mischaracterization both of that the *Mitchell* plurality was doing and the extent to which the proffered position broke with the past jurisprudence. That said, however, the decision is now part of the jurisprudence, and the way it may be characterized or used in the subsequent case law is frightening to contemplate.

When is Sectarian Support Reasonably Attributed to the State?

The *Mitchell* plurality and concurrence disagreed about whether state funding given directly to sectarian schools that supported religious teaching could reasonably be described as state support of religion. The existence of this disagreement did not convince these Court members that the standard itself was not suitable in this context. Nor did it convince them that their own intuitions about what reasonable people might say needed some fine-tuning. Instead, the Court in *Zelman v.*

---

107   See *id.* at 911 (Souter, J., dissenting).
108   Viteritti, *supra* note 29, at 138.

Simmons-Harris[109] adopted the position articulated by the *Mitchell* plurality and concurrence that state aid channeled through private individuals that was used to promote sectarian objectives could not reasonably be attributed to the state.

Regrettably, the Court again used the reasonable person standard to uphold a program that at least one (unreasonable?) member of the Court understood to involve government support of religion. In *Zelman*, the Court considered an Establishment Clause challenge to the Ohio voucher program that offered financial assistance to parents of children in the Cleveland public schools. Most of the children participating in the program went to religiously affiliated schools. The Court upheld the program, distinguishing between, on the one hand, direct aid to religious schools and, on the other, programs of true private choice, where the government funds reach private schools as a result of independent choices by individuals.

One of the issues dividing the Court was whether in fact the Ohio program provided true private choices. Justice O'Connor was confident that a true choice was offered, because the nonreligious schools were adequate, whereas Justice Souter suggested that the fact that "almost two out of three families using vouchers to send their children to religious schools did not embrace the religion of those schools"[110] indicated that there was a lack of true choice.

Reasonable people might disagree about whether the Cleveland program gave parents enough choices so that it could not be struck down on that account. Given the jurisprudence since *Everson*, however, it is at the very least surprising that the constitutionality of the program would turn on whether the choices presented were adequate. As Justice Stephen Breyer pointed out in his dissent, at issue was the financing of "a core function of the church: the teaching of religious truths to young children."[111] Even Justice O'Connor noted that this case was unlike prior cases involving indirect financing of sectarian schools "because a significant portion of the funds appropriated for the voucher program reach religious schools without restrictions on the use of these funds."[112] The *Zelman* Court had moved very far from the jurisprudence of *Everson*, *Allen*, and *Nyquist*, which had suggested that it was permissible for a state to give aid to parents whose children were attending private schools only if the aid would promote secular rather than sectarian objectives. Regardless of whether one accepts Justice Souter's assessment that *Zelman* represents all that has gone wrong in the development of Establishment Clause jurisprudence, since it is not only incompatible with *Everson*, but betrays "every objective underlying the prohibition of religious establishment,"[113] there is some difficulty in understanding how *Zelman* can be thought to be part of the same jurisprudence that includes *Allen* and *Nyquist*.

---

109   536 U.S. 639 (2002).

110   *Id.* at 704 (Souter, J., dissenting).

111   *Id.* at 726 (Breyer, J., dissenting).

112   *Id.* at 663 (O'Connor, J., concurring).

113   *Id.* at 711 (Souter, J., dissenting).

Viteritti suggests that *Zelman* is defensible, because a "bad education would do more harm to children than religion could."[114] But this simply cannot be the relevant test as a matter of constitutional theory or common sense. If the doctrine of true private choice is to do any work, one cannot boil the question down to whether a parent would prefer her child to be exposed to religious doctrine offensive to her beliefs or to receive an education that is deficient in a number of other respects.

Ravitch describes the *Zelman* Court's position in the following way:

> If a program is neutral on its face—it does not specify religious entities as beneficiaries—and there is some government or nonreligious private entity that the recipients could conceivably choose to go to for the service, the test is met because the program is neutral on its face and provides "true private choice," even if virtually all funding going to private organizations goes to religious organizations.[115]

If this is the Court's current position, then Ravitch is correct to suggest that "the Court's new test [is] an exercise in almost pure formalism."[116] If instead the Court is offering a more nuanced and plausible test, then everyone would be helped were the Court to spell out the kinds of limitations on public funding of parochial education that are currently in place.

Reasonable people may disagree about whether the parents in *Zelman* had a true private choice. Further, reasonable people may disagree about whether the use of state funds to promote religious indoctrination in schools is ever constitutionally permissible. But it is much more difficult to see how one can plausibly maintain that *Zelman* is consistent with modern Establishment Clause jurisprudence, and simply pointing out that parents preferred that their children receive religious teaching contrary to their faith to the conditions to which the children would have been subjected in other schools simply does not further the constitutional analysis. The currently articulated jurisprudence is simply unfathomable, especially if it is supposed to be following rather than replacing the prevailing jurisprudence of the past half-century.

Conclusion

While *Everson* is sometimes characterized as being stridently separationist, that neither captures the majority opinion nor even the dissent. Rather, the *Everson* Court was trying to strike a balance so that the state would neither be favoring religion nor antagonistic towards it. The *Allen* Court likely modified the *Everson* standard from whether the aid at issue promoted health and safety rather than

---

114 Viteritti, *supra* note 29, at 139.
115 Ravitch, *supra* note 26, at 25.
116 *Id.*

education to whether the aid promoted secular rather than sectarian education. For the next few decades, the Court would uphold or strike programs based at least in part upon whether there seemed to be too great of a risk of promoting sectarian education. During this period, the Court articulated special concerns about the dangers posed by direct aid to sectarian schools.

In the 1980s, the Court reversed course. That, in itself, is unremarkable. What is more remarkable is that the Court consistently seemed to misrepresent past opinions, for example, suggesting in *Mueller* that channeling monies through individuals would immunize state funding rather than simply remove a source of additional constitutional concern. What is still more remarkable is that the *Agostini* Court implied that the *Zobrest* majority had knowingly created a sea-change in the jurisprudence while expressly claiming to be following it.

The pattern of misrepresentation continued when, for example, the Court claimed that its jurisprudence has long held that benefits conferred without reference to religion are not readily subject to Establishment Clause challenge when, until fairly recently, that was true only where the conferred benefits were secular. The requirement that the benefits be secular was not only that the aid itself be secular but also that state funds could only be used to purchase products or services that were themselves secular. Even *Zobrest* stands for this proposition if the sign language interpreter is likened to a (secular) hearing aid.

Mitchell and *Zelman* offer a radically different way to understand Establishment Clause guarantees. Reasonable people might disagree about whether that very forgiving version of the Establishment Clause better captures what the Clause should do. Yet, it is difficult to believe that members of the Court upholding the programs in those decisions took the past jurisprudence very seriously, even when claiming to do so.

Figuring out the appropriate test to determine whether Establishment Clause guarantees have been violated is a daunting task even for those who are either following the existing jurisprudence or, when necessary, overruling it. However, the task is simply impossible when members of the Court consistently misrepresent what the Court has already done, whether intentionally or inadvertently. While the Court's having severely weakened the Establishment Clause's protections will be welcome to some, the Court's having done so in a way that undermines the Court's honesty, credibility, and integrity should be welcome to no one. Regrettably, the same pattern of retroactive reformulation of the past jurisprudence is present in other areas involving the Establishment Clause and the schools.

Chapter 2
Religion in Public Schools

In cases ranging from challenges to programs providing on-site religious education during school hours to challenges of school refusals to permit after-school lectures from a religious perspective, the Court has had several opportunities to clarify the respects in which religious education may be associated with public schools without violating constitutional guarantees. The Court's analysis of the implicated issues has been remarkably inconsistent, both in tone and in substance. Indeed, the reasoning most recently embraced by the Court not only invalidates much of what had seemed foundational just a short time ago, but sets the stage for a repudiation of one of the central tenets of the jurisprudence, namely, that certain kinds of religious activities have no place in the public schools while classes are in session.

While establishing that federal constitutional guarantees require some separation of church and state, *Everson* nonetheless permits states to subsidize transportation to and from religious schools. A separate issue involves the degree to which religion and the state must be separate in the public school arena. Over the past several decades, the Court has attempted to lay out the relevant jurisprudence, sometimes interpreting the Clause to require strict separation between church and state, at other times to accord states great discretion with respect to the kinds of assistance they afford to religious instruction, and at still other times to impose an affirmative obligation on states to permit religious views to be expressed within the public schools. In short, the current jurisprudence in this area is simply incoherent.

The Release-Time Cases

Shortly after *Everson* was decided,[1] the Court heard a case challenging the constitutionality of a program permitting on-site religious instruction at a public school. At issue in *McCollum v. Board of Education*[2] was a program of release time during which students would receive religious instruction by privately paid religious teachers in classrooms in public school buildings. Attendance would be taken at these classes, and the secular teachers would receive the attendance reports. Students not wishing to attend these religious classes would leave their classrooms to go to another room within the same building to further their secular studies.

---

1   For a discussion of *Everson*, see Chapter 1, third section.
2   333 U.S. 203 (1948).

After noting that students were required by law to go to school and that they would be released from that duty contingent upon their attending the religious classes, the *McCollum* Court struck down the program as a violation of constitutional guarantees. Because the program used a tax-supported public school system to help religious groups disseminate their beliefs, the Court held that the program was barred by *Everson*. Two reasons were offered: (1) public buildings were being used to disseminate religious doctrine, and (2) the state was helping to provide pupils for religious classes through the use of compulsory school attendance policy.[3]

Yet, the fact that the school buildings were tax-supported was not as important as the Court had implied. The buses used to transport the students in *Everson* were also tax-supported, and that did not suffice to make the New Jersey program unconstitutional. Further, not only were tax-supported buses being used, but the state was reimbursing the cost of the fares, making the state even more directly involved in helping students to receive religious instruction. Thus, claims to the contrary notwithstanding, it was not obvious after *Everson* that the program at issue in *McCollum* was unconstitutional just because taxes helped pay for the building in which the instruction took place.

Even the fact that the Illinois compulsory school law was viewed as aiding religious instruction in *McCollum* was not as important as the Court implied. Many states had compulsory schooling laws that required parents to send their children to approved public or private schools. For example, New Jersey required that students attend approved schools, which included public and parochial schools. Yet, this law aided religious instruction in that the law provided an incentive to attend approved parochial schools. Parochial schools were given further aid when the Court upheld that state's decision to authorize the reimbursement of the costs of transporting the children to those approved institutions providing religious education. Nonetheless, New Jersey's having provided invaluable aids in helping children to receive religious instruction did not thereby make its transportation funding unconstitutional.

While there are ways to analogize the New Jersey and Illinois programs for constitutional purposes so that the Court's upholding the travel expense reimbursement in *Everson* would suggest that the Illinois program also passed muster, almost all members of the Court believed that the Establishment Clause precluded Illinois from permitting religious teaching in public school buildings. One way to understand the difference between *Everson* and *McCollum* is in the kind of aid afforded by the state—*Everson* upheld the constitutionality of the state's promoting health and safety, while *McCollum* struck down the state's promoting religious instruction. Yet, interpreting the decisions as representing this categorical distinction is misleading, if not simply wrong. In his *McCollum* concurrence, Justice Felix Frankfurter noted:

---

3   *Id.* at 212.

Different forms which "released time" has taken during more than thirty years of growth include programs which, like that before us, could not withstand the test of the Constitution; others may be found unexceptionable. We do not now attempt to weigh in the Constitutional scale every separate detail or various combination of factors which may establish a valid "released time" program. We find that the basic Constitutional principle of absolute separation was violated when the State of Illinois, speaking through its Supreme Court, sustained the school authorities of Champaign in sponsoring and effectively furthering religious beliefs by its educational arrangement.[4]

Thus, it was not at all clear that the Court was willing to paint the different program with a broad brush, and then uphold or strike down the programs at issue in light of whether the program was designated as "instructional" rather than as "promoting health or safety." Justice Frankfurter implied that the constitutionality of release-time programs depended upon unspecified factors or combinations of factors. While he did not thereby communicate which factors were important for constitutional purposes, he nonetheless suggested that some release-time programs might or did pass muster. Yet, if all of the release-time programs involved religious instruction and some of them (based on the unspecified factors) did not violate constitutional guarantees, then it seems clear that the fact that a release program involved religious instruction rather than the promotion of health or safety did not alone suffice to establish the program's unconstitutionality.

That the Court did not believe all release-time programs unconstitutional was made clear in *Zorach v. Clauson*, where the Court considered a New York City program releasing students during the school day so that they could go off-campus to receive religious instruction or engage in "devotional exercises."[5] Students who did not attend these religious classes would remain in school. The Court contrasted the New York program with the Illinois program at issue in *McCollum*, noting that the latter had permitted religious teachers to use the public classrooms, whereas the former involved "neither religious instruction in public school classrooms nor the expenditure of public funds."[6]

Of course, it is not as if public funds were being used in *McCollum* to pay the religious instructors. Rather, the public funds expended were the de minimis funds involved in permitting tax-supported public property to be used for religious instruction. While there was no religious instruction on public school grounds in *Zorach*, *McCollum* had been written in such a way as to suggest that this was not an important distinction. For example, the *McCollum* Court had suggested that the reporting of attendance at the religious classes to the secular teachers integrated the public and religious education in a way that was prohibited by the Establishment

---

4   *Id.* at 231 (Frankfurter, J., concurring).
5   343 U.S. 306, 308 (1952).
6   *Id.* at 308–9.

Clause. But the same kind of attendance reporting and, thus, integration was present in *Zorach*, which would make *Zorach* constitutionally vulnerable as well.

The *Zorach* Court rejected that students were coerced into taking the religion classes, reasoning that the school authorities "do no more than release students whose parents so request."[7] Yet, no one had been forced to take the religion classes in *McCollum*. While the students who had chosen not to participate in the Illinois religious instruction program felt alienated and humiliated, that could hardly have been attributed to the state.

Justice Frankfurter suggested in *McCollum* that it was mistaken to analyze the state's role in the release-time program solely in terms of whether the state had coerced attendance. Before the initiation of the program at issue, after-school religious classes had been conducted during the week. However, the results had been disappointing, because children had resisted attending religious instruction classes during playtime. Church leaders had decided that religious schooling during the week would only be successful if it could take place during regular school hours. But making the religious instruction available during regular school hours made the public school personnel more actively involved in the success of the program, although not in the sense that teachers were actively attempting to persuade or force students to receive the religious instruction. Rather, the school personnel were involved in the sense that but for the willingness of the schools to give students the constrained choice between remaining in school to pursue secular studies or, instead, having the opportunity to receive religious instruction during school hours so that valued after-school playtime would not be diminished, the religious instruction program would have foundered.

Yet, *Zorach* also involved releasing students during regular school hours to receive religious instruction. As Justice Frankfurter noted in his *Zorach* dissent, there is a difference between closing the schools as a general matter, thereby freeing the children to attend religious schools or other activities, and in effect closing the school for some children but keeping it in session for others.

When analyzing whether the state is violating Establishment Clause guarantees by participating in a release-time program, one should consider how individuals who do not receive the religious instruction will be spending their time. Some commentators suggest that the students who did not participate in the religious programming might have found the secular alternative rather uninteresting, which would have incentivized attendance at the religious classes. Justice Frankfurter implied that there was a kind of coercion involved in the program, suggesting that "formalized religious instruction is substituted for other school activity which those who do not participate in the released-time program are compelled to attend."[8] He noted that if the school's "doors are closed, they are closed upon those students who do not attend the religious instruction, in order to keep them within

---

7   *Id.* at 311.

8   *Id.* at 321 (Frankfurter, J., dissenting).

the school."[9] It was this element of coercing or, to put it another way, incentivizing the religious instruction that worried Justice Black, who viewed the relevant issue as "whether New York can use its compulsory education laws to help religious sects get attendants presumably too unenthusiastic to go unless moved to do so by the pressure of this state machinery."[10] He argued that "New York is manipulating its compulsory education laws to help religious sects get pupils. This is not separation but combination of Church and State."[11]

The *Zorach* Court disputed Justice Black's analysis, explaining that the Constitution requires complete and absolute separation between church and state *insofar as an establishment of religion is at issue.*[12] However, as long as an establishment of religion is not at issue, the First Amendment does not require separation of church and state in every respect. The Court reasoned that if the release program were unconstitutional, a whole host of other practices would also be unconstitutional.

> Churches could not be required to pay even property taxes. Municipalities would not be permitted to render police or fire protection to religious groups. Policemen who helped parishioners into their places of worship would violate the Constitution. Prayers in our legislative halls; the appeals to the Almighty in the messages of the Chief Executive; the proclamations making Thanksgiving Day a holiday; "so help me God" in our courtroom oaths-these and all other references to the Almighty that run through our laws, our public rituals, our ceremonies would be flouting the First Amendment. A fastidious atheist or agnostic could even object to the supplication with which the Court opens each session: "God save the United States and this Honorable Court."[13]

Yet, the Court's recounting this parade of horribles undercuts its own analysis in two different respects. First, it is not at all clear that it would be so terrible if indeed some of the practices discussed by the Court were discontinued. For example, it is not so clear that great costs would be incurred were the Court to stop opening each session with "God save the United States and this Honorable Court," although it might be argued that the Court's opening each session that way does not impose a great harm on anyone.

Second, the Court had just been suggesting that the jurisprudence at issue carefully considers aspects of each case. If that is true, however, the guiding principles might well allow the Court to make distinctions among practices, permitting some and prohibiting others. It would thus not be at all clear that the Court's holding that the New York system violated constitutional guarantees

---

9 *Id.* (Frankfurter, J., dissenting).
10 *Id.* at 318 (Black, J., dissenting).
11 *Id.* (Black, J., dissenting).
12 *Id.* at 312.
13 *Id.* at 312–13.

would mean that other practices, for example, permitting a student in accord with her parents' wishes to attend a religious service rather than school on a particular day, would also be constitutionally objectionable.

In his dissent, Justice Black noted some of the ways in which the systems at issue in *Zorach* and *McCollum* were similar. For example, in *McCollum*, the state used its power to get the children into the schools and, further, would only release from school those who attended the religious classes. The same might have been said of the program at issue in *Zorach*. Indeed, Justice Black suggested that the sole difference between the programs upheld in *Zorach* and struck down in *McCollum* was where the program was taking place.[14] Greenawalt reaches a similar conclusion.[15]

Justice Jackson seemed particularly incensed by the suggestion that anyone who would strike the New York plan was hostile to religion, because his children attended privately supported religious schools.[16] Regrettably, the charge that those who would strike a religious program must be hostile to religion has been made repeatedly since then.

Substantively, it is not clear how to read *Zorach*. Perhaps, as Justice Jackson suggests, the *Zorach* Court is emphasizing the importance of the location of the religious teaching, although that factor will become less important in the subsequent case law. Perhaps *Zorach* is suggesting that the Illinois program at issue in *McCollum* was struck down because it included several factors: the state used its coercive power to get the students in the schools and to keep them there unless they opted to participate in the religious program, the programs were integrated in that the religious school teachers were reporting attendance to the secular teachers, the students who did not attend the religious classes were required to remain in school and perform secular work, the program occurred while public school was in session, and the program was on-site. Because the teaching took place off site in the New York program at issue in *Zorach*, not all of the *McCollum* factors were present in *Zorach* and thus the New York and Illinois programs were distinguishable.

Regrettably, the *Zorach* Court did not specify why the New York but not the Illinois program passed constitutional muster. The Court did explain that "Government may not finance religious groups nor undertake religious instruction nor blend secular and sectarian education nor use secular institutions to force one or some religion on any person."[17] However, these points were not particularly helpful, because neither Illinois nor New York financed religious groups or blended secular and sectarian education or used secular institutions to impose religion on anyone. So, too, while the Court suggested that striking down the New York

---

14 *Id.* at 316 (Black, J., dissenting).

15 *See* Kent Greenawalt, *Does God Belong in Public Schools?* 19 (2005) (suggesting that the different between the two programs is that one was conducted off site).

16 *Zorach*, 343 U.S. at 324 (Jackson, J., dissenting).

17 *Id.* at 314.

program would mean that the Constitution was hostile to religion, the Court failed to explain why striking down the New York program would evidence hostility to religion whereas striking down the Illinois program did not manifest hostility to religion but, instead, simply the recognition that "both religion and government can best work to achieve their lofty aim if each is left free from the other within its respective sphere."[18]

One of the many confusing aspects of the *Everson–McCollum–Zorach* line of cases is how or whether they can be reconciled or, perhaps, explained. A factor that is tempting to consider is how the composition of the Court had changed during the period. The Justices deciding *Everson* and *McCollum* were Justices Joseph Vinson, Black, Stanley Reed, Frankfurter, Douglas, Frank Murphy, Jackson, Rutledge, and Harold Burton. There were two changes on the Court by the time that *Zorach* was decided—Justice Sherman Minton replaced Justice Rutledge and Justice Tom Clark replaced Justice Murphy.

Yet, the changes on the Court will not alone explain the different results in *McCollum* and *Zorach*, since there was only one dissent in *McCollum*. Three Justices in the majority in *McCollum* were also in the majority in *Zorach*—Justice Douglas (who wrote the opinion), Chief Justice Vinson, and Justice Burton.

Some suggest that *Zorach* is best understood as responding to the public outcry produced by *McCollum*, implying that the Court simply modified its position to quell the uprising in public opinion. Or, perhaps the Court was taking into account that many were not following *McCollum*—Viteritti notes that many communities simply ignored the decision.[19] Still other commentators focus in particular on the opinion written by Justice Douglas, suggesting that Douglas was motivated by the political ambition to run for president, although there is reason to reject that interpretation. Justice Douglas expressly claimed that he did not see *McCollum* and *Zorach* as incompatible:

> Three of us—The Chief Justice, Mr. Justice Douglas and Mr. Justice Burton—who join this opinion agreed that the "released time" program involved in the *McCollum* case was unconstitutional. It was our view at the time that the present type of "released time" program was not prejudged by the *McCollum* case, a conclusion emphasized by the reservation of the question in the separate opinion by Mr. Justice Frankfurter in which Mr. Justice Burton joined.[20]

There is some irony in Justice Douglas's citing Justice Frankfurter's *McCollum* concurrence, given Frankfurter's dissent in *Zorach*. However, Justice Frankfurter's failure to specify the conditions that would make a release-time program constitutionally permissible may have been the product of a tactical decision on his part. Precisely because those signing onto his concurrence might

---

18 *McCollum*, 333 U.S. at 212.

19 Joseph P. Viteritti, *The Last Freedom: Religion from the Public School to the Public Square* 100 (2007).

20 *Zorach*, 343 U.S. at 315 n.8.

not have been in agreement about which factors were significant for constitutional purposes, he might have refused to specify what those factors were in order to get the others to sign onto his opinion. Justice Reed in his *McCollum* dissent explicitly mentioned the New York program, suggesting that while he believed that program constitutional the *McCollum* opinion implied that it was not.

Both Chief Justice Vinson and Justice Douglas were part of the majority opinion in *Everson*, so it might be tempting to think that their votes to uphold the program at issue in *Zorach* were easier to predict than Justice Burton's, who was in the dissent in *Everson*. However, some suggest that Justice Burton believed all along that *McCollum* and *Zorach* were compatible.

A separate question is why. While it is true that the teaching occurred in the school in *McCollum* and off site in *Zorach*, it is not clear why that was constitutionally significant. The extra cost to the state in *McCollum* cannot plausibly account for the difference. Perhaps it was the symbolism of having such classes held in a public school, although the Court would not find that rationale particularly compelling in subsequent cases.

Whether *Zorach*, *Everson* and *McCollum* are reconcilable substantively is controversial. What is uncontroversial is that *Zorach* sets a much different tone than do *Everson* and *McCollum*. Both the *Everson* and *McCollum* Courts discussed the impregnable wall between church and state, while the *Zorach* Court wrote, "We are a religious people whose institutions presuppose a Supreme Being."[21] Lest the implications of its view be unclear, the *Zorach* Court suggested that when the "state encourages religious instruction or cooperates with religious authorities by adjusting the schedule of public events to sectarian needs, it follows the best of our traditions."[22] Indeed, the Court explained that prohibiting the program at issue "would be to find in the Constitution a requirement that the government show a callous indifference to religious groups," which would amount to "preferring those who believe in no religion over those who do believe."[23] Thus, whether or not the Court's substantive position had changed, the tone in *Zorach* signaled that the Court might be adopting a much different approach to the accommodation of religion within the public school setting. As Greenawalt points out, *Zorach's* accommodationist reading "gave temporary encouragement to those who favored a more permissive understanding of the Establishment Clause."[24]

Prayer in School

Zorach and *McCollum* involved religious programs taught by religious school teachers whether on or off site. A different but related issue involved prayer

---

21 *Id.* at 313.
22 *Id.* at 313–14.
23 *Id.* at 314.
24 Greenawalt, *supra* note 15, at 40.

in schools. At issue in *Engel v. Vitale* was the required daily recitation in New York public schools of a nondenominational prayer composed by the Board of Regents.[25] The Court struck down the practice, noting that "the constitutional prohibition against laws respecting an establishment of religion must at least mean that in this country it is no part of the business of government to compose official prayers for any group of the American people to recite as a part of a religious program carried on by government."[26] Yet, the Constitution prohibiting states from composing official prayers to be recited at state functions does not impose much of a limitation on the states, and the important issue for purposes of understanding the coercion test involves determining what else *Engel* and other cases have to say about the constraints imposed by the Establishment Clause.

Suppose that the state had not composed the prayer but, instead, had merely encouraged the daily recitation of a nondenominational prayer in the classroom. Even so, the *Engel* Court suggested that the state would have been overstepping the limitations imposed by the Establishment Clause, explaining that "government in this country, be it state or federal, is without power to prescribe by law any particular form of prayer which is to be used as an official prayer in carrying on any program of governmentally sponsored religious activity."[27] Thus, the state would not have been allowed to require the recitation of a prayer at a state-sponsored event, even had the prayer been composed by a private citizen rather than by the Regents, themselves.

The difficulty with the New York program was not that students were being forced to say the prayer or even to remain in the room while it was said, since they had the option of absenting themselves from the room during the recitation of the prayer. The *Engel* Court explained that the Establishment Clause "does not depend upon any showing of direct governmental compulsion and is violated by the enactment of laws which establish an official religion whether those laws operate directly to coerce nonobserving individuals or not."[28] Yet, merely because direct governmental compulsion need not be shown does not mean that Establishment Clause guarantees can be violated even absent a showing of any compulsion at all. Instead, the *Engel* Court may merely have meant that although it is necessary to show some sort of governmental compulsion, a showing of indirect compulsion will suffice.

The New York practice imposed some pressure on the students to participate: "When the power, prestige and financial support of government is placed behind a particular religious belief, the indirect coercive pressure upon religious minorities

---

25 For the text of the prayer, see 370 U.S. 421, 422 (1962) ("Almighty God, we acknowledge our dependence upon Thee, and we beg Thy blessings upon us, our parents, our teachers and our Country.").

26 *Id.* at 425

27 *Id.* at 430.

28 *Id.*

to conform to the prevailing officially approved religion is plain."[29] By requiring the recitation of a prayer, the state placed non-adherents in a difficult position—either they could leave and risk the potentially adverse consequences that might result from refusing to remain in the room while the prayer was recited, for example, ostracism by peers, or they could remain in the room and be forced to confront the fact that their religious beliefs did not coincide with those endorsed by the state. Yet, after noting that the New York program indirectly coerced students to accept prevailing religious views, the Court failed to explain whether that coercion was necessary or, instead, sufficient to show that constitutional guarantees had been violated.

The *Engel* Court's discussion of the purposes behind the Establishment Clause might be interpreted to support either of two competing positions: (1) the state cannot be shown to have violated Establishment Clause guarantees unless there is proof of at least indirect coercion, or (2) the state may be shown to have violated Establishment Clause guarantees even absent proof of either direct or indirect coercion. After suggesting that one of the goals of the Establishment Clause was to prevent the imposition of indirect pressure on non-adherents, the Court explained that the purposes behind the Establishment Clause go much further than that. But the Court did not make clear whether those further purposes were totally divorced from preventing religious coercion or, instead, could all be understood in terms of the negative effects associated with forcing individuals to subscribe to religious orthodoxy.

Consider the point that the Clause's "first and most immediate purpose rested on the belief that a union of government and religion tends to destroy government and to degrade religion," because "whenever government ... allie[s] itself with one particular form of religion, the inevitable result [is] that it incur[s] the hatred, disrespect and even contempt of those [holding] contrary beliefs."[30] It is simply unclear whether these feelings of contempt and disrespect arise from the mere fact that the state has endorsed particular religious views or, instead, from the state imposing pressure on its citizens to adopt those views. By the same token, the Founders' understanding that government-established religion and religious persecutions go hand in hand speaks to a recognition that the government endorsement of religion can lead to state pressure to adhere to religious orthodoxy. But if the result to be avoided is religious persecution and not government endorsement of particular religious views per se, then the Constitution's precluding both direct and indirect coercion would seem to do all of the necessary work to achieve the desired goal.

Nonetheless, the *Engel* Court implied that the Establishment Clause was designed to do more than prevent governmental coercion. When suggesting that government should neither write nor sanction official prayers, the Court was not solely focused on coercion. Rather, it was suggesting that the Constitution reserves

---

29 *Id.* at 431.
30 *Id.*

religious functions for the people or, perhaps, members of the clergy, and that the state is simply not to get involved in religion, much less coerce people to adopt or reject particular religious views.

It might seem that the danger posed by the short, nondenominational prayer at issue in *Engel* was so trivial as to pose no real danger. Yet, as Joan Delfattore suggests, "the Regents' Prayer was not, as its advocates suggested, dogma-free."[31] Further, the Court feared that permitting this incursion on religious liberty might permit much more serious incursions in the future. Still, it was unclear what kind of incursions the Court was envisioning—more coercive measures, for example, the imposition of sanctions on those who were unwilling to recite a nondenominational prayer, or more sectarian, albeit noncoercive practices, for example, state-sponsored prayers invoking the name of a particular religious figure.

After focusing on the coercive aspect of the practice at issue, Justice Douglas noted that a variety of other state practices imposed that same sort of indirect religious coercion:

> It is said that the element of coercion is inherent in the giving of this prayer. If that is true here, it is also true of the prayer with which this Court is convened, and of those that open the Congress. Few adults, let alone children, would leave our courtroom or the Senate or the House while those prayers are being given. Every such audience is in a sense a "captive" audience.[32]

When making this point, he was arguing that all of these practices offended constitutional guarantees. His point at least suggests that in many cases involving alleged violations of Establishment Clause guarantees, the requirement that there be proof of indirect coercion may not pose much of a bar. If indirect coercion is interpreted rather broadly and, for example, occurs whenever religious activities take place at state-sponsored events, the relevant question in many cases will not be whether there was indirect coercion but, instead, whether something in addition to coercion must be shown in order for the Court to find that Establishment Clause guarantees have been violated.

Given that the state itself had composed the prayer for which daily recitation in the public schools was mandated, there were several different bases upon which the *Engel* Court could rest the practice's unconstitutionality. That said, it should not be thought that the *Engel* decision was unanimous. In his dissenting opinion, Justice Potter Stewart not only suggested that permitting but not requiring students to pray did not constitute an establishment of religion, but also suggested that denying "the wish of these school children to join in reciting this prayer is to deny

---

31 Joan Delfattore, *The Fourth R: Conflicts over Religion in America's Public Schools* 70 (2004).

32 *Engel*, 370 U.S. at 441–2 (Douglas, J., concurring).

them the opportunity of sharing in the spiritual heritage of our Nation."[33] Justice Stewart thereby foreshadowed a different argument that would be offered with some frequency in the context of prayer in schools, namely, that some students fervently wish to recite such prayers and that by denying those students such an opportunity the state seemed to be denying them something that they valued rather highly.

The Court further developed its coercion analysis in *School District of Abington Township v. Schempp*,[34] in which the Court considered the constitutionality of a Pennsylvania law requiring the reading of Bible verses at the beginning of each school day. As was true in *Engel*, the law at issue in *Schempp* provided that children could be excused from the reading. As was also true in *Engel*, the Court struck down the law as a violation of religious guarantees. The *Schempp* Court reaffirmed that it was not necessary to make a showing of coercion under the Establishment Clause, noting that the "distinction between the two [Religion] clauses is apparent—a violation of the Free Exercise Clause is predicated on coercion while the Establishment Clause violation need not be so attended."[35]

It might seem that by unequivocally stating that coercion was not an element of Establishment Clause analysis, the *Schempp* Court made clear what the *Engel* Court had left uncertain. Yet, one might argue that implicit in the *Schempp* discussion of coercion was the term "direct." After all, pressure and coercion were discussed in *Schempp*, at least in that the Court mentioned that the father had not sought to have his children excused from these exercises because he had feared that his doing so would adversely affect his children's relationships with their teachers and with the other students. Thus, *Schempp* might be thought compatible with an interpretation of Establishment Clause jurisprudence suggesting that there must be at least indirect coercion in order for the relevant guarantees to be triggered. That said, however, such a reading would also imply that there is a very low threshold for finding that there is indirect coercion, because the only coercion mentioned in *Schempp* is the possibility that students or teachers might react negatively were the children to absent themselves from the classroom during the daily prayer recitation.

The *Schempp* Court suggested that there is an important difference for constitutional purposes between talking about God and engaging in religious worship or indoctrination.

> Nothing we have said here indicates that such study of the Bible or of religion, when presented objectively as part of a secular program of education, may not be effected consistently with the First Amendment. But the exercises here do not fall into those categories. They are religious exercises, required by the States in

---

33 *Id.* at 445 (Stewart, J., dissenting).
34 374 U.S. 203 (1963).
35 *Id.* at 223.

violation of the command of the First Amendment that the Government maintain strict neutrality, neither aiding nor opposing religion.[36]

One infers from *Schempp* that Establishment Clause guarantees would not have been violated by a school program in which Comparative Religion was the first class of the day. Yet, if starting the school day each day with a Bible reading and prayer is prohibited by the Establishment Clause but starting the day with Comparative Religion is not, then there must be something special about prayer or religious worship that must be taken into account in First Amendment analyses. Regrettably, it appears that some members of the current Court do not appreciate the distinction recognized by the *Schempp* Court.

Any discussion of the coerciveness of prayer in the classroom setting should include *Wallace v. Jaffree*,[37] which involved an Alabama minute-of-silence-or-voluntary-prayer statute. The Court held the statute unconstitutional, because it was enacted to promote religion and, indeed, had no secular purpose. Because the state already had a statute permitting meditation, the Court viewed the new statute, which permitted meditation or prayer, as an attempt to return prayer to the public schools.

Wallace is of interest, at least in part, because several members of the Court stated or implied that the constitutional difficulty was not prayer in school per se, but some of the other features of the case. For example, the *Wallace* Court distinguished what was before it from the state merely protecting the right of each student to engage in voluntary prayer during a moment of silence. The Court did not explore why a student praying during the moment of silence was permissible, although in her concurrence in the judgment Justice O'Connor offered several ways to distinguish between state-sponsored prayer and the state instituting a moment of silence during which students might pray or reflect.

She began her analysis by explaining how both *Engel* and *Schempp* might be understood in terms of indirect coercion by the state. In both of those cases, "a student who did not share the religious beliefs expressed in the course of the exercise was left with the choice of participating, thereby compromising the non-adherent's beliefs, or withdrawing, thereby calling attention to his or her nonconformity."[38] Justice O'Connor contrasted the constitutionally problematic scenarios presented in *Engel* and *Schempp* with a scenario where the state has merely set aside a moment of silence during the day. She noted that a moment of silence is not intrinsically religious, since that time can be used for nonreligious reflection or meditation. Further, an individual taking part in a moment of silence need not thereby compromise her beliefs, because "a student who objects to prayer is left to his or her own thoughts, and is not compelled to listen to the prayers or

---

36 *Id.* at 225.
37 472 U.S. 38 (1985).
38 *Id.* at 72 (O'Connor, J., concurring in the judgment).

thoughts of others."[39] For these kinds of reasons among others, Justice O'Connor believed that state provision of an opportunity for prayer during a moment of silence was constitutionally distinguishable from state implementation of a policy whereby prayers are periodically offered.

Religious Students Groups Using School Facilities

While *Wallace* focused on prayer during the school day, a separate analysis is required for student groups wishing to use school facilities after school for prayer among other activities. In *Board of Education of Westside Community Schools v. Mergens*,[40] the Court examined a Nebraska high school refusal to permit students to form a Christian club. At issue was whether federal law precluded the high school from denying recognition to this student group and, if so, whether that federal law violated Establishment Clause guarantees.

The *Mergens* plurality construed the statute as prohibiting the school from recognizing some non-curricular student clubs such as a chess club or stamp collecting club, and then refusing to recognize other clubs based on the content of that group's speech. After finding that the school did recognize some non-curricular clubs, the plurality found that the school's refusal to grant the student club official recognition violated the federal act.

The next question was whether the Act violated Establishment Clause guarantees. The *Mergens* plurality interpreted the principal argument against permitting recognition of the student group to be that:

> [B]ecause the student religious meetings are held under school aegis, and because the State's compulsory attendance laws bring the students together (and thereby provide a ready-made audience for student evangelists), an objective observer in the position of a secondary school student will perceive official school support for such religious meetings.[41]

The plurality rejected that argument, noting that the state is permitted to accord incidental benefits to religious groups and suggesting that a state refusing to permit religious groups to use facilities open to others would demonstrate hostility rather than neutrality toward religion. Students would be unlikely to mistake the school recognizing the student group with the school endorsing that group and, in any event, steps could be taken to make sure that students did not mistakenly believe that the religious group had received the school's endorsement.

---

39 *Id.* (O'Connor, J., concurring in the judgment).
40 496 U.S. 226 (1990).
41 *Id.* at 249.

Yet, the plurality's assurances to the contrary notwithstanding, even adults might be tempted to interpret the school's actions somewhat differently than the plurality would have one believe. Justice Anthony Kennedy wrote:

> I should think it inevitable that a public high school "endorses" a religious club, in a commonsense use of the term, if the club happens to be one of many activities that the school permits students to choose in order to further the development of their intellect and character in an extracurricular setting.[42]

He believed that the program did not violate constitutional guarantees, however, because no coercion had been established, that is, no students had been coerced into joining such a club.

In his concurrence in the judgment, Justice Marshall argued that schools permitting religious clubs on campus had the affirmative duty to disassociate themselves so that their endorsement of the club would not be inferred. The plurality dismissed this objection by noting that the school could do more to assure that students would not infer endorsement. Basically, the plurality understood Justice Marshall's point but did not want to permit a school to refuse to recognize a religious club because of its own failure to disassociate itself from that club. However, the plurality could have made clear that schools had to take affirmative steps to prevent even mistaken endorsement. By not doing so, the plurality implied that it was not taking the problem of perceived endorsement very seriously, an attitude that would be reinforced in subsequent cases.

Justice Marshall also objected that the *Mergens* plurality was not appreciating the role that the state was playing when requiring students to attend school and then permitting these clubs to meet on school grounds:

> When the government, through mandatory attendance laws, brings students together in a highly controlled environment every day for the better part of their waking hours and regulates virtually every aspect of their existence during that time, we should not be so quick to dismiss the problem of peer pressure as if the school environment had nothing to do with creating and fostering it. The State has structured an environment in which students holding mainstream views may be able to coerce adherents of minority religions to attend club meetings or to adhere to club beliefs. Thus, the State cannot disclaim its responsibility for those resulting pressures.[43]

When making this point, he was echoing concerns articulated in *McCollum* and, indeed, he cited *McCollum* for support of his position. After all, the religious activities in *McCollum* also were not run by school officials. However, *McCollum* differed from *Mergens* in that the only non-curricular activity was the religious

---

42 *Id.* at 261 (Kennedy, J., concurring in part and concurring in the judgment).
43 *Id.* at 269 (Marshall, J., concurring in the judgment).

studies class, whereas in *Mergens* there were numerous activities such as chess club, photography, and so on.

Ironically, the *Mergens* analysis suggested that *Zorach* was wrongly decided. Given that the release-time at issue in *Zorach* could only be used to attend classes in religious instruction, it would seem that New York was endorsing the religion classes, even though they were conducted off site, and thus that the state was violating Establishment Clause guarantees.

As suggested by Justice Jackson in his *Zorach* dissent, one of the few ways to reconcile *Zorach* and *McCollum* was to suggest that the location of the classes was important—they could not be conducted on site but could be conducted off site. But in *Mergens* the club meetings were occurring on site rather than off site. Thus, *Mergens* seems difficult to reconcile as a constitutional matter with the previous cases most directly on point. While neither *McCollum* nor *Zorach* established that *Mergens* was wrongly decided, both cases suggest that the *Mergens* plurality needed to do much more to justify its position as a constitutional matter.

The *Mergens* plurality briefly mentioned one of the purposes of the club—to engage in prayer—but then offered the same analysis that it would have offered had the club been formed so that it could discuss matters of interest from a religious perspective. Yet, much of the jurisprudence has distinguished prayer and inherently religious activities from other sorts of activities. If, for example, Justice Douglas is correct that the Establishment Clause is violated when "public funds, though small in amount, are being used to promote a religious exercise,"[44] then it does not matter whether the provision of those funds would be construed by an objective observer as an endorsement of religion. So, too, if Justice O'Connor is correct to distinguish between inherently religious activities and other activities that might be secular, then one would need some analysis of the different functions performed by the club. Thus, it might have been argued that while discussions from a religious perspective could not be precluded, paradigmatically religious activities like prayer were subject to different treatment. Thus, it is at best misleading for Viteritti to suggest that *Mergens* is simply about preventing discrimination against speech from a religious perspective,[45] where religious speech might on the one hand involve a descriptive claim about which practices a particular religion permits or prohibits and on the other a prayer to God.

The *Mergens* plurality gave short shrift to the claim that student peer pressure might have adverse effects on the high schoolers. "[T]he possibility of student peer pressure remains, but there is little if any risk of official state endorsement or coercion where no formal classroom activities are involved and no school officials actively participate."[46] Yet, it had been the student peer pressure that had motivated the challenges in *McCollum* and *Schempp*, and the Court had done nothing in those cases to undercut the seriousness of the difficulty thereby presented.

---

44 *Schempp*, 374 U.S. at 229 (Douglas, J., concurring).

45 See Viteritti, supra note 19, at 131–2.

46 *Mergens*, 496 U.S. at 251.

An important part of the *Mergens* analysis involved the view that permitting the club to meet on campus provided only incidental benefits to religion. Yet, these benefits could only be construed as incidental if one rejected much of the preceding jurisprudence. Nonetheless, this understanding of "incidental" would become further entrenched a few years later when the Court heard another case challenging a school's refusal to allow its facilities to be used for religious purposes.

In *Lamb's Chapel v. Center Moriches Union Free School District*,[47] the Court examined a New York law authorizing local school boards to adopt reasonable regulations for the use of school property for designated purposes while school was not in session. Religious purposes were not included among the permissible designated purposes.

At issue in particular was a request by an evangelical church to show a six-part film series containing lectures on family by James Dobson. The request was denied because it was church-related, notwithstanding that school property was permissibly used for social, civic and recreational purposes. Regrettably, there was no further discussion of what was meant by "church-related." For example, it could have involved a film in which viewers were called to prayer or, instead, might merely have been discussing family issues from a particular Christian perspective.

The Court of Appeals had held that the rule at issue was viewpoint neutral, because it was applied in the same way to any use of school property for a religious purpose. However, the *Lamb's Chapel* Court noted:

> That all religions and all uses for religious purposes are treated alike … does not answer the critical question whether it discriminates on t. basis of viewpoint to permit school property to be used for the presentation of all views about family issues and child rearing except those dealing with the subject matter from a religious standpoint.[48]

A few points might be made about the Court's analysis. First, there are a few different ways to understand "dealing with the subject matter from a religious standpoint." It might be thought to suggest that there is a uniform view among all religions about a particular matter, for example, family matters, although that would be false. There are widely divergent religious views about the role of women in the family, whether same-sex marriage should be recognized, et cetera. Yet, a different way to understand the point is that the religious standpoint does not stand for a particular substantive position; rather, such a standpoint is compatible with a whole range of views on particular matters. The religious viewpoint is distinctive in that it seeks to incorporate these varying substantive positions within a world view.

---

47 508 U.S. 384 (1993).

48 *Id.* at 393.

By precluding discussions from a religious viewpoint, the district was not precluding liberal or conservative discussions of family matters, since either kind of view might be presented from a nonreligious perspective. Nonetheless, the school district was excluding certain kinds of views—those seeking to locate positions on particular issues within a (religious) world view. Because of this type of exclusion, it might be argued that there was viewpoint discrimination in *Lamb's Chapel*, although the Court never made clear that this was the constitutional defect in the school policy.

The school district had worried that its permitting the use of school property for religious purposes would violate Establishment Clause guarantees. However, the Court noted, the "showing of this film series would not have been during school hours, would not have been sponsored by the school, and would have been open to the public, not just to church members."[49] Further, a wide variety of groups had repeatedly used the facilities. Under these circumstances, the Court reasoned, any benefits to a religious group would be "incidental."

The film series might be contrasted with worship services—the *Lamb's Chapel* Court noted that the church had also asked to use school facilities for Sunday School and for Sunday morning church services for a year. That request had been denied and the church had not challenged that denial in court. The Court did not intimate how it would have viewed such a challenge, instead merely noting that the validity of the denial was not before it. One thus could not tell whether the *Lamb's Chapel* Court was distinguishing the film series from the religious services or, instead, was suggesting that they were the same for constitutional purposes.

Part of the difficulty in analyzing *Lamb's Chapel* is that the Court merely suggested that the church had "conceded that its showing of the film series would be for religious purposes."[50] Yet, it would serve religious purposes to discuss a matter from a particular perspective just as it might also serve religious purposes to pray. Without further specification of which or what kind of religious purposes would be served, it is not even clear what the *Lamb's Chapel* Court was suggesting must be permitted.

The statute at issue did not permit use of the facilities for religious worship or instruction. Yet, "religious instruction" is amenable to different interpretations. For example, does a course in World Religions amount to religious instruction because those taking the course learn about different religious beliefs and practices? The *Schempp* Court had expressly rejected that a course on world religions was the equivalent of engaging in religious prayer, notwithstanding that the content might be thought to involve religious instruction.

Would it promote religious purposes to present religious views on the family? Presumably. But there would seem to be a big difference between discussing what a particular religious group suggests is its ideal picture of a family and an exhortation to prayer. Precisely because religious purposes and religious instruction might be

---

49 *Id.* at 395.
50 *Id.* at 389.

thought to cover such a wide range of topics and practices, the *Lamb's Chapel* opinion is compatible with a variety of views about what the Establishment Clause requires, permits, and prohibits. For example, the decision is quite compatible with the view that while a school district "discriminates on the basis of viewpoint ... [if] permit[ting] school property to be used for the presentation of all views about family issues and child rearing except those dealing with the subject matter from a religious standpoint,"[51] the school district acts permissibly when permitting expressions of religious viewpoints but prohibiting prayer. For the Court to suggest that the "film series involved here no doubt dealt with a subject otherwise permissible under Rule 10, and its exhibition was denied solely because the series dealt with the subject from a religious standpoint"[52] is by no means the equivalent of suggesting that if discussions of matters of public interest are permitted on school grounds then prayer must also be permitted. Otherwise, the decisions striking down prayer in school but permitting discussion of secular matter would be much harder to justify. Indeed, because prayer might simply be described as presenting material from a religious viewpoint and because teachers in public schools present much material from nonreligious viewpoints, it might be argued that by representing multiple viewpoints (including the viewpoint represented by prayer) the school could not be inferred to be endorsing any of them.

Depending upon how *Lamb's Chapel* and other decisions are read, the Court's position would seem to permit a whole host of practices previously thought impermissible, because the school could not reasonably be thought to be endorsing a particular (religious) position. Regrettably, subsequent analyses offered by the Court have done little if anything to cabin what might be taught in public schools without offending Establishment Clause guarantees.

In *Good News Club v. Milford Central School*,[53] the Court examined whether a school district offended constitutional guarantees when denying recognition to an after-school club where students would engage in religious worship among other activities. The district court had found that the club was not merely discussing secular matters from a religious point of view but instead was dealing with a subject matter that was clearly religious in nature. Indeed, Ravitch describes the group at issue as "designed to proselytize and influence young children."[54]

At issue was whether the limited public forum created by the school could exclude the group because of their religious focus. The Court noted that viewpoint discrimination is not permitted even in a limited public forum, and that any content restrictions must be reasonable in light of the forum's purpose. The Court then reviewed its past cases, suggesting that it had struck down policies effecting viewpoint discrimination against religious groups. The Court concluded that the

---

51 *Id.* at 393.
52 *Id.* at 394.
53 533 U.S. 98 (2001).
54 Frank S. Ravitch, *Masters of Illusion: The Supreme Court and the Religion Clauses* 96 (2007).

refusal to recognize the Good News Club based on the religious nature of their practices was indistinguishable from the exclusions struck down in past cases, and held that the Milford school was engaging in viewpoint discrimination, thereby obviating the need to decide whether the exclusion was reasonable in light of the limited public forum's purpose.

The Court did not seem to appreciate that *Lamb's Chapel* and *Good News Club* were very different cases. *Lamb's Chapel* involved a refusal to air a discussion of family issues from a religious perspective. *Good News Club* did not involve an attempt to remove a topic from discussion. Rather, this restriction was on particular types of expression, such as prayer or religious proselytizing. Thus, no viewpoints were excluded by the regulation at issue in *Good News Club* unless it is argued, for example, that prayer offers a distinctive viewpoint that cannot be expressed in other types of discourse. But the Court was not suggesting that. Indeed, the Court rejected that "something that is 'quintessentially religious' or 'decidedly religious in nature' cannot also be characterized properly as the teaching of morals and character development from a particular viewpoint,"[55] suggesting that for Free Speech Clause purposes there is "no logical difference in kind between the invocation of Christianity by the Club and the invocation of teamwork, loyalty or patriotism by other associations to provide a foundation for their lessons."[56]

At least two points might be made about this alleged equivalence. First, claims to the contrary by the Court notwithstanding, it suggests that no viewpoints were excluded by the regulation at issue in *Good News Club*. Whatever had been excluded by the limitation on prayer could have been expressed in a discussion of the relevant topic from a sectarian perspective. Second, the Court has offered a non sequitur to support its position. By suggesting that religion provides as valid a foundation as patriotism, the Court is suggesting that there is no legitimate reason to discriminate against discussions from a sectarian perspective. But this is exactly what the district court had found was not occurring. Rather, such perspectives could be presented, as long as method did not involve an inherently religious form such as prayer.

The *Good News Club* Court also rejected that the fact that elementary schoolchildren were involved made this case distinguishable from other cases, noting that the instructors were not schoolteachers and that young schoolchildren were not loitering around the classroom after the school day had ended. Presumably, the Court was thinking that the children would not hear the Club's discussions or prayers from the hallway, and thus would not be induced to misperceive the inclusion as an endorsement by the school. Yet, children would come to know of the programs in other ways than through loitering, and young children might not be sophisticated enough to reject endorsement merely because the schoolteachers were not the instructors.

---

55 *Good News Club*, 533 U.S. at 111.
56 *Id.*

The *Good News Club* Court worried that the state's refusal to permit the club to use the school facilities would be perceived as hostility to religion, suggesting that "we cannot say the danger that children would misperceive the endorsement of religion is any greater than the danger that they would perceive a hostility toward the religious viewpoint if the Club were excluded from the public forum."[57] It is unclear whether the Court intended to contrast the misperception of endorsement with the perception of hostility, as if the failure to permit the club to use the facilities would rightly be perceived as hostile, whereas the inclusion might be misperceived as endorsement. In any event, the Court's mischaracterization of the policy at issue as viewpoint discrimination coupled with its failure to see that this case differed from those cases previously decided in ways that had been previously described as significant suggest that some members of the Court will not permit legal distinctions to stand in the way of prayer resuming its "rightful" place in the schools.

The Court understood that *McCollum* had precluded the use of school facilities for religious instruction, but distinguished that case because in *Good News Club* there was "simply no integration and cooperation between the school district and the Club."[58] Yet, given that the integration/cooperation factor was downplayed or ignored so that the Court could uphold the program at issue in *Zorach*, and given all of the other arguments offered by the Court, for example, that prayer should not be distinguished for constitutional purposes from discussions from a religious perspective, it would seem that *Good News Club* might be used to justify a whole range of religious practices on site during school time in the name of neutrality. Indeed, given all of the secular instruction that occurs during the day, it would be unsurprising for some members of the Court to claim that the failure to include religious instruction or prayer should be viewed as manifesting hostility to religion.

When commenting about *Widmar* and subsequent cases, Viteritti suggests that "the only thing more remarkable than the way the Supreme Court embraced the Free Speech Clause to hold off Establishment Clause claims is that it did so with little consideration of the Free Exercise Clause."[59] Viteritti's comment is telling. The Court has long held that prayer is different from other kinds of speech, and that it does not belong in the public schools, free exercise guarantees notwithstanding. Now, at least some members of the Court refuse to recognize the special nature of prayer, instead treating it as just another kind of speech.

---

57 *Id.* at 118.
58 *Id.* at 116 n.6.
59 Viteritti, *supra* note 19, at 114.

Prayer at School Functions

A different strand of the jurisprudence involves the kinds of prayers, invocations, or orations that are permissible at school ceremonies. Whether the students were being coerced to attend or pray has proven to be a key consideration, although the jurisprudence involving voluntary after-school prayer is suggestive of some of the reasons that the Court's jurisprudence with respect to school ceremonies is in flux.

The seminal case in this area is *Lee v. Weisman*,[60] which involved a challenge to a school policy in which local members of the clergy were invited to give invocations and benedictions at public school graduations.[61] The Court noted that the controlling precedents regarding prayer and religious exercise in primary and secondary public schools require that the practice at issue be declared unconstitutional, and then tried to explain why that was so.

The Court first explained the numerous ways in which the state had been implicated. For example, a school official had decided that an invocation and a benediction should be given, which was treated as the equivalent of a state

---

60 505 U.S. 577 (1992).

61 For the content of the remarks, *see id.* at 581–2

Invocation

God of the Free, Hope of the Brave:

For the legacy of America where diversity is celebrated and the rights of minorities are
    protected, we thank You. May these young men and women grow up to enrich it.

For the liberty of America, we thank You. May these new graduates grow up to guard it.

For the political process of America in which all its citizens may participate, for its
    court system where all may seek justice we thank You. May those we honor this
    morning always turn to it in trust.

For the destiny of America we thank You. May the graduates of Nathan Bishop Middle
    School so live that they might help to share it.

May our aspirations for our country and for these young people, who are our hope for
    the future, be richly fulfilled.

Amen

Benediction

O God, we are grateful to You for having endowed us with the capacity for learning
    which we have celebrated on this joyous commencement.

Happy families give thanks for seeing their children achieve an important milestone.
    Send Your blessings upon the teachers and administrators who helped prepare them.

The graduates now need strength and guidance for the future, help them to understand
    that we are not complete with academic knowledge alone. We must each strive to
    fulfill what You require of us all: To do justly, to love mercy, to walk humbly.

We give thanks to You, Lord, for keeping us alive, sustaining us and allowing us to
    reach this special, happy occasion.

Amen

statute mandating prayer.[62] Further, a state actor had chosen the individual (at this ceremony, a rabbi) who would offer the invocation and benediction. Finally, the principal had provided the rabbi with guidelines, suggesting that the prayers should be nonsectarian. However, the Court reasoned that by offering guidelines, "the principal directed and controlled the content of the prayers."[63]

Not only did the Court construe the case as involving state-sponsorship of prayer that the state itself had a hand in directing and controlling, but the Court also mentioned additional aspects making the school policy constitutionally suspect. After noting that attendance at the graduation was voluntary, the Court nonetheless suggested that student "attendance and participation in the state-sponsored religious activity are in a fair and real sense obligatory."[64] Because attendance at the activity was obligatory in the relevant sense, the students were being coerced into attending a state-run exercise during which prayers would be offered.

The Court did not impute bad motivation to the state, accepting that offering guidelines for the prayers involved a good faith attempt to avoid sectarianism at the graduation ceremony. However, the Court noted that this did not settle the issue:

> The question is not the good faith of the school in attempting to make the prayer acceptable to most persons, but the legitimacy of its undertaking that enterprise at all when the object is to produce a prayer to be used in a formal religious exercise which students, for all practical purposes, are obliged to attend. By characterizing this as an attempt to make the address non-offensive to most students, the Court implied that the state was imposing prayers on some, however few, for whom this would be most unwelcome. By requiring attendance at an event at which there would be unwelcome prayers, the state was proselytizing and, perhaps, engaging in some form of religious coercion.[65]

Noting that the Religion Clauses preclude the state from prescribing or proscribing religious beliefs and expression, the Court explained that school officials are not permitted to assist in the composition of prayers to be offered at a formal student exercise. This prohibition is especially stringent when younger children are involved, because "there are heightened concerns with protecting freedom of conscience from subtle coercive pressure in the elementary and secondary public schools."[66] These concerns are greater still when prayers are involved, because such "exercises in public schools carry a particular risk of indirect coercion."[67]

---

62 *Id.* at 587.
63 *Id.* at 588.
64 *Id.* at 586.
65 *Id.* at 588–9.
66 *Id.* at 592.
67 *Id.*

There are at least two different ways to understand the constitutional concerns implicated here, depending upon whether one emphasizes the state role in the composition of the prayers or, instead, in assuring that (possibly young) children will be present at an exercise where the prayers will be offered. If the focus is only on the former, then it should not matter whether prayers are offered at a state-sponsored exercise as long as the state does not have a role in composing or providing guidelines for the prayers.

But if there are heightened concerns involving the freedom of conscience of young children, especially when prayers are being offered at a public school exercise, then state practices should not be immunized from review merely because the state does not shape the prayers to be offered at compulsory public functions. The coercive pressure on children in primary and secondary schools is present regardless of who authored the prayers. If the goal is to prevent the imposition of such coercion rather than merely to prevent students from being involuntarily exposed to state-authored prayers, then prayer at public school functions must be scrutinized whether or not the state has a hand in fashioning what the children will hear.

The *Lee* Court was not implying that the state intended to coerce individuals into adopting particular religious beliefs. Nor was the Court implying that most individuals would perceive the exercise as coercive. However, the Court suggested, those were not the relevant issues to consider; instead, the prayer exercises should be examined from the perspective of the dissenter. From that person's point of view, standing during an invocation or benediction might not simply be characterized as standing in respectful silence; it might instead be thought to signify much more: "What to most believers may seem nothing more than a reasonable request that the nonbeliever respect their religious practices, in a school context may appear to the nonbeliever or dissenter to be an attempt to employ the machinery of the State to enforce a religious orthodoxy."[68] The dissenter would feel coerced, both in that she might feel that she could not leave and in that she might feel forced to stand during the prayer. Further, she might not feel as if she were merely getting out of her seat as a sign of respect but, instead, as if she were thereby being forced to signify her support of or participation in the religious exercise.

The Court explained that "the school district's supervision and control of a high school graduation ceremony places public pressure, as well as peer pressure, on attending students to stand as a group or, at least, maintain respectful silence during the invocation and benediction."[69] Here, the Court's focus is on the state control of the graduation ceremony as a whole rather than on its influence with respect to the contents of the invocation and benediction. Further, the Court did not minimize the degree to which the ceremony would be experienced as coercive, since this "pressure, though subtle and indirect, can be as real as any overt compulsion."[70]

---

68 *Id.*
69 *Id.* at 593.
70 *Id.*

By offering this analysis, the Court seemed to be making two distinct points: (1) the type of pressure qualified for constitutional purposes; and (2) the amount of pressure sufficed for constitutional purposes. By the same token, *Engel* and *Schempp* had both involved coercion, notwithstanding that the students in both of those cases had not been required to be present for the religious presentations. While the *Engel* and *Schempp* context might be differentiated from that of *Lee* in that the former involved an instructional and the latter a ceremonial setting, they all involved a kind of psychological coercion to be present at a state-sponsored school activity.

The Court has never offered a detailed analysis of how much pressure must be exerted in order for Establishment Clause guarantees to be violated, and it would be unsurprising for a member of the Court to suggest that the coercion, if any, in a particular case was de minimis and hence not enough to violate constitutional guarantees. Justice Antonin Scalia noted in his *Lee* dissent that there was "nothing in the record to indicate that failure of attending students to take part in the invocation or benediction was subject to any penalty or discipline."[71] Such a point might have been directed both to the type and to the amount of pressure that had been imposed. He clearly believed that the amount was de minimis, having described the ceremony as a minimal inconvenience for dissenters.

The *Lee* Court recognized that many of the students did not feel at all pressured to participate in this ceremony; on the contrary, they welcomed the prayer and might have felt that the ceremony would be incomplete without some kind of acknowledgment of the divine. The Court further recognized that many of those preferring not to have an invocation and benediction included in the ceremony nonetheless did not feel compromised by standing while others took part in the prayer. However, the Court did not focus on those who had no objections to the practice but, instead, on the individual who had strong reservations about participating in such an exercise: "But for the dissenter of high school age, who has a reasonable perception that she is being forced by the State to pray in a manner her conscience will not allow, the injury is no less real."[72]

Yet, the state was not forcing anyone to pray. For example, no one was monitoring the students to make sure that they said, "Amen," or engaged in other symbolic behavior that might be construed as participating in prayer. Rather, the dissenter was merely being pressured to stand. The Court understood this point, but noted that "for many, if not most, of the students at the graduation, the act of standing or remaining silent was an expression of participation in the rabbi's prayer."[73] Because that was so, the dissenter's act of standing would be indistinguishable from the standing and participation performed by most of the other students.

---

71 *Id.* at 643 (Scalia, J., dissenting).

72 *Id.* at 593.

73 *Id.*

While correct that an external observer might not be able to distinguish between what the dissenter and the non-dissenter were doing during the invocation and benediction, the Court overstates the point when suggesting that the dissenter was being forced to pray. She would know that she was standing and not praying. Further, even were a speaker to intone, "Let us bow our heads and pray," and even were the dissenter to bow her head, she would still know that she was not praying, although she might be pretending to do so. It would not be reasonable for a dissenter to have suggested that she had been forced to pray, at least if prayer is a kind of internal activity.

Nonetheless, pressuring individuals to appear to be praying violates constitutional guarantees. That is not because the individual would think that she was praying when in fact she was only standing there with head bowed. Instead, it would be for other reasons, including that individuals cannot be forced by the state to articulate particular positions. As the Court explained in *West Virginia State Board of Education v. Barnette*, "If there is any fixed star in our constitutional constellation, it is that no official, high or petty, can prescribe what shall be orthodox in politics, nationalism, religion, or other matters of opinion or force citizens to confess by word or act their faith therein."[74]

The *Lee* Court explained that it would be of "little comfort to a dissenter ... to be told that for her the act of standing or remaining in silence signifies mere respect, rather than participation."[75] Basically, the Court believed it unimportant for these purposes to distinguish between (1) actually praying, and (2) being viewed as praying: "What matters is that, given our social conventions, a reasonable dissenter in this milieu could believe that the group exercise signified her own participation or approval of it."[76] While the Court understood that some who did not wish to participate might nonetheless not have been averse to being viewed as participating, others might have found it quite offensive.

Suppose, however, that standing did not signify participation, perhaps because those who participated would not only stand but would also bow their heads. Or, perhaps included in the program was a disclaimer specifically noting that those who stood during the invocation and benediction should not be assumed to be participating. The question would be whether the policy would still violate constitutional guarantees. By implying that public graduation invocations or benedictions should be analyzed as forced speech cases, the Court suggests that there are ways to remove the constitutional taint without omitting the invocation or benediction. Yet, someone who felt psychologically coerced because of the inclusion of an invocation or benediction in a public school graduation ceremony would likely still feel coerced by such practices, even were there a note in the program suggesting that an individual's standing quietly during the invocation or benediction did not signify agreement or participation. If the constitutional evil

74 319 U.S. 624, 642 (1943).
75 *Lee*, 505 U.S. at 593.
76 *Id.*

is state facilitation of religious coercion, then the difficulty is not removed by a simple notation in the program.

Although the Court mentioned that Deborah Weisman attended her graduation, the Court did not mention what she did during the graduation. Suppose, for example, that she had remained seated during the invocation and benediction. No one could have mistaken her actions as involving participation or approval of the invocation and benediction. Would there then have been no harm to her? Would the only harm have been to those who had unwillingly stood and "participated?" Greenawalt suggests that students "may well feel offended in conscience at having to sit through religious practices to which they object."[77]

The Court noted that Deborah was enrolled in high school and would likely have to confront the same choice during her high school graduation that she had been forced to make during her middle school graduation. But the Court's analysis suggests that it is not the fact that there will be an invocation and benediction that is relevant; rather, the constitutional injury lies in her being pressured to stand and unwillingly signify her approval of the prayers. But if that is the injury, then what she did during her middle school graduation would at least seem relevant to the constitutional inquiry.

Certainly, some on the Court believed that the emphasis should not have been on whether the student's standing constituted participation. For example, while arguing that the student's being pressured to participate in a state-sponsored religious activity was a sufficient condition for its constitutional invalidity, Justice Blackmun also suggested in his concurring opinion that the state taking a religious position was constitutionally objectionable whether or not dissenters were forced to participate. Given that Justices O'Connor and John Paul Stevens joined Justice Blackmun's concurring opinion, and given Justice Blackmun's express denial that coercion had to be shown if a state practice was to be struck down on Establishment Clause grounds, it might seem surprising that *Lee* stands for the proposition that some form of the coercion test best captures the Establishment Clause guarantees. Indeed, the other Justice signing onto Justice Kennedy's opinion, Justice David Souter, also made clear in his concurring opinion (joined by Justices Stevens and O'Connor) that coercion was not a necessary element of an Establishment Clause violation.

Nonetheless, these Justices did write or sign onto concurring opinions rather than, for example, opinions that were concurring in part or only concurring in the judgment. Further, a different way of counting the *Lee* opinions seems to yield a majority view about coercion. Justice Scalia in his dissent, joined by Chief Justice William Rehnquist and Justices Clarence Thomas and White, argued that a more restricted notion of coercion should be the constitutional standard. Thus, Justice Kennedy plus the dissenting Justices seem together to suggest that proof of coercion is a necessary element of an Establishment Clause claim.

---

77 Greenawalt, *supra* note 15, at 46.

The *Lee* majority suggested that the graduation prayers placed dissenters in an unenviable position: "participating, with all that implies, or protesting."[78] While refusing to comment whether imposing such a forced choice on adults violates the Constitution, the Court suggested that the Constitution does preclude the imposition of such a choice on students in primary and secondary schools. Individuals of that age are more subject to peer pressure than are older individuals, and thus the Court presumably felt that such pressure constituted sufficient coercion as to be constitutionally cognizable.

Lee would have been much easier to understand and apply if the Court had made clear whether the constitutional difficulty was that dissenters were being compelled to participate in a religious exercise or, instead, that they were being subjected to prayer at a public ceremony. To the extent that it was the latter, it would have been helpful had the Court made clear whether the state's having had a hand in the composition of the prayer was the constitutional difficulty rather than, for example, the state having had a hand in assuring attendance at a public function at which prayers would be offered.

The *Lee* Court understood that dissenting students could simply not attend the ceremony and thereby avoid being subjected to the unwanted choice of appearing to participate on the one hand or objecting on the other. However, the Court refused to characterize skipping the graduation as a viable option, at least in part, because of the importance of the occasion.

The occasion's importance and the relative ease with which the respective prayers might be avoided distinguished *Lee* from a previous case, *Marsh v. Chambers*,[79] where the Court had upheld the Nebraska Legislature's practice of beginning sessions with a prayer. The "atmosphere at the opening of a session of a state legislature where adults are free to enter and leave with little comment and for any number of reasons cannot compare with the constraining potential of the one school event most important for the student to attend."[80] Thus, the Court implied, nothing would be signified by one's leaving the chamber before the legislative prayer was offered, whereas one's leaving before the graduation invocation or benediction would signify dissent.

The Court also distinguished the two cases by emphasizing the ages of those who might be forced to make a difficult choice, noting:

> We do not address whether that choice [that is, being forced to choose between protesting or unwillingly participating in a religious exercise] is acceptable if the affected citizens are mature adults, but we think the State may not, consistent with the Establishment Clause, place primary and secondary school children in this position.[81]

---

78 *Lee*, 505 U.S. at 593.
79 463 U.S. 783 (1983).
80 *Lee*, 505 U.S. at 597.
81 *Id.* at 593.

There are various ways to read *Lee*. Perhaps it is suggesting that the coercion test determines whether the Establishment Clause has been violated, although the standard advocated by Justice Kennedy is much broader than the standard articulated by Justice Scalia. On the other hand, most members of the *Lee* majority argued that the Establishment Clause could be violated even absent proof of coercion. Thus, *Lee* might be read as offering either a necessary or a sufficient condition for a finding that the Establishment Clause has been violated.

An additional confusing aspect of *Lee* is that the Court discussed numerous respects in which the state was implicated in the creation and presentation of the benediction and invocation. It also discussed the various ways in which dissenting students were being coerced into participating in or witnessing a religious activity at a state-sponsored event. However, the Court did not offer any guidance with respect to which of the state practices at issue sufficed for a finding of unconstitutionality. But this meant that some courts might view *Lee* as precluding a wide range of practices, whereas other courts would view *Lee* as precluding only those practices that mirrored the policies and procedures struck down in *Lee*. As was eminently foreseeable, very different interpretations of *Lee* have been offered in the circuits, resulting in relevantly similar cases being decided differently.

Lee left a number of issues unresolved. For example, one issue is whether the same rules respecting religious coercion apply if the students attending the public function are older, for example, are in college. *Lee* also failed to determine whether the individuals who are the focus of concern at a graduation are the students or, instead, all who might reasonably be expected to attend. A different issue that was raised but not decided involved what the state could do, if anything, to immunize itself from the charge that it was responsible for the offering of a prayer at a public function. Would the state immunize school prayer from constitutional challenge if the state played no role in the composition of the benediction? Or would the state's coercing attendance at a school event at which it was known that a prayer would be offered suffice for a showing that Establishment Clause guarantees had been violated?

Engel involved indirect coercion because the state put its seal of endorsement behind a particular nonsectarian prayer. If that were the kind of coercion making the practice in *Lee* unconstitutional, then focusing on whether Deborah Weisman felt coerced into falsely signifying approval was misleading, because the practice at issue would have been unconstitutional even had there been no danger that her standing respectfully would be misinterpreted.

The *Lee* Court suggested that "in our society and in our culture high school graduation is one of life's most significant occasions."[82] Yet, for at least some of those graduating from college or whose family members are graduating from college, college graduation is as significant as or more significant than high school graduation. Some individuals feel more compelled to attend their own college

---

82 *Id.* at 595.

graduation or that of a family member than they do the same person's high school graduation.[83]

Individuals could attend their high school graduations without being present for the invocation and benediction, but the *Lee* Court implied that the Constitution forbade states from imposing such a choice: "It is a tenet of the First Amendment that the State cannot require one of its citizens to forfeit his or her rights and benefits as the price of resisting conformance to state-sponsored religious practice."[84] However, one could not tell from the *Lee* opinion whether presenting such a choice was prohibited because so few students would take advantage of it or, instead, because the state was precluded from imposing such a choice regardless of how many would exercise that option.

The *Lee* Court had recognized that graduations often involve family celebrations: "Graduation is a time for family and those closest to the student to celebrate success and express mutual wishes of gratitude and respect."[85] Families might involve the graduate's parents, siblings, children, and extended family, among others. When the graduation is from college or professional school, it is even more likely that the graduate might have children attending. Yet, this means that the constitutional concerns implicated when impressionable young people are present at a graduation are still implicated in the college and post-graduate setting, even if the children present are not themselves graduating but instead are the children or nephews and nieces of the graduates.

The *Lee* Court downplayed the importance of the number of young and impressionable individuals who might be affected by a benediction or invocation, suggesting instead that the fact that most individuals would not be offended by an invocation would not immunize that prayer, given that there still might be some who would be offended or improperly influenced. Nonetheless, the Court did not explain whether it had some minimum number of objectors in mind that would trigger the constitutional protections. The Court seemed to recognize the issue: "We do not hold that every state action implicating religion is invalid if one or a few citizens find it offensive. People may take offense at all manner of religious as well as nonreligious messages, but offense alone does not in every case show a violation."[86] However, the Court neither addressed nor even seemed interested in how many were adversely affected by the ceremony.

It is simply unclear whether the Court would say that including a benediction and invocation coerced those who were graduating but did not coerce family members who were attending. While recognizing that graduations are important for family members too, the Court never explored whether there were constitutional implications if some of the invited guests had qualms about the prayers. However,

---

83 For a discussion of the Court's Establishment Clause jurisprudence with respect to public universities, see Chapter 4.

84 *Lee*, 505 U.S. at 596.

85 *Id.* at 595.

86 *Id.* at 597.

given the likelihood that there would be impressionable children present at graduations either because they were graduating or because they had a family member who was graduating, the *Lee* Court's comments about the importance of not indoctrinating impressionable youth would seem to have implications for many kinds of graduations.

Arguably, it might seem more of a burden for a graduating student than a guest with a small child to leave before the benediction could be offered. Perhaps the Court was thinking that the departure of a graduate before a prayer would be so obvious that it would signify disagreement, whereas a parent in the audience who left with a small child at such a time might be thought to be trying to find a bathroom rather than signifying disagreement. Or, perhaps the Court was suggesting that the state should not have a hand in religiously educating impressionable young children whether they were there as guests or graduates.

Yet, even the qualification that one person being offended may not suffice for a finding of an Establishment Clause violation should be understood in light of the context in which it was offered. The *Lee* Court did not name any other student in addition to Deborah who had been offended by the practice at issue. Instead, the Court either assumed that they existed or that the offense to one student sufficed.

One of the reasons that the *Lee* Court worried about coercing younger children to attend primary and secondary school graduations where there would be graduation prayers was the fear that students would thereby have their religious beliefs changed. Were that the sole rationale, however, then it should not have mattered whether the young persons were sitting quietly in their seats or, instead, were being asked to stand to signify their approval of something that they did not believe. Rather, the focus should simply have been on whether the dissenting children had been coerced into being present at a state function where prayers would be offered. Further, if the relevant issue is that government should not be shaping religious beliefs, then there should have been little or no analysis of whether dissenters would feel offense. Individuals can feel offended even when there is no likelihood that the offending practice will cause a change of belief. Indeed, there was no discussion whatsoever of whether Deborah Weisman's religious beliefs were likely to be changed by being exposed to the invocation and benediction.

Not only might individuals feel offended by prayers having no likelihood of changing their beliefs, but prayers might not cause offense even if they did have some likelihood of changing particular religious beliefs. The very impressionable child who may be quite open and have no fixed opinions on a particular subject would seem less likely to take offense were particular religious views presented, even if there was a significant likelihood that exposure to those views would result in a change in religious beliefs.

If the focus of concern was that children should not be coerced into signifying something that they do not believe, then the *Lee* Court should not have emphasized how impressionable young children are. The state forcing individuals to communicate something which they do not believe is problematic, even if they are not at all impressionable and are steadfast in their religious beliefs.

Some of the *Lee* analysis did not focus on whether the individuals were being coerced into communicating something that they did not believe but, instead, on their being coerced into attending a state-sponsored event where they would be confronted by an unwelcome, religious message. But this is problematic for both children and adults. Presumably, the *Lee* Court mentioned these different aspects of the case because it believed that they all were problematic. Yet, the Court never said that each of these state practices was precluded by the Establishment Clause. Nor did the Court identify which element or combination of elements, if present, would suffice for invalidation under the Establishment Clause. But by failing to do so, the Court left lower courts with wide discretion to uphold state practices as long as one of the offending features in *Lee* was not present.

The prayer at issue in *Engel* did not seem likely to promote conversion or to increase the faith of the faithful, and the Court nonetheless suggested that this kind of religious activity implicated Establishment Clause concerns. So, too, the prayers at issue in *Lee* did not seem likely to result in conversions or increases in faith.

Consider a different issue discussed by the *Lee* Court, namely, that the state should not be arranging to have a prayer at a school graduation. Suppose, instead, that the students vote to have a graduation invocation and benediction. A religiously dissenting student knowing that such prayers will be offered as a result of a student vote will have to decide whether to attend. At least one question is whether such a student would feel less coerced than, say, Deborah Weisman felt.

Permitting the majority to impose its will on the minority violates at least the spirit of *Lee*. The *Lee* Court rejected the legitimacy of the high school producing a "prayer acceptable to most persons ... [when it would] be used in a formal religious exercise which students, for all practical purposes, are obliged to attend."[87] While the students voting for graduation prayers might signify that the prayer would be acceptable to many, it would nonetheless be true that the prayer would be part of a formal religious exercise that students would feel pressure to attend. If including the nonsectarian prayer at issue in *Lee* put dissenting students in a difficult position and forced them to make choices that they should not be forced to make, the same would be true even were the prayer authorization a result of a student vote.

From the dissenting student's perspective, graduations involving state-chosen or student-chosen prayers might seem equally coercive. Or, perhaps, the latter graduation would seem even more coercive, because the prayers might have been inferred to have the stamp of approval of both the district and the majority of the graduating student body. Further, the *Lee* Court emphasized the view of the reasonable dissenting student, and it would be reasonable for dissenting students to believe their views in conflict with those of the state and those of the majority of the student body.

---

87 *Id.* at 588–9.

It might be argued that coercion should not be attributed to the state simply by virtue of a school having authorizing the students to vote. That issue was addressed in *Santa Fe School District v. Doe*,[88] where the Court made clear that a school permitting student elections to determine whether there would be a prayer at a state-sponsored event would not immunize the practice from review. However, the Court did not make clear what additional actions or nonactions by the state would preclude a finding that offering a prayer at a public function violated Establishment Clause guarantees. These and other issues have been left to the lower courts to figure out, resulting in the foreseeably confusing and confused jurisprudence that governs the law in this area.

At issue in *Santa Fe* was a high school policy authorizing two student elections, the first to determine whether there would be messages, statements, or invocations at football games and the second, if necessary, to determine the identity of the orator. The specific question before the Court was whether the local policy permitting student-initiated and student-led prayers at football games violated constitutional guarantees. In concluding that the policy violated the Establishment Clause, the Court suggested that the principles articulated in *Lee* governed the case, as if those principles were clear.

The first question addressed by the *Santa Fe* Court was whether the speech at issue was public or private. The Court noted that the invocations were authorized by the school policy and took place at a state-sponsored event on state property. Further, one person would be chosen to deliver the message or invocation for the entire season, and that message was regulated with respect to subject matter and content. The Court explained that the "alleged 'circuit-breaker' mechanism of the dual elections and student speaker do not turn public speech into private speech."[89] The Court also noted that this mechanism would not immunize the school policy from constitutional review when students were coerced into being present for unwelcome religious messages.

The Court analogized *Santa Fe* to *Lee* in a few different respects. For example, while the school district had argued in *Lee* that its requiring nonsectarian prayers minimized the message's coercive effect, the *Lee* Court responded that protecting the sensibilities of most people would not minimize and might even aggravate the dissenters' feelings of isolation and affront. So, too, the *Santa Fe* Court reasoned, while one student being chosen as the speaker at each of the football games "might ensure that most of the students are represented, it does nothing to protect the minority; indeed, it likely serves to intensify their offense."[90]

Of course, it was not as if the stated criterion for election involved the contents of the prayers or even whether the speaker would offer prayers. Instead, individuals might be chosen based on popularity, grades, or oratory skills. However, the Court examined the context in which this election took place—first, there was a decision

---

88 530 U.S. 290 (2000).

89 *Id.* at 310.

90 *Id.* at 305.

about whether there would be an invocation or message, and second, assuming that the first vote yielded a positive response, an election to determine who would deliver the oration—and concluded that "the policy, by its terms, invites and encourages religious messages."[91]

One of the noteworthy aspects of the *Santa Fe* opinion was the way that it addressed the regulations regarding content and topic. The message was "to solemnize the event, to promote good sportsmanship and student safety, and to establish the appropriate environment for the competition."[92] But, the Court noted, a religious message is one of the most obvious methods of solemnizing an event. Further, because the term "invocation" had always been used in the past to refer to a religious message, the Court reasoned that the policy encouraged and was understood by the students to encourage a religious message. Indeed, the Court noted that it was not clear what kind of message would be nonreligious and yet appropriately solemnizing.

Santa Fe was similar to *Lee* in that a religious message would be delivered and in that attendees were being coerced into attending. While accepting that the pressure to attend a football game was not as great as the pressure to attend a graduation ceremony, the *Santa Fe* Court noted that some students—such as cheerleaders, band members, and members of the football team—had to attend. Even bracketing those for whom attendance was required, the Court suggested that to "assert that high school students do not feel immense social pressure, or have a truly genuine desire, to be involved in the extracurricular event that is American high school football is formalistic in the extreme."[93] For at least some students, "the choice between attending these games and avoiding personally offensive religious rituals is in no practical sense an easy one [and the] Constitution, moreover, demands that the school may not force this difficult choice upon these students."[94]

Suppose, however, that the choice to attend a football game was viewed as purely voluntary. Even so, the Court reasoned, "the delivery of a pregame prayer has the improper effect of coercing those present to participate in an act of religious worship."[95] The Court refused to "turn a blind eye to the context in which this policy arose, and that context quells any doubt that this policy was implemented with the purpose of endorsing school prayer."[96]

Part of what drove this decision may have been that there had already been allegations of proselytizing, and so it might have seemed eminently reasonable to expect that this mechanism would be used to engage in similar activity. Yet, the *Santa Fe* Court did not rely on this factor, instead offering what might be viewed as a relatively forgiving standard for what would qualify as being too coercive.

---

91 *Id.* at 306.
92 *Id.*
93 *Id.* at 311.
94 *Id.* at 312.
95 *Id.* at 315.
96 *Id.*

After all, in *Santa Fe*, the students chose the speaker, whereas in *Lee* the speaker had been chosen by the school administration. In *Lee* the policy limitations were to promote non-sectarianism, which nonetheless might be characterized as promoting religion over non-religion, whereas in *Santa Fe* the policy limitations on the content of the oration were designed to promote allegedly secular goals.

Santa Fe at least seemed to clear up some of the questions raised in *Lee*. *Santa Fe* suggests that it is not necessary to show that the state is promoting certain religious views over others (for example, nonsectarian rather than sectarian) for the state having had a hand in the content of an oration to trigger Establishment Clause guarantees. However, it is unclear whether a state refusal to speak to the content of an oration immunizes that message from an Establishment Clause challenge. On the one hand, it seems less plausible to argue that the state caused a religious message to be delivered if the state provided no content guidelines. On the other hand, the state refusal to take an oversight role, especially where there was reason to believe that a religious message would be delivered, might be thought to contribute to the degree to which the message delivered at a state-sponsored event might feel coercive.

The *Lee* Court recognized that the state guidelines had involved a good-faith attempt to remove sectarianism from the graduation ceremony, and at least one of the purposes behind the adoption of the Establishment Clause was the reduction or prevention of religious strife. Yet, interpreting the Establishment Clause to encourage states to have a hands-off policy might have the perverse result that the Clause would make it more likely that there would be sectarian flashpoints for religious animosity.

The *Santa Fe* Court suggested that an examination of the context revealed that the "policy involve[d] both perceived and actual endorsement of religion."[97] The Court's willingness to consider the realities of the situation (whether the policy was understood by the students to be a way of promoting prayer, even if the policy was structured in such a way as to give the district cover) suggests that the Court will look behind the policies adopted by school boards. *Santa Fe* might be read to suggest that the Constitution does not permit the state to avoid Establishment Clause guarantees by adopting policies that foreseeably and actually result in students praying before large audiences at either public football games or graduations, even if those prayers are composed by individual students.

Yet, *Santa Fe* might not be read so broadly. There were various reasons to believe that the state was trying to promote prayer. For example, at one point the district adopted a policy permitting only nonsectarian and non-proselytizing prayer, but then subsequently removed that restriction. As if realizing that removal of this provision might make the policy more constitutionally vulnerable, the district also added a provision suggesting that if the latter policy were struck down, the former would automatically become effective. But if *Santa Fe* is read to

---

97 *Id.* at 305.

apply only to cases in which the state is obviously trying to promote prayer, then it may be viewed as having limited application.

Viteritti notes that the "idea of a nonreligious prayer is an oxymoron,"[98] and that it is increasingly difficult to devise prayers that are both meaningful and non-offensive, given our increasingly diverse society both religiously and culturally.[99] Further, as Ravitch points out, even allegedly nonsectarian prayers can be offensive both to atheists and to those who do not believe in public prayer.[100] Thus, if offense is the key consideration, it is difficult to see how a prayer at a public school event can withstand constitutional scrutiny.

Greenawalt suggests that the special nature of prayer must be acknowledged,[101] and that prayer should not be allowed at public school ceremonies,[102] although he faults the Court for failing to expressly recognize that many families believe something of significance is lost by not including prayers to solemnize the occasion.[103] However, as Ravitch correctly points out, such ceremonies can be quite solemn without prayer,[104] and that solemnity can be achieved without incurring many of the costs associated with prayer at such events. The state simply should not have a hand in arranging to have prayers at school events or in arranging to have parents and children attend school events where prayers will be offered.

Conclusion

The Court's Establishment Clause jurisprudence as applied to religion in the schools has varied greatly over the past several decades. The articulated understanding of the Clause's restraints has run the gamut from strict separation to required accommodation. Members of the Court have suggested on the one hand that prayer can of course be kept out of school and on the other that prayer must be treated in the same way for constitutional purposes as discussions of secular subjects whether from a religious or nonreligious perspective.

The endorsement test has sometimes appeared to offer robust protections, precluding the state from favoring one religion over another or religion over non-religion. Yet, at other times, that test has seemed infinitely malleable, both in that the states could take simple steps to avoid imputations of endorsement and in that a state refusal to permit prayer might be interpreted as an attitude of hostility towards religion. Thus, while at one point it was absolutely clear that

---

98   Viteritti, *supra* note 19, at 113.

99   *Id.*

100   See Frank S. Ravitch, *School Prayer and Discrimination: The Civil Rights of Religious Minorities and Dissenters* 54 (1999).

101   Greenawalt, *supra* note 15, at 48–9.

102   *Id.* at 50.

103   *Id.*

104   See Ravitch, *supra* note 100, at 54.

certain religious activities could not take place on site during school hours, the rationales recently articulated by the Court suggest that such a position should now be viewed as at best controversial.

Good News Club does not stand for the proposition that because secular subjects are taught, prayers must be included during the school day—the school curriculum is not a limited public forum. Yet, presumably, states might be tempted to include prayer within the school day even if they are not constitutionally required to do so, and it is hardly clear that the Court would now say that the Establishment Clause forbids states from doing so.

The Court has offered broad outlines of what is prohibited at school functions, for example, the state cannot itself compose a prayer to be recited at a graduation involving primary or secondary school students. While it is clear that the age of those hearing the orations is relevant, the Court has not made clear why this is so. If it is because young children are more likely to have their religious views changed, then the Court should not focus on whether such children are feeling coerced into appearing to pray or actually praying. Rather, the Court should simply suggest that the state should not facilitate the presence of prayer where young children are present. If age is relevant because children are more likely to succumb to pressure to signify what they do not believe, then the discussion of the malleability of children is misplaced. Rather, the Court should simply focus on forced speech issues.

Regardless of why age is important, the Court should explain which group is the proper focus of concern. The Court never explains, for example, whether at a graduation the constitutional focus is on the dissenting graduates who are unwillingly being subjected to prayer or, instead, on all dissenting individuals who might reasonably feel pressured to attend, including employees and the graduates' friends and family, young and old.

The Court focuses on offense but does not explain how many or what kind of people must be offended for Establishment Clause guarantees to have been violated. Both adults and children might be offended if their religious convictions are being challenged at a public graduation, and the Court never explains why offense to children is more constitutionally problematic than offense to adults. Nonetheless, the Court does not focus on the religious offense to adults, even though there presumably would have been adults who might have felt offended by the prayers at both the graduation ceremony at issue in *Lee* and the pre-game address at issue in *Santa Fe*.

The Court focuses on coercion but never explains whether the coercion at issue is to attend the event or participate in the prayer. For example, in both *Lee* and *Santa Fe*, the Court does not even discuss whether the plaintiffs had "participated," and one simply cannot tell whether this was an oversight or instead meant that the coerced attendance was the constitutionally significant feature of the cases.

Much of the prayer jurisprudence involves state participation in the composition or presentation of prayers at school ceremonies. But the Court never explains whether a truly "hands-off" policy immunizes the state. Nor does the

Court explain or even suggest what the state should or must do if it is not to have prayer imputed to it.

Perhaps all of these factors are relevant. Even if that is so, the Court should explain whether the presence of one, some, or all is either necessary or sufficient for a finding of a violation of Establishment Clause guarantees. Circuits are left with so much discretion that the jurisprudence cannot help but be in hopeless disarray.

The Court's willingness to consider context is to be applauded. Nonetheless, the Court must offer clearer guidelines with respect to what the Establishment Clause prohibits and permits. As currently described, it is impossible to know whether the coercion test is very forgiving, very demanding, or somewhere in between. Nor is it clear whether coercion is a necessary or a sufficient condition for a finding that Establishment Clause guarantees have been violated. The lack of clarity on these issues has led to an intolerably high level of confusion and disagreement in the circuits, which will only be intensified unless the Court is much clearer about both what the test permits and what it is designed to discourage.

The United States is becoming more and more religiously diverse. As a matter of public policy, this is hardly the time to permit certain inherently religious activities back in the schools while classes are in session—doing so would only lead to further alienation and fragmentation within the general populace. Further, as a constitutional matter, the kinds of specious reasoning and mischaracterizations of past decisions that would have to be offered to achieve that result would lead to the gutting of the Establishment Clause. Regrettably, however, some of the Court's recent decisions and rationales provide the basis for a radical reinterpretation of the Establishment Clause, thereby strengthening the suspicion that, in the words of Justice Scalia, "principle and logic have nothing to do with the decisions of this Court."[105]

The religious, the areligious, and the antireligious may disagree about the desirability of having prayer during the school day. However, no one should approve of the Court's mischaracterizations both of past decisions and of the local policies at issue in particular cases as a way of promoting a greater sectarian presence in the schools. The Court's current approach to Establishment Clause guarantees will only lead to a growing loss of confidence in the efficacy of constitutional protections and in the Court's own integrity, results that all can agree should be avoided at great cost.

---

105   *Lawrence v. Texas*, 539 U.S. 558, 605 (2003) (Scalia, J., dissenting).

Chapter 3
Public Funding of Sectarian Higher Education

The Court's attitude toward the public funding of religious studies can best be described as ambivalent. Not long ago, religious education was viewed as one of the few kinds of study that the state clearly could not fund. Then, the Court did an about-face, implying that public funding of such studies does not violate constitutional guarantees, because that kind of study cannot be distinguished for constitutional purposes from other kinds of permissibly funded areas of study. Still more recently, the Court changed course yet again, suggesting that states may but need not refuse to fund such studies, reverting to the position that there is something about such studies that distinguishes it from other kinds of study for constitutional purposes, while nonetheless reaffirming that this area of study is not so different that the Establishment Clause bars its being funded, at least indirectly. While the most recently articulated position seems to be a kind of compromise that neither prohibits nor requires states to provide funds for religious studies, this newest formulation of the parameters of the Establishment Clauses is neither stable nor satisfying. The Court's current position will likely undergo yet another transformation, making the constitutional limitations and protections in this area even murkier and more confusing.

State Funding of Sectarian Colleges and Universities

In the 1970s, the Supreme Court decided three cases involving public aid to sectarian colleges and universities. The Court clearly articulated the conditions under which the Constitution precluded state aid to such institutions. The difficulty posed by these three cases was not in understanding what the criteria were, but in how they were applied. Factors thought important in one case were ignored in another and the rationales deemed practically dispositive in these cases would have been viewed as irrelevant in other Establishment Clause contexts. The Court thereby not only offered very little helpful guidance to lower courts but belied its own commitment to apply the relevant criteria and undercut its own credibility in an important area of law.

Tilton v. Richardson

The first important case in this area *Tilton v. Richardson*[1] in which the Court examined a provision of the Higher Education Facilities Act (HEFA) providing funds for the construction of academic facilities at institutions of higher learning. HEFA was challenged as a violation of Establishment Clause guarantees because federal funds were being used for projects at four institutions, each of which was sponsored by a religious organization. The Court employed the *Lemon* test to determine whether the funding passed muster, focusing on whether the act was motivated by a secular legislative purpose, whether the primary effect of the act was to advance or inhibit religion, or whether administering the act would bring about excessive entanglement with religion.[2]

The *Tilton* Court dispensed with the purpose prong rather quickly, finding that Congress's desire to expand opportunities for the growing number of young men and women seeking a higher education was a legitimate, secular purpose. The Court saw no need to second-guess Congress's rejection of the proposition that the relevant educational needs could be served by providing funds to public and to private, nonsectarian, nonprofit institutions. Rather, the Court accepted that there was a growing need for educational services and that the federal government providing funds to aid construction projects at colleges and universities was well-suited to promote that end. After all, the Court noted, the funds were only to be used for secular educational purposes, which suggested that it was not Congress's purpose to circumvent constitutional limitations by underwriting religious instruction.

While the Court was confident that Congress's purposes were legitimate, a separate issue involved whether the effects of the legislation would pass constitutional muster. First, the Court clarified the "effect" inquiry. To establish that Congress's providing financial support had a constitutionally impermissible effect, it would not suffice to point out that religious institutions would receive some benefit from the financial outlay. Rather, the relevant concern was whether the principal or primary effect of the program was to advance religion.

To justify its conclusion that there was no constitutional violation, the Court noted that the act at issue had been drafted carefully to assure that only secular and not religious functions would be subsidized. Indeed, HEFA expressly prohibited the use of funds for religious instruction, training, or worship. While the Court recognized that construction grants would benefit any recipient institution in that the new buildings would help institutions perform various functions, the provision of secular aid to religious institutions had previously been upheld by the Court, and the Court saw nothing making this kind of aid constitutionally objectionable.

Even a well-crafted statute might have effects which violate constitutional guarantees—the Court recognized that legitimate goals might be undercut by

---

1   403 U.S. 672 (1971).
2   For a discussion of *Lemon*, see Chapter 1, third section.

"conscious design or lax enforcement."[3] However, the mere possibility that abuses might occur would not justify striking down the legislation. Rather, the Court implied, there would have to be some evidence that the legitimate purposes were being undermined before HEFA could be invalidated as a violation of constitutional guarantees.

The Court offered two reasons to justify its confidence that HEFA's secular purposes were in fact being served. First, the oversight mechanism incorporated within the act seemed to be working, because some institutions not before the Court had been forced to return monies that had been used improperly. Second, there was no evidence that the institutions before the Court had engaged in prohibited activities. For example, the Court expressly noted that there had been no religious services conducted in the federally financed buildings, no religious symbols or plaques on the walls, and no evidence that the buildings had been used for anything other than nonreligious purposes. The Court concluded that as far as the record was concerned, the buildings were indistinguishable from what one might find at a typical state university.

Of course, the mere fact that there were no religious symbols on the walls and that no religious services had been held in the rooms would not end the inquiry if the courses incorporated religious instruction. Indeed, the plaintiffs argued that the education at these institutions was pervasively religious and that all classes promoted the religious objectives of the schools, which meant at the very least that the government's funding the building of any classrooms would support the schools' religious mission.

The Court rejected the contention that federal funds were being used to support religious instruction in the schools at issue, noting that two of the five financed buildings were libraries in which no classes were held. Thus, even had it been true that the schools at issue were pervasively sectarian, it could not have been claimed that federal funds were being used to support religious instruction if those funds were only used for buildings in which no classes were conducted. Of course, there are other ways in which religious instruction might be aided in a library, for example, if the institution imposed severe restrictions on the acquisition of books. However, no evidence was presented establishing or even implying the existence of institutionally imposed restrictions on the books that these libraries could acquire.

There was no discussion in the *Tilton* opinion about whether an institution that did impose restrictions on library acquisitions would thereby make itself ineligible for federal funding of its library construction. The Court's reticence on this subject was unsurprising, given the lack of evidence of any such restrictions at these schools. What might seem more surprising, however, was that the Court did not consider any other factors when deciding whether the library construction funding violated constitutional guarantees. Suppose, for example, that there had been only religious books in the collection. Even were this limited selection a result of

---

3   *Tilton*, 403 U.S. at 679.

something other than institutional mandate—for example, it was due instead to the choices consistently made by those who had been selected to be in charge of book acquisitions—it nonetheless might suggest that the government's providing funds for a new library would in fact promote the religious mission of the school. The point here is not to claim that these institutions in particular would or did in fact limit their holdings to religious books, but merely that the Court might have engaged in a more searching inquiry before concluding that federal guarantees had not been violated. Lower courts considering analogous cases in the future would look to the Court's analysis for guidance, and the guidance provided suggested that a cursory examination of the local practices was all that was required.

A different issue not even considered by the Court was whether the library might be used in other ways to further religious objectives. Libraries might house administrative offices and those offices might be used in ways that promote a school's religious objectives. While there was no suggestion that the school libraries at issue had housed offices promoting religious goals, the Court's having explicitly considered this possibility would have alerted lower courts to the kinds of uses that would be constitutionally precluded, and also would have suggested that the Court was taking its constitutional role seriously.

The other buildings whose construction was at least partially funded by federal monies did have classes in them. One of these buildings was a language laboratory, which was to be used to help students with their pronunciation of modern foreign languages. The Court was confident that this building would not be used in a way which would violate constitutional guarantees, because its function was "peculiarly unrelated and unadaptable to religious indoctrination."[4] Yet, the Court offered no reason to support its belief that a modern language laboratory would be immune from abuse. For example, students might be taught to say prayers in modern foreign languages, and this would presumably violate constitutional guarantees. The point here is not that Albertus Magnus College was using its language laboratory to perform religious indoctrination, but that the Court offered a merely cursory analysis when attempting to determine whether federal funds were being used in ways that violate the Establishment Clause. The Court's having considered the ways in which a language laboratory might be misused and then having noted that there was no evidence of such misuse by the college both would have made the Court's analysis more persuasive and would have been more helpful to lower courts faced with similar challenges in the future.

The Court's analysis of the constitutionality of the funding of the other two buildings—a science building and a building for music, drama, and arts—was no less disappointing. The appellants had introduced several documents into evidence specifying some of the religious restrictions on what could be taught. However, the Court noted that there was some evidence indicating that the restrictions were not enforced and that academic freedom was respected. After all, each of the institutions subscribed to the 1940 Statement of Principles on Academic Freedom

---

4   *Id.* at 681.

and Tenure (Principles), which had been endorsed by the American Association of University Professors and the Association of American Colleges.

Yet, the Court's citing to the Principles is not particularly reassuring when one considers that the following is included:

> Teachers are entitled to freedom in the classroom in discussing their subject, but they should be careful not to introduce into their teaching controversial matter which has no relation to their subject. Limitations of academic freedom because of religious or other aims of the institution should be clearly stated in writing at the time of the appointment.[5]

The *Tilton* Court noted that the schools at issue had written policies imposing religious restrictions on what could be taught, so it would not have violated the Principles for a school to have disciplined an individual for expressing disfavored views in the classroom. Discipline might be especially likely to be imposed if the expressed views had been characterized by the institution as "controversial" and having had no relation to the subject of the course.

On first blush, it might seem eminently reasonable to discipline someone for articulating views having no relation to the course subject matter. Why, it might be thought, should there be irrelevant discussions of social issues in a mathematics class? Yet, relevance must be understood in light of the background principle announced by these schools that religion should be incorporated into the courses as a general matter. Thus, religious views would appropriately be included in any class, but antireligious or other kinds of nonreligious views would not.

Suppose, however, that there had been nothing in the record about the imposition of discipline for "irrelevant," nonreligious discussion in the classroom. Even so, the very possibility that such discipline could be imposed might increase the likelihood that certain, but not other, views would be expressed. While schools are, of course, free to encourage views in accord with their religious mission and discourage views contrary to that mission, a separate issue is whether the state should be offering institutions financial support to aid them in pursuing those goals.

The *Lemon* Court discussed some of the dangers that arise in the context of secondary religious education, for example, "the danger that a teacher under religious control and discipline poses to the separation of the religious from the purely secular aspects of precollege education."[6] The Court was not suggesting that teachers would consciously violate their professional obligations and mix the secular with the religious—the Court did not "assume that teachers in parochial schools will be guilty of bad faith or any conscious design to evade the limitations

---

5   American Association of University Professors (AAUP), *1940 Statement of Principles on Academic Freedom and Tenure with 1970 Interpretive Comments* 3 (1990).

6   *Lemon*, 403 U.S. at 617.

imposed by the statute and the First Amendment."[7] Instead, the Court recognized that a "dedicated religious person, teaching in a school affiliated with his or her faith and operated to inculcate its tenets, will inevitably experience great difficulty in remaining religiously neutral."[8] Thus, a teacher even with the best of intentions might find it difficult to completely separate religious doctrine from secular teaching. Further, the relevant line between these might not be so clear, because what might "appear to some to be essential to good citizenship might well for others border on or constitute instruction in religion."[9] Many of these same points might analogously be made about instructors in religious colleges or universities.

Given the difficulties in ascertaining the line between the secular and the sectarian, even for those who have the best of intentions, the *Tilton* Court's justification for its conclusion that the funding did not violate Establishment Clause guarantees was at best surprising. Even if particular courses were taught according to the "academic requirements intrinsic to the subject matter and the individual teacher's concept of professional standards,"[10] the individual teacher's concept of professional standards might not provide a bulwark against religious indoctrination. Indeed, it may well be that an individual teacher's concept of professional standards would correspond to those of the institution, and that both concepts would permit or require the infusion of religious teaching into all aspects of the curriculum.

Suppose that federal funds were used to construct a building including classrooms, and that classes in that building included religious instruction. It should not matter for constitutional purposes whether that religious teaching occurred because it was viewed as permissible in light of the teacher's own professional standards or, instead, because the institution believed such instruction in keeping with its mission. In either case, federal funds were being used to promote religious teaching.

The *Tilton* Court noted that all four of the schools were "governed by Catholic religious organizations, and the faculties and student bodies at each [were] predominantly Catholic."[11] However, the Court seemed to think it relevant that non-Catholics were admitted as students and hired as faculty. Yet, even were there non-Catholic teachers who were not including religious instruction within their courses, that would hardly speak to whether Catholic teachers were promoting the mission of the school by including religious teaching within their courses. The Establishment Clause precludes state funding of religious instruction, and there is no waiver of that requirement merely because some teachers choose not to include religious indoctrination within their courses. *Lemon* had already warned against

---

7   *Id.* at 618.
8   *Id.*
9   *Id.* at 619.
10 *Tilton*, 403 U.S. at 681.
11 *Id.* at 686.

ignoring "the danger that a teacher under religious control and discipline poses to the separation of the religious from the purely secular."[12]

Nor can it be claimed that *Lemon* had simply slipped the *Tilton* Court's mind. First, the decisions were argued on the same day and issued on the same day. Second, *Tilton* specifically referred to *Lemon* in several places, differentiating what was at issue in *Tilton* from what was at issue in *Lemon*.

Consider the issue of the potential political divisiveness resulting from the funding of sectarian education. While the *Lemon* Court had noted that "political debate and division, however vigorous or even partisan, are [ordinarily] normal and healthy manifestations of our democratic system of government," that same Court had cautioned that "political division along religious lines was one of the principal evils against which the First Amendment was intended to protect."[13]

If the *Lemon* Court was worried about political divisiveness at the local level that might be caused by funding religious education, one would think that the Court would also have been concerned about potential political divisiveness caused by Congress's appropriating monies on the national level to help fund religious schooling. Yet, the *Tilton* Court dismissed the political divisiveness concern out of hand, simply noting that the appellants had not pointed to continuing religious division on this issue and hypothesizing that perhaps the "potential for divisiveness inherent in the essentially local problems of primary and secondary schools is significantly less with respect to a college or university whose student constituency is not local but diverse and widely dispersed."[14]

One might have inferred from reading the *Tilton* justification for worrying about political divisiveness on the local but not on the national level that the *Lemon* Court had pointed to evidence of continuing political divisiveness along religious lines and that this divisiveness had been particularly evident in certain localities. Yet, the *Lemon* Court had not pointed to evidence of political divisiveness of any sort, instead merely suggesting that where many pupils attend church-affiliated schools, "it can be assumed that state assistance will entail considerable political activity."[15] That activity will likely occur, the Court suggested, because those promoting state support of parochial schools, "understandably concerned with rising costs and sincerely dedicated to both the religious and secular educational missions of their schools, will inevitably champion this cause and promote political action to achieve their goals."[16] In contrast, those who oppose state support of parochial schools, "whether for constitutional, religious, or fiscal reasons, will inevitably respond and employ all of the usual political campaign techniques to prevail."[17]

---

12 *Lemon*, 403 U.S. at 617.

13 *Id.* at 622.

14 *Tilton*, 403 U.S. at 689.

15 *Lemon*, 403 U.S. at 622.

16 *Id.*

17 *Id.*

Yet, all of the points made by the *Lemon* Court might analogously be made about funding of sectarian schools on the national level. Further, the same points might be made whether the funding of sectarian elementary or secondary schools— or, instead, the funding of sectarian institutions of higher education—was at issue. Colleges and universities also face rising costs and they, too, have supporters employing political methods to promote their goals. Individuals who opposed Congress's supporting religiously affiliated colleges and universities, whether for constitutional, religious, or financial reasons, would also marshal support for their cause. In short, the political divisiveness factor is no less persuasively employed on the national level than it is on the local level.

As a way of bolstering its view that Establishment Clause guarantees were not being violated, the Court explained:

> Although all four schools require their students to take theology courses, the parties stipulated that these courses are taught according to the academic requirements of the subject matter and the teacher's concept of professional standards. The parties also stipulated that the courses covered a range of human religious experiences and are not limited to courses about the Roman Catholic religion. The schools introduced evidence that they made no attempt to indoctrinate students or to proselytize. Indeed, some of the required theology courses at Albertus Magnus and Sacred Heart are taught by rabbis.[18]

Here, one cannot tell whether the Court is seeking to establish that the schools do not promote a particular religion or that the schools do not promote religion generally. That courses cover a range of religious experiences might give one confidence that the theology course would not cover one religion exclusively, although one still might want to know whether one religion was privileged over the others, for example, by the teacher's discussing several religions but then concluding that there was only one true religion.

Even were the course not designed to privilege certain religions over others, a separate question would be whether the course was designed to promote religion generally rather than make it a subject of academic focus. If so, then the Establishment Clause would still be violated, even if no one religion was promoted at the expense of others. As the Court explained in *Capitol Square Review and Advisory Board v. Pinette*: "The establishment clause does not merely prohibit the state from favoring one religious sect over others. It also proscribes state action supporting the establishment of a number of religions, as well as the official endorsement of religion in preference to nonreligion."[19] Thus, even if the Court were correct that the theology courses at these institutions were not designed to promote Catholicism in particular, that would not settle the issue. The question still would be whether the courses were promoting rather than merely

---

18 *Tilton*, 403 U.S. at 686–7.
19 515 U.S. 753, 809 (1995).

discussing religion. The Court simply refused to address the more difficult issue for Establishment Clause purposes.

The *Tilton* Court also considered whether the Act would cause excessive entanglement between church and state. As part of its justification for why it did not, the Court noted that "college students are less impressionable and less susceptible to religious indoctrination," reasoning that the "skepticism of the college student is not an inconsiderable barrier to any attempt or tendency to subvert the congressional objectives and limitations."[20] Yet, this is an unusual interpretation of both constitutional and congressional objectives and limitations, because it implies that the Constitution's and Congress's focus of concern is to prevent successful indoctrination. Were the focus of concern instead that public funds not be used to promote religious teaching or worship, that concern would not be allayed merely because the target audience was hard to persuade. Thus, while it may well be true that college students are not as impressionable as schoolchildren, that point relates to whether the religious teaching will alter the views of the students rather than to whether the state should be supporting an attempt to indoctrinate religion.

Suppose that a particular town were to erect a cross on top of city hall.[21] Would that only be impermissible if doing so was thought likely to change individuals' beliefs? Presumably, this would violate Establishment Clause guarantees even if no one's religious views were affected and the only result had been that certain people seeing the display had felt like political outsiders.

The Court contrasted *Lemon* and *Tilton* by suggesting that because "teachers are not necessarily religiously neutral, greater governmental surveillance would be required to guarantee that state salary aid would not in fact subsidize religious instruction."[22] However, because "the Government provides facilities that are themselves religiously neutral, ... [t]he risks of Government aid to religion and the corresponding need for surveillance are therefore reduced."[23] Yet, this analysis simply will not stand. The Court has suggested that classrooms whose construction was funded in part by the federal government cannot be used to indoctrinate religion. If that is so, then the fact that teachers are not necessarily religiously neutral would speak to the necessity of greater governmental surveillance of those federally funded classrooms, precisely because the teachers might use those classrooms to engage in religious instruction.

The Act specified that "no part of the project may be used for sectarian instruction, religious worship, or the programs of a divinity school,"[24] and the Court noted that the "restrictions have been enforced in the Act's actual

---

20 *Tilton*, 403 U.S. at 686.

21 See *County of Allegheny v. ACLU Greater Pittsburgh Chapter*, 492 U.S. 573, 661 (1989) (Kennedy, J. concurring in part, dissenting in part) (offering this example).

22 *Tilton*, 403 U.S. at 687–8.

23 *Id*. at 688.

24 *Id*. at 675.

administration, and the record shows that some church-related institutions have been required to disgorge benefits for failure to obey them."[25] Yet, this suggests that the buildings might well be misused and that oversight might well be required. Precisely because instructors might feel implicit or explicit institutional pressure to include religion within their courses or might feel that they should include such materials either because of their internalized professional standards or, perhaps, their individual consciences, there is a danger that religious indoctrination would take place. Without oversight, that indoctrination might well occur in federally financed buildings. While all else being equal a reduction in entanglement between church and state is better for all concerned, all else is not equal if the entanglement reduction would increase the likelihood that federal funds would be misused to promote religious indoctrination.

There are at least two distinct ways in which federal funds might be misused: (1) the building whose construction was made possible by federal funds might be used in ways prohibited by statute, or (2) the funds themselves might be misappropriated. Not only was the *Tilton* Court confident that the buildings would be used for their intended purposes, but the Court seemed relatively confident that the funds would be used to help fund the cost of the buildings, noting that another reason that there would be less entanglement required was that "the Government aid here is a one-time, single purpose construction grant."[26]

Consider two kinds of grants: (1) a one-time grant, and (2) a grant involving partial payments over several years. The Court suggested that there was less need to monitor the former than the latter, perhaps thinking that the one-time grant would immediately be dispensed to those responsible for designing and constructing the buildings at hand. However, if the one-time allocation was put into an account and the funds were dispensed from that account over several years, then the one-time grant would be functionally equivalent to the grant involving partial payments over several years, at least with respect to the need to monitor those funds to make sure that they were going towards the construction of buildings rather than other expenses not contemplated within the purposes for the provision of the grant.

Once the federal funds had been spent, it would no longer be necessary to continue surveillance to assure that the funds had been used for their designated purpose, but it still would be necessary to continue to monitor to assure that the building constructed with federal funds would be used only for the designated purposes. Justice Douglas explained in his *Tilton* dissent that "surveillance creates an entanglement of government and religion which the First Amendment was designed to avoid."[27] However, he noted, using federal funds to pay for the construction of buildings at religious institutions would require surveillance lasting for the useful life of the building. Indeed, the *Tilton* Court implicitly recognized

---

25　*Id.* at 680.

26　*Id.* at 688.

27　*Id.* at 694 (Douglas, J., dissenting in part).

the force of Justice Douglas's point when striking down one provision of the Higher Education Facilities Act.

The Act had provided that the government would receive a partial refund if an institution violated the terms of the agreement by using a building for religious purposes, notwithstanding that the construction of the building had been supported by federal funds. However, the government was entitled to receive monies back only if the violation occurred within 20 years of the completion of the building. This meant that a building whose construction was made possible through the use of federal funds could be used for religious worship as long as 20 years had elapsed since its completion. Because the useful life of the building would probably extend for more than 20 years, the provision would in effect permit the use of government funds to construct buildings to be used for religious purposes as long as the institution waited the requisite 20 years. The Court noted, "If, at the end of 20 years, the building is, for example, converted into a chapel or otherwise used to promote religious interests, the original federal grant will in part have the effect of advancing religion."[28] This, the Court held, violated constitutional guarantees. Yet, if the Court understood that it would be impermissible for the buildings to be used for religious purposes during the life of the building, then it is not clear why Justice Douglas was incorrect in asserting that supervision—and the accompanying entanglement—would also be necessary during those years.

The claim here is not that the schools at issue in *Tilton* used the monies in a way that violated Establishment Clause guarantees, but that the Court's justifications for why the Establishment Clause had not been violated sent a signal that the relevant test in the context of higher education was so weak that colleges and universities might be eligible to receive state funding even if those funds would indeed be used to promote religion. The Court did little to undermine that signal in subsequent cases.

Hunt v. McNair

Hunt v. McNair[29] involved a South Carolina program in which the state created an Educational Facilities Authority (EFA) to assist colleges and universities in financing their construction projects. The advantage for higher education institutions in making use of the EFA was that the interest on the bonds used to raise money was tax exempt, thereby enabling the school to market the bonds at a significantly lower rate of interest than the school would be forced to pay if borrowing the money through private financing. Basically, the EFA would issue bonds for the desired building improvements for which the state assumed no direct or indirect obligation. The institution would convey without charge the portion of the campus to be improved to the EFA, and the EFA would lease back that part of

---

28 *Id.* at 683.
29 413 U.S. 734 (1973).

the campus to the institution. After the bonds had been paid in full, the EFA would convey the property back to the institution.

The act creating the EFA included a provision specifying that monies raised by the issuance of these bonds could not be used to construct buildings where there would be sectarian instruction or religious worship. To assure that the property would not be used for sectarian purposes once the institution had regained title to it, the EFA was authorized by the agreement to conduct inspections to assure that the property was not being used improperly.

The *Hunt* Court began its analysis by reaffirming that the *Lemon* test would determine whether there had been an Establishment Clause violation, quickly dispensing with the purpose prong. After all, the "benefits of the Act are available to all institutions of higher education in South Carolina, whether or not having a religious affiliation."[30] Thus, there was no claim that the South Carolina Legislature was secretly trying to aid religious institutions by passing the act in question.

When deciding what the primary effect was, the Court did not consider the primary effect of the statute generally, for example, providing lower cost loans for construction projects to colleges and universities in the state. Rather, to ascertain the primary effect of the statute, the Court narrowed its focus to the transaction at issue in the litigation.

On first blush, it might seem that the Court's narrowing its focus to the primary effect of the statute with respect to the Baptist College of Charleston would almost necessitate a finding that the statute's primary effect would be to promote religion. After all, the monies saved by offering a lower return for tax-exempt bonds would give the college the opportunity to use those monies for other, more sectarian uses. Yet, the *Hunt* Court expressly rejected that funding was prohibited merely because it would allow an institution to spend other resources to promote religious ends. Indeed, the Court offered a rather narrow definition of what would constitute the primary effect of advancing religion: "Aid normally may be thought to have a primary effect of advancing religion when it flows to an institution in which religion is so pervasive that a substantial portion of its functions are subsumed in the religious mission or when it funds a specifically religious activity in an otherwise substantially secular setting."[31] Thus, aid will have the primary effect of advancing religion only when it is actually used to promote religion either because the aid is specifically used to fund a sectarian program or because it goes to an institution that is so pervasively religious that the aid to that institution cannot help but promote religion.

The Court considered whether the institution before it was pervasively sectarian, noting that no evidence had been presented that would justify so categorizing that institution. While the members of the Board of Trustees were elected by the South Carolina Baptist Convention, the approval of the Convention was required for certain financial transactions, and the college's charter might

---

30 *Id.* at 741.
31 *Id.* at 743.

only be amended by the Convention, there were no religious qualifications for faculty or students. The Court concluded that on the record there was "no basis to conclude that the College's operations are oriented significantly towards sectarian rather than secular education,"[32] although that may have been because there was relatively little in the record. Nonetheless, because the institution had not itself been found to be pervasively sectarian and because the statute expressly excluded any buildings or facilities used for religious purposes, the Court rejected that the statute would be providing aid to religious rather than secular college activities. The Court compared the record before it to the record before the *Tilton* Court, noting that there was "no evidence here to demonstrate that the College is any more an instrument of religious indoctrination than were the colleges and universities involved in *Tilton*."[33] Thus, given the deferential stance adopted in *Tilton* combined with the scant record before the *Hunt* Court, the Court did not have enough evidence to support the contention that the Baptist College of Charleston was pervasively sectarian.

The entanglement issue implicated in *Hunt* differed from that in *Tilton* because, in *Hunt*, the South Carolina EFA was empowered to:

> determine the location and character of any project financed under the act; to construct, maintain, manage, operate, lease as lessor or lessee, and regulate the same; to enter into contracts for the management and operation of such project; to establish rules and regulations for the use of the project or any portion thereof; and to fix and revise from time to time rates, rents, fees, and charges for the use of a project and for the services furnished or to be furnished by a project or any portion thereof. In other words, the College turns over to the State Authority control of substantial parts of the fiscal operation of the school—its very life's blood.[34]

Thus, the EFA in *Hunt* might become "deeply involved in the day-to-day financial and policy decisions of the College"[35] in a way that was not even potentially implicated in *Tilton*. However, the *Hunt* Court rejected that these EFA powers would likely be exercised, instead accepting that the EFA would only step in if "the College fails to make the prescribed rental payments or otherwise defaults in its obligations."[36]

There were two different respects in which the EFA might be thought to be too deeply entangled in the affairs of the college—one involved the day-to-day financial decisions and the other involved decisions about the inclusion of religious materials in particular. Justice Brennan argued in his dissent that the

---

32 *Id.* at 744.
33 *Id.* at 746.
34 *Id.* at 751 (Brennan, J., dissenting).
35 *Id.* at 747.
36 *Id.* at 748.

"content of courses taught in facilities financed under the agreement must be closely monitored by the State Authority in discharge of its duty to ensure that the facilities are not being used for sectarian instruction."[37] However, the Court reasoned that the required entanglement in *Hunt* would be no more burdensome than the required entanglement in *Tilton*, and that the statute could therefore not be struck down on these grounds.

Almost as an afterthought, the *Hunt* Court implied that the fact that the state was not contributing any monies directly to the school militated in favor of the constitutionality of the program. However, that factor seemed to play no role in the analysis, and the same result would likely have been reached even had the monies been loaned or given directly to the school. Further, the Court having mentioned this and nonetheless having analyzed whether the funds would be used for sectarian purposes undercuts the claim that the state not contributing public monies to the school should play an important role in the analysis of whether such bond programs comport with constitutional requirements.

The Court's mere mention of the fact that the state had not directly given or loaned money to the school should be contrasted with the role that this factor played in the South Carolina Supreme Court decision in which the constitutionality of the statute was upheld. When that court first heard the case, the court was considering a challenge to the statute based on the supposition that public funds were being used to benefit the school. However, the South Carolina Supreme Court noted that no public monies were involved and, further, that the state's credit could never be adversely affected. In this opinion, the South Carolina Supreme Court disposed of the Establishment Clause objection in one paragraph, basically suggesting that because "neither the credit of the State nor the property of the State is involved, it follows that this constitutional provision is not violated."[38]

The United States Supreme Court vacated and remanded the decision for reconsideration in light of *Lemon* and *Tilton*. On remand, the South Carolina Supreme Court reiterated its belief that there was no Establishment Clause violation because neither the credit nor the property of the state was involved. The court distinguished *Lemon*, including an analysis downplaying the state's oversight role:

> The surveillance on the part of the State, obviously abhorred by the Court, is not necessary under the proposed financing plan of the college. The Court contemplates execution of a contract which definitely establishes the rights of all parties to the agreement. The State plays a passive and very limited role in the implementation of the Act, serving principally as a mere conduit through which institutions may borrow funds for the purposes of the Act on a tax-free basis.[39]

---

37 *Id.* at 752 (Brennan J., dissenting).

38 *Hunt v. McNair*, 177 S.E.2d 362, 370 (S.C. 1970), *vacated* 403 U.S. 945 (1971).

39 *Hunt v. McNair*, 187 S.E.2d 645, 650–51 (S.C. 1972).

Yet, there are numerous respects in which it is inaccurate to describe the state as a mere conduit. First, it is not as if individuals were merely using the state as a conduit as they would by sending checks through the mail. Rather, the state was making it possible for the college to market bonds at a much lower interest rate, thereby resulting in substantial savings for the school. More important for purposes here, however, is that while the South Carolina Supreme Court was correct that the Court seemed to abhor some of the difficulties caused by intrusive surveillance, that abhorrence cannot justify the state's failing to fulfill its constitutional obligation to make sure that the funds at issue are being used properly. It should hardly be thought a virtue for a state to fail to oversee whether state support is being used to promote religious indoctrination, and Establishment Clause jurisprudence is turned on its head if a state's refusal to take an active role in overseeing whether funds are being used properly is what enables the funding to pass muster.

The South Carolina Supreme Court noted that the college would convey most of the campus to the state of South Carolina, although a few buildings were excluded from that conveyance including the Physical Education Building, where the religious worship facilities were located. The state supreme court did not examine whether classes included religious indoctrination. The closest that the court came to examining whether the college was pervasively sectarian or to whether there would be impermissible instruction in the classrooms was to note that there was "less potential for experiencing the substantive evils which the religious clauses were intended to protect than in [*Tilton*]."[40] Part of that conclusion may have rested on the composition of the faculty and student body, which the court had noted in a prior opinion was 60 percent Baptist, mirroring the ratio of Baptists to non-Baptists in that part of the state.

It is not surprising that the state supreme court did not include an analysis of the ways that the classes were taught. In that court's view, the Establishment Clause affords "protection against sponsorship, financial support and active involvement of the government in religious activity."[41] However, the court implied that those protections were not even triggered, given the state's passive and very limited role. Yet, one infers from the *Hunt* Court's analysis that the state was sufficiently involved in the funding to require an analysis of whether there was religious indoctrination in the classroom.

That the South Carolina Supreme Court did not address whether there was religious instruction in the classroom was understandable, given its view that the funding program did not trigger Establishment Clause protections. However, the *Hunt* Court made clear that those protections were triggered and thus that Establishment Clause guarantees would be violated were the funds used to promote religious instruction. At the very least, the United States Supreme Court might have remanded the case to get a more developed record with respect to what was going on in the classroom, although that may not have been viewed as

---

40 *Id.* at 651.

41 *Id.* at 648.

a particularly attractive alternative given that the Court had already remanded the case once before.

Tilton and *Hunt* together suggest that the Court takes a very deferential view with respect to state funding of religious higher education. Absent evidence of pervasive sectarianism, the Court will likely uphold the constitutionality of state funding of religious schools of higher education as long as there has been no showing that the funds are being used to promote religious instruction or worship. Yet, this gives the state great incentive not to engage in much oversight. There will then be no evidence of impermissible indoctrination and the funding can be upheld. Indeed, by noting that the record about how classes were taught was rather sparse but nonetheless upholding the funding rather than remanding the case for further fact-finding, the *Hunt* Court sent an important message to the states. Basically, the Court implied that it would not insist that the state do much to assure that state funds were not used to promote sectarian activities and that the funding of non-pervasively-sectarian institutions would be upheld, absent evidence that the funds were being used to promote religious indoctrination or worship.

In both *Tilton* and *Hunt*, the Court implied that there was little need for much oversight of postsecondary school practices, presumably because college students were less vulnerable to indoctrination. However, the Court did not make clear whether the students being less subject to indoctrination somehow immunized the attempts to indoctrinate or, instead, made it less likely that schools would try to indoctrinate, thereby obviating the need to maintain strict supervision over the classes. The Court helped answer that question in *Roemer v. Board of Public Works*.[42]

Roemer v. Board of Public Works

At issue in *Roemer* was a statute authorizing annual grants to private colleges, provided that the funds were not used for sectarian purposes. To assure that the monies were used for their stated purposes, the state employed two safeguards. First, it would simply exclude schools primarily awarding theological or seminary degrees. Second, with respect to those schools still potentially qualifying for a grant, the chief executive officer would have to sign an affidavit stating that the funds would not be used for sectarian purposes and describing the purposes for which the monies would be used. Further, a report would have to be filed by the end of the fiscal year describing how the funds had been used. The chief executive officer would then have to certify that report and also file a supporting affidavit stating that the funds had not been used for sectarian purposes.

Questions of sectarian use would be resolved on the basis of affidavits, if possible. If that would not resolve this issue, then the school might be subjected to a quick and non-judgmental audit that would take no more than a day. The *Roemer* plurality noted that "religious institutions need not be quarantined from

---

42 426 U.S. 736 (1976).

public benefits that are neutrally available to all,"[43] emphasizing that "[n]eutrality is what is required."[44] Basically, the plurality suggested that as long as the state has a secular purpose and does not promote or undermine religion, the state's funding religious institutions will not violate the Establishment Clause. That said, however, facial neutrality and a secular purpose provide no guarantee that state funding will pass constitutional muster. After all, the state is constitutionally precluded from paying for religious education.

The Court explained that state funding that accords an incidental benefit to a religious institution is not barred by the Establishment Clause. Rather, the Clause merely requires that the state have a policy of "neutrality." Yet, the Court's neutrality requirement is open to misinterpretation. The *Roemer* Court was not suggesting, for example, that neutrality requires the state to fund religious programs if nonreligious programs are also being funded. On the contrary, religious programs cannot be funded. As the *Roemer* Court explained, "The State must confine itself to secular objectives, and neither advance nor impede religious activity."[45]

When suggesting that neutrality is required, the *Roemer* Court meant that the Establishment Clause does not prohibit the state from providing funds to religiously affiliated institutions providing secular services. The required neutrality is with respect to the identity of the provider of the secular service—not with respect to the kind of service provided. The *Roemer* Court would never have agreed with the plurality in *Mitchell v. Helms* that the state may provide aid to pervasively sectarian institutions as long as secular institutions are also receiving that aid.[46]

Even when this potentially confusing point about Establishment neutrality is clarified, it may not always be easy to tell what the neutrality principle requires, permits, or prohibits. The Court has given some guidance, however, explaining that the "State may not, for example, pay for what is actually a religious education, even though it purports to be paying for a secular one, and even though it makes its aid available to secular and religious institutions alike."[47] Thus, while some of the implications of the Court's neutrality policy may not be clear, the *Roemer* Court made very clear that the state could not pay for a religious education and, presumably, ministerial studies would be a paradigmatic example of religious education.

Roemer suggests that the constitutionally required protections against religious indoctrination at the university level are minimal at best. For example, the Court understood that some of the classes at these institutions began with a prayer and, indeed, that a majority of the classes at one of the institutions began with prayer. However, the Court did not hold that these institutions therefore could not receive

---

43 *Id.* at 746.

44 *Id.* at 747.

45 *Id.*

46 See 530 U.S. 793, 809 (2000). For a discussion of *Mitchell*, see Chapter 1, seventh section.

47 *Roemer*, 426 U.S. at 747.

public funding, reasoning instead that the funding was constitutional because there was no institutional policy of encouraging prayer and the decision by an instructor to begin class with a prayer was a matter of academic freedom. The Court thereby suggested that a teacher's beginning her class with prayer in a publicly funded classroom was not constitutionally significant as long as this was not mandated by school policy.

In addition, the Court noted that some of the instructors wore clerical garb when teaching, and that some of the classrooms had religious symbols. These very factors were the kinds of factors that the *Tilton* Court implied would militate in favor of a finding of pervasive sectarianism. Nonetheless, the *Roemer* Court upheld the district court, finding that the colleges were not pervasively sectarian, because the curriculum covered a wide spectrum of liberal arts courses and because religious indoctrination was not a substantial purpose of the schools.

The Court accepted the finding below that the secular could be separated from the sectarian, and then was willing to assume that the funds would be used correctly. The Court did not seem to believe that much monitoring was required, suggesting that secular activities could mostly be taken at face value. For example, the plurality believed that there was "no danger, or at least only a substantially reduced danger, that an ostensibly secular activity—the study of biology, the learning of a foreign language, an athletic event—will actually be infused with religious content or significance."[48] Yet, it would not be surprising that a biology class might include religious content by discussing whether or when human embryos had become ensouled. Further, while athletic events might not seem particularly religious, prayers for victory might be recited before or during such events, and prayers of thanksgiving afterwards. Indeed, it might be noted that one of the few buildings on the Baptist College of Charleston campus that was not eligible for state funding was the physical education building, which also housed the chapel.

The *Roemer* plurality did not believe that the subsidy being annual rather than a one-time contribution should be dispositive, even though that had played an important role in *Tilton*. Nor did the Court believe it important that the funds at issue here went directly to the institution. The *Roemer* Court noted that the funds could be used for any nonsectarian purpose, although the Court was particularly unhelpful with respect to what uses would be impermissible. Indeed, rather than give criteria to determine what would count as sectarian, the *Roemer* Court instead deferred to the Council to develop the appropriate safeguards, apparently endorsing some of the requirements imposed by the Council. For example, the Council precluded the use of state funds "to pay in whole or in part the salary of any person who is engaged in the teaching of religion or theology, who serves as chaplain or director of the campus ministry, or who administers or supervises any program of religious activities."[49] Yet, this does not seem to preclude paying

---

48 *Id.* at 763.
49 *Id.* at 761 n.22.

individuals who start their classes with a prayer, as long as they do not, in addition, teach religion or theology.

Another provision was that state funds could "not be used to pay any portion of the cost of maintenance or repair of any building or facility used for the teaching of religion or theology or for religious worship or for any religious activity."[50] Yet, it was not clear whether this limitation only referred to those buildings that were primarily used for religious worship such as a building housing a chapel, or any building in which religious worship might take place. One infers that this limitation only meant the former, given that at one institution over half of the classes began with a prayer and thus on the latter interpretation many of the buildings containing classrooms would then be off limits for state maintenance or support. The same point might be made about state support for the payment of utilities or capital construction or improvements.

Roemer is extremely deferential with respect to what religiously affiliated institutions of higher learning can do without offending the Establishment Clause. The Court seemed to accept almost wholesale the district court's conclusion that the religious programs were separable from the secular programs at each school, notwithstanding that many classes began with a prayer.

The district court reasoned that "prayer in class is as peripheral to the subject of religious permeation of an institution as are the facts that some instructors wear clerical garb and some classrooms have religious symbols."[51] Perhaps that is so with respect to the *institution*. For example, the practices in a particular classroom might not carry over to classes in a different building, especially if the students in the latter classes had no classes in which there were prayers or religious symbols on the walls or instructors in religious garb. Yet, to say that these practices would not be enough to establish institutional permeation hardly suggests that these practices would not contribute to or even constitute religious permeation in the very classes in which these practices were occurring. Certainly, in a classroom with religious symbols on the walls, it would be unsurprising that the dynamic of the class would be affected as a general matter if the instructor were dressed in religious garb or were to begin the class with a prayer. Further, it would also be unsurprising were there a kind of carryover effect so that classes in which these practices did not occur might nonetheless be affected if many of the students in those classes were also taking classes in which these religious practices frequently occurred.

The district court had noted that there was "convincing evidence that courses at each defendant are taught according to the academic requirements intrinsic to the subject matter and the individual teacher's concept of professional standards."[52] Yet, given the qualifier involving the individual's concept of professional standards, it might well be that some individual instructors felt that they would

---

50 *Id.* n.22.
51 *Roemer v. Board of Public Works*, 387 F. Supp. 1282, 1293 (D. Md. 1974).
52 *Id.* at 1294.

be failing to live up to their responsibilities were they not to include within their classes the appropriate religious perspective. While the district court might have been correct that the plaintiffs had failed to establish that a professor's "beginning a class with prayer in any way diminishes the atmosphere of intellectual freedom which marks these colleges"[53] as a whole, it is hard to believe that the same could be said about many of those classes in particular. Presumably, at least one of the purposes or foreseeable effects of starting a class with a prayer is to change that class's atmosphere in a way that the professor believes would be desirable.

At issue is not whether infusing classes with religion should be permissible in a religiously affiliated school but, instead, whether the state would be violating the Establishment Clause, for example, by effectively paying the instructor's salary. Judge Bryan noted in his district court dissent that the "payment of the grants directly to the colleges [is] unmarked in purpose."[54] He worried that grants could "go into secular and sectarian areas at the same time."[55] This danger existed not only with respect to theology departments—until the Council had changed its regulations—but also with respect to classes where an individual instructor's professional judgment required that she infuse her class with religious instruction.

Some of the institutions whose practices were at issue in *Roemer*—College of Notre Dame, Mount Saint Mary's College, Saint Joseph College and Loyola College—had been subject to a similar suit earlier. *Horace Mann League v. Board of Public Works*[56] involved a challenge to state funding of Western Maryland College, Notre Dame College and St. Joseph College, each of whom was found by the Maryland Supreme Court to be sufficiently sectarian that it could not receive state funding. While it is not surprising that courts over time might reach different conclusions about whether particular institutions were sufficiently sectarian to be precluded from receiving funds, for example, because the jurisprudence or the institutions' practices had evolved in the interim, it is somewhat surprising that institutions that had been thought so sectarian that they could not receive aid were subsequently thought sufficiently unlikely to infuse religious doctrine into their secular classes that close surveillance would not be necessary, even when such classes started with a prayer by an instructor dressed in religious garb.

The trilogy of aid-to-religious-higher-education cases makes a mockery of Establishment Clause jurisprudence. Factors that had been thought relevant, for example, whether teachers were in fact incorporating religious teaching into the curriculum, would suddenly not be relevant, allegedly because the students were less vulnerable to indoctrination. Indicia that an institution was pervasively sectarian—for example, whether the school included religious symbols in the classroom or whether classes began with prayers—were suddenly less important or, perhaps, irrelevant as long as these religious practices were not a result of

---

53 *Id.* at 1293.

54 *Id.* at 1298 (Bryan, J., dissenting).

55 *Id.* at 1299 (Bryan J., dissenting).

56 220 A.2d 51 (Md. 1966).

institutional command. Basically, the Court has created a jurisprudence that makes it very difficult to successfully challenge state aid to colleges and universities on Establishment Clause grounds as long as those institutions are not pervasively sectarian. Even aid to pervasively sectarian institutions may be protected, although that conclusion is based on several cases decided after the *Tilton–Roemer* lines of cases.

Impermissible Burdening of the Clergy

In *McDaniel v. Paty*,[57] which was decided a mere two years after *Roemer*, the Court examined whether a Tennessee statute precluding members of the clergy from serving as delegates to the state's limited constitutional convention violated free exercise guarantees. The Tennessee Supreme Court examined the clergy disqualification and held that it imposed no burden on religious belief and that it restricted religious action only in the lawmaking process, where religious action was barred by the Establishment Clause. The court concluded that the state interests in preventing establishment and in avoiding religious divisiveness justified the disqualification. The Tennessee decision was appealed.

When explaining why the Tennessee decision had to be reversed, the *McDaniel* Court began by noting that if the "provision were viewed as depriving the clergy of a civil right solely because of their religious beliefs, [the] … inquiry would be at an end. The Free Exercise Clause categorically prohibits government from regulating, prohibiting or rewarding religious beliefs as such."[58] However, it did not seem accurate to suggest that the beliefs as such were being penalized—an individual who was not a member of the clergy but who had religious beliefs identical to her minister's was not barred by Tennessee law from serving as a delegate to the convention. By the same token, Tennessee would not bar an individual who renounced his ministry from being a legislator, even if his religious beliefs had not changed. The *McDaniel* Court reasoned that it was not the individual's beliefs as such that were targeted by the Tennessee statute; rather, the Tennessee disqualification was based on McDaniel's status as a minister or priest. For that reason, "the Free Exercise Clause's absolute prohibition of infringement on the 'freedom to believe' [was] inapposite,"[59] and the Tennessee disqualification provision could not be struck down as a violation of constitutional guarantees safeguarding religious belief.

That said, however, the state still needed to justify the disqualification. The state asserted that its interest was in preventing the establishment of a state religion. However, the Court rejected the implicit characterization of the clergy as individuals who would be less faithful to their oaths of office than their

---

57 435 U.S. 618 (1978).

58 *Id.* at 626.

59 *Id.* at 627.

non-ordained counterparts. Thus, the Court rejected that the means adopted by the state—disqualifying members of the clergy from acting as legislators— was sufficiently closely tailored to achieve the desired end of preventing the establishment of a state religion. Justice White pointed out in his concurrence in the judgment that all of the states were constitutionally required to maintain separation of church and state but no state other than Tennessee felt it necessary to prevent ministers from running for office.

Yet, the fact that Tennessee was employing a method no longer used by other states did not establish that method's unconstitutionality. After all, there was no suggestion that the clergy disqualification provision had been adopted out of animus toward religion. Indeed, the *McDaniel* Court noted that "at least during the early segment of our national life, those [clergy disqualification] provisions enjoyed the support of responsible American statesmen and were accepted as having a rational basis."[60] After making clear that it would "not lightly invalidate a statute enacted pursuant to a provision of a state constitution which has been sustained by its highest court,"[61] the *McDaniel* Court explained that "the right to the free exercise of religion unquestionably encompasses the right to preach, proselyte, and perform other similar religious functions, or, in other words, to be a minister of the type McDaniel was found to be."[62]

By noting the deference that would normally be accorded to such a constitutional provision and by suggesting that the disqualification was considered reasonable at the time of its adoption, the Court implied that it would not have reversed the judgment of the Tennessee Supreme Court if it merely was employing rational basis scrutiny under the Equal Protection Clause. The Court has been willing to make assumptions in other contexts about how an individual's religious beliefs might alter her perceptions of what the Constitution requires, so it would have been surprising for the Court to have treated Tennessee's having done so as irrational and thus not passing muster under rational basis scrutiny. Nonetheless, because McDaniel's activity enjoyed significant First Amendment protection, the Tennessee clergy disqualification could not pass muster. In his concurrence in the judgment, Justice Brennan offered the following criticism:

> [C]haracterization of the exclusion as one burdening appellant's "career or calling" and not religious belief cannot withstand analysis. Clearly freedom of belief protected by the Free Exercise Clause embraces freedom to profess or practice that belief, even including doing so to earn a livelihood. One's religious belief surely does not cease to enjoy the protection of the First Amendment when held with such depth of sincerity as to impel one to join the ministry.[63]

---

60 *Id*. at 625
61 *Id*.
62 *Id*. at 626.
63 *Id*. at 631 (Brennan, J., concurring).

Of course, Tennessee did not seek to preclude all devoutly religious individuals from serving as legislators, so it is not as if that was the state's goal. While one might expect a correlation between the depth of sincerity of religious belief and the decision to enter into the ministry, there would be many individuals with deeply held religious beliefs who would not be members of the clergy, and there might be members of the clergy whose religious beliefs were not deeply held.

In any event, even if the statute was viewed as implicating religious status rather than religious belief, the Court held that the Tennessee statute impermissibly interfered with McDaniel's Free Exercise rights. Eight years later in *Witters v. Washington Department of Services for the Blind*[64] the Court would hold that states could help individuals study for the ministry without violating Establishment Clause guarantees.

Public Support for Becoming a Minister

Witters was an important case in part because of what it did not, rather than what it did, say. The petitioner, who was suffering from a progressive eye condition, was eligible for rehabilitation assistance. He was attending a private Christian college and was studying to become a pastor, missionary, or youth director. At issue was whether the Establishment Clause precluded his receipt of the rehabilitation assistance.

The Court explained that Establishment Clause guarantees are not necessarily violated merely because money once in the possession of the state has been given to a religious institution. After all, the Court reasoned, a public employee could donate all of her paycheck to a religious institution without offending constitutional guarantees, even if the state knew about the employee's intention to make that donation prior to her receipt of the paycheck.[65] Of course, the analogy is not entirely apt. When paying an employee for services rendered, the state cannot put conditions on those monies, for example, say that they must be used to buy food or clothing. Rather, it is entirely up to the recipient to decide what she shall do with the money—it is not for the state to distinguish among the myriad legal uses to which the monies might be put. In contrast, the funds at issue in *Witters* were specifically designated to provide visually handicapped individuals with "special education and/or training in the professions, business or trades."[66] They could not be used for just any purpose. While a variety of programs, almost all of which were secular, were permissible in light of the relevant limitations, recipients were not given the kind of freedom of choice with respect to the use of funds that an individual would have with respect to how she would spend her paycheck.

---

64 474 U.S. 481 (1986).

65 *Id.* at 486–7

66 *Id.* at 483.

When the state pays an employee for services rendered, the state is paying a debt owed. The state is not offering a gift whose acceptance can be conditioned on that gift being used for certain purposes and not others. Thus, while it is true that in both scenarios the state once possessed the monies that eventually would have ended up in the hands of the pervasively religious charity, that does not make the situations comparable. Otherwise, one would expect the Court to say that because a government employee would be free to donate her salary to a church to spread God's Truth, the state should be free to do so as well.

For the state to preclude an individual from using earned monies to contribute to any and all pervasively religious charities would itself violate the Establishment Clause. But the Court made quite clear in the *Tilton–Roemer* line of cases that there was no Establishment Clause violation by the state's refusing to fund pervasively sectarian institutions. Were the *Witter* Court's analogy to private choices apt, either the Establishment Clause would impose limitations on private donations to pervasively sectarian institutions or the Establishment Clause would impose no limitations on state aid to pervasively sectarian institutions. But neither of those positions is correct. The Establishment Clause of course imposes no limitations on private donations, and the Establishment Clause does impose limitations on state aid to pervasively sectarian institutions. A separate issue is whether the Washington statute passed muster, but the analogy to private choices is simply unhelpful.

The *Witters* Court refused to characterize the aid going to the Inland Empire School of the Bible as involving state sponsorship or subsidizing of religion. However, the Court was not particularly clear about why that was so, and numerous explanations might be offered.

The Court began its discussion of what was central to its analysis by noting that the assistance is "paid directly to the student, who transmits it to the educational institution of his or her choice," reasoning that any aid that flows to "religious institutions does so only as a result of the genuinely independent and private choices of the recipient."[67] The *Witters* Court also noted that the state could not give an in-kind grant of money to a religious institution, where that would be a direct subsidy of religious teaching. It might be thought, then, that the constitutional parameters are clear—state monies that go directly to religious institutions implicate constitutional limitations, whereas state monies that go to students and then indirectly to the schools do not implicate those limitations.

Yet, this analysis does not represent the relevant limitations as explicated by *Witters*. First, after explaining that the state cannot give an in-kind grant of money to a religious institution, where that would be a direct subsidy of religious teaching, the *Witters* Court also noted that an impermissible in-kind grant might take place even where a student or the student's parents were the conduit for that grant. An important issue thus became how to distinguish among the different kinds of indirect aid, some of which were permissible and others of which were not.

---

67 *Id.* at 488.

One way to distinguish is to seek to determine whether the student's decision to direct the funds to a sectarian rather than secular institution is a result of the recipient's independent and private choice. Yet, it is unclear why the fact of independent and private choice should immunize a decision from Establishment Clause review rather than simply be a factor in determining whether the funds could be directed to a sectarian institution without offending constitutional guarantees. For example, at issue in *Nyquist*[68] were New York programs whereby parents sending their elementary school children to nonpublic schools might receive some reimbursement or state income tax deduction. Eighty-five percent of these schools were religiously affiliated. These schools were Roman Catholic, Jewish, Lutheran, Episcopal, and Seventh-Day Adventist, among others.

The *Nyquist* Court noted that the grants could not be given directly to the sectarian schools and then explained that the "controlling question ... is whether the fact that the grants are delivered to parents rather than schools is of such significance as to compel a contrary result."[69] Rejecting that the question was settled when the parents rather than the schools received the funds, the Court explained that the existing jurisprudence established that "far from providing a per se immunity from examination of the substance of the state's program, the fact that aid is disbursed to parents rather than to the schools is only one among many factors to be considered."[70]

Other factors to be considered included an examination of what would be done with the money. The *Nyquist* Court noted with disapproval that there had been "no endeavor to guarantee the separation between secular and religious educational functions and to ensure the state financial aid supports only the former."[71] Indeed, the Court suggested that by "reimbursing parents for a portion of their tuition bill, the state seeks to relieve their financial burdens sufficiently to assure that they continue to have the option to send their children to religion-oriented schools," concluding that the Establishment Clause would not permit this, because "the effect of the aid is unmistakably to provide desired financial support for nonpublic, sectarian institutions."[72]

Yet, it might be argued that the tuition reimbursement at issue in *Nyquist* was not really going to the schools. The tuition had already been paid, and the reimbursement might be used for a variety of purposes. Thus, because "New York's program calls for reimbursement for tuition already paid rather than for direct contributions which are merely routed through the parents to the schools, in advance of or in lieu of payment by the parents,"[73] the Court understood that the parent was absolutely free to spend the money in any way desired. That these

---

68 For a discussion of *Nyquist*, see Chapter 1, third section.
69 *Nyquist*, 413 U.S. 781.
70 *Id.*
71 *Id.* at 783.
72 *Id.*
73 *Id.* at 785–6.

monies were not simply being directed through the parents to the schools militated in favor of the program's constitutionality. However, the *Nyquist* Court noted that if the funds were being offered as an incentive to parents to send their children to sectarian schools, then the Establishment Clause was violated whether or not the actual dollars were received by those schools. Indeed, the Court explained, the impact is the same whether the grant is called a reimbursement, a subsidy, or a reward.

The *Nyquist* Court implicitly offered a way to understand the difference between those parents acting as a conduit and those who were not. Basically, the question was whether the contributions were being routed through the parents or, instead, could be used for any purpose. The Court implied that where the funds were simply routed through the parent, the constitutionality of the funding would be analyzed in the same way as would any direct funding by the state. If the funding was not simply being routed through the parents, then a different analysis was in order—the question would be whether the monies were being offered as an incentive to or inducement for the parents to send their children to sectarian schools. If so, then the provision of the funds would still violate constitutional guarantees; if not, then the funding might pass constitutional muster.

It might be noted that using this definition of "conduit," the *Witters* program should have been analyzed in the same way that a direct subsidy to the school would have been analyzed, because the monies would have gone to the school via the student. Indeed, the *Witters* Court acknowledged that aid might be a direct subsidy to a school even though it had gone through the student, citing *Nyquist*,[74] but then seemed to think that this *Nyquist* point governed a different factual scenario. Adding to the confusion, the *Witters* Court incorporated language from *Nyquist* to describe the program at issue, namely, that the program was "made available generally without regard to the sectarian-nonsectarian, or public-nonpublic nature of the institution benefited,"[75] as if the fact that aid was made available generally would preclude aid from being a direct school subsidy. But that is not what *Nyquist* said or implied. Even if generally available, the aid at issue would be direct aid if it was simply passed through to the schools.

Much of the *Witters* discussion involved a laundry list of what the Washington program was not. For example, the program was not skewed towards religion or an ingenious method by which the state could channel aid to sectarian schools. The program did not provide greater or broader benefits for those who were using the aid for religious education. Nor were the full benefits limited in large part to students at sectarian institutions. But these considerations might come into play when analyzing a program where the money had not gone directly to the school via a student conduit. They simply were not relevant where the recipient was functioning as a mechanism through which the funds were being transferred to the school, because the appropriate analysis in that kind of case is simply whether

74 *Witters*, 474 U.S. at 487–8.
75 *Id.* at 488.

the funding would have passed muster were it going directly to the educational institution.

It is not exactly clear why the Court was spelling out all of these things that were untrue of the Washington program. It may be that Justice Marshall (who wrote the opinion) was trying to undermine a previous opinion, *Mueller v. Allen*,[76] in which the Court had upheld a tax deduction for expenses incurred in providing tuition, textbooks, and transportation for children attending primary and secondary schools. In his *Mueller* dissent, Justice Marshall had noted that "the vast majority of the taxpayers who are eligible to receive the benefit are parents whose children attend religious schools,"[77] that the Minnesota program would give a financial incentive to parents to send their children to religious schools, and that the bulk of the tax benefits afforded by the program went to parents of children attending parochial schools. These are exactly the kinds of considerations that the *Witters* opinion suggests would support a finding that the program violated Establishment Clause guarantees.

Thus, one way to read *Witters* is as a debate about a previously decided opinion rather than about the issue at hand. Several members of the Court had noted the majority's glaring failure to discuss *Mueller*, and Justice Powell implied that an explanation should have been offered for that omission. Indeed, in his *Witters* concurrence, Justice Powell implicitly recognized that many of the criteria cited in *Witters* militating against the constitutionality of a program indirectly aiding sectarian schools were not applicable in *Witters* but were applicable in *Mueller*.

In *Witters*, one of the debates occurring among the Court members sub silentio might have been about whether *Mueller* was compatible with *Nyquist*. The *Mueller* Court had distinguished *Nyquist* by suggesting that the Minnesota deduction was available to parents whose children attended public schools as well as parents whose children attended private schools. Of course, the fact that all parents would be entitled to some deduction did not establish that all parents would receive roughly comparable deductions. On the contrary, parents sending their children to public schools would receive a benefit that paled in comparison to the benefits received by parents sending their children to private schools. Further, about 95 percent of the Minnesota students attending private schools were attending sectarian schools, so if the effect of the New York statute at issue in *Nyquist* had been to promote religious schooling, the same was true of the Minnesota program at issue in *Mueller*. Indeed, it might have been thought that the program at issue in *Mueller* could not be upheld without overruling *Nyquist*. Thus, one way to read *Witters* is as an admonishment of certain members of the Court for having issued a decision in *Mueller* that seemed to contradict *Nyquist* in particular and the existing jurisprudence more generally.

In retrospect, however, it might have been better had Justice Marshall discussed some of the respects in which the program at issue in *Mueller* was less

---

76 463 U.S. 388 (1983). For a discussion of *Mueller*, see Chapter 1, fourth section.
77 *Id.* at 405.

constitutionally suspect than the program at issue in *Witters*. For example, because *Mueller* involved a tax deduction for education expenses, the Court suggested that parochial schools were receiving an attenuated financial benefit. After all, one simply could not tell where the monies saved through the tax deduction would be spent. It might be that the parochial school costs would be paid in any event and that other expenses would not have been incurred but for the tax deduction. In contrast, the monies at issue in *Witters* would have to go to the religious institution.

Surprisingly, the *Witters* Court did not mention the *Tilton–Roemer* line of cases at all. But those cases established that the state could not promote religious education. Further, it will not do to say that because the funding was going to the student rather than to the school directly, *Witters* did not fall into the *Tilton–Roemer* line of cases. *Witters*, itself, rejected the direct versus indirect argument, noting that funneling funds to religious institutions was impermissible even if parents or students were the means by which the funds were funneled to the schools. Further, using the notion of "conduit" suggested in *Nyquist*, monies are funneled to the schools through the conduit of a student or parent when those monies are routed "to the schools, in advance of or in lieu of payment"[78] by the student or her parent. Because the monies at issue in *Witters* would not have been paid to reimburse Witters for expenses already paid but, instead, would have been directed by him to the school, Witters would be acting as a conduit (using the *Nyquist* notion of "conduit").

The claim here is not that the *Nyquist* Court's analysis of what constitutes a conduit is beyond reproach. While it may be that a paradigmatic example of parent-acting-as-conduit would involve a parent who signs over to a religious institution a check from the state that is intended to pay this year's tuition at the institution, the analysis becomes much murkier after that. Suppose, for example, that a parent receives reimbursement for the tuition payment made during the previous year. That parent then signs over that check to a religious institution for this year's tuition payment. There was no requirement that the check be signed over to the school—it could have been used for other expenses—but the religious school tuition bill was nonetheless paid with a check from the state.

If the fact that the money could have been used elsewhere would suffice to free the parent from being designated as a conduit, then we would have a seemingly anomalous result. The parent would be a mere conduit if signing over to the school the check received from the state to cover this year's tuition. However, the parent would not be viewed as a mere conduit if paying this year's tuition by signing over to the school the check received from the state to cover last year's tuition. In both cases, state monies would simply be signed over to a religious school, but the Establishment Clause would be offended in one but not the other case.

If signing over the reimbursement check for last year's tuition was too conduit-like even though the parent could have used the money for anything, then suppose instead that the parent deposits the reimbursement for last year's tuition payment

---

78 *Nyquist*, 413 U.S. at 785–6.

in a checking account and then writes a check drawing on that account for this year's tuition. If this would still count as a conduit, then it might be argued that the parent must use the reimbursement check for other purposes, for example, making one or several mortgage payments. The parent could then use the monies that would have been used for the mortgage payments to pay tuition. Because the Court has rejected the reduction-of-opportunity-cost theory of Establishment Clause jurisprudence, this use of the monies would presumably pass muster.

Yet, requiring this kind of segregation of funds would impose an insurmountable burden on some of those whom such grants were designed to help. Many of the potential recipients simply would not have the resources to be able to pay the tuition bills in a particular year without making use of the government grants to do so. Thus, were individuals receiving government grants constitutionally required to segregate the grant funds to make sure that they were not used to promote sectarian activities, many deserving but poor recipients might be viewed as ineligible for the grants, whereas someone with access to greater resources might be able to pay religious school tuition with non-government funds and use the government funds to pay other expenses. But this would mean that the most needy and deserving might be constitutionally barred from taking advantage of the program that had been designed to help them.

It is by no means clear where the line between being a mere conduit and not being a mere conduit should be drawn, although it is clear that the mere act of signing over a state check to a religious school would not make the parent a conduit. Else, the public employee who signs over a paycheck would be viewed as a mere conduit. Certainly, we can distinguish between the individual who receives a check from the government to pay religious school expenses and the individual who receives a check from the government for services rendered. The point is merely that drawing the relevant line may be somewhat more difficult than might first appear. Presumably, any analysis should capture two points: (1) a public employee who uses a paycheck to send a child to a religious school is not somehow violating Establishment Clause guarantees, and (2) a parent who simply signs over a check that could only be used for a religious school education is acting as a mere conduit.

The Court has never offered an account of what would constitute a parent or student merely acting as a conduit. That said, however, *Witters* was not a particularly difficult case along the continuum suggested by *Nyquist*, because Witters would have signed over the monies to the school "in advance of or in lieu of payment."

Suppose, however, that one rejects the invitation to distinguish between individuals who are acting as mere conduits and those who are not, because of the difficulty in drawing a line that persuasively distinguishes between these two groups. The *Nyquist* Court suggested a different kind of limitation on the use of government funds, namely, that state monies only be used for secular purposes. However, it might be noted that such a principle would have precluded the award at issue in *Witters*, unless that grant were permitted as a kind of de minimis exception.

It may be that the *Witters* Court did not offer a detailed analysis of the jurisprudence, because the opinion was really designed to uphold the grant without encapsulating the jurisprudence. Basically, all members of the Court agreed that the program at issue did not violate constitutional guarantees. However, they may well have had very different reasons for thinking so, and *Witters* may have been written in a way that was designed to smooth over those differences. By not forcing members to sign onto particular descriptions of the jurisprudence, the Court may have been leaving the hard work of carefully working out the relevant jurisprudence for another day with, perhaps, a fact scenario that was more conducive to offering a clear and careful exposition of the relevant principles.

Justice Marshall apparently believed the program constitutional as a kind of de minimis exception. He noted in the opinion both that a very insignificant amount of the total grant monies supported religious education, and that no one else had sought to use grant monies in the same way as Witters had. In contrast, several Justices believed *Mueller* was strongly supportive of the outcome, if not controlling, notwithstanding that *Mueller* involved reimbursement for expenses paid and *Witters* involved the state's providing fund that would go directly through the student to the school, and that *Mueller* involved a more generalized program rather than a one-time use of the vocational funds to pursue sectarian training.

Witters is a disappointing decision more because of what it did not say rather than because of what it did say. The opinion is compatible with a variety of approaches to Establishment Clause jurisprudence. One infers, for example, that Justice Marshall did not believe *Mueller* controlling in that he seemed to believe that the grant at issue in *Witters* was permissible, perhaps as a de minimis exception, while the program at issue in *Mueller* was not. However, by not discussing *Mueller*, including the fact that the monies received by the parents in *Mueller* might not in fact have gone to religious schools, the *Witters* Court created the possibility that *Witters* would be viewed as a watershed opinion in which a private individual's receipt of funds would immunize what was done with those funds, even if the individual might be thought a mere conduit through which the funds were being directed to the pervasively sectarian school.

Viteritti notes that "Justice Powell, the author of *Nyquist*, used the occasion to outline an emerging set of standards that was moving the Court in a more accommodationist direction. According to the guidelines, a program passes constitutional muster if (1) it is facially neutral regarding religion, (2) funds are made equally available to students in public and nonpublic schools (3) any aid flowing to religious schools result from the private decisions of individuals."[79] But at least one difficulty with this analysis is that it does not represent the view put forward in *Nyquist*, which had suggested that monies funneled through private

---

79   Joseph P. Viteritti, *The Last Freedom: Religion from the Public School to the Public Square* 136 (2007).

individuals to parochial schools should be treated as if the funds had been paid directly to the schools.

The *Witters* opinion could have emphasized the differences between the facts of *Mueller* and *Witters*, while nonetheless upholding the use of the grant in *Witters* after emphasizing that there were no other reported instances in which this grant would be used for ministerial training. That way, the Court could have suggested that the Establishment Clause did not bar this grant in particular, but that the Clause nonetheless does not permit state support of religious functions as a general matter and does not immunize state funding of pervasively sectarian schools via parent or student conduits. By offering such an analysis, the subsequent effect of the opinion might have been more limited and, for example, it would not have been used to provide support for *Zelman v. Simmons-Harris*,[80] in which the Court upheld state funding of religious schools via vouchers that were simply signed over to the school without restrictions on the use of those funds.

Witters suggests that state funding of devotional studies is permissible, past jurisprudence notwithstanding. Further, by failing to emphasize that Witters had been the only individual to seek to use the funding that way, the Court seemed to imply that there were no constitutional worries implicated by such funding. Given some of the Court's other statements with respect to the neutrality required by the Establishment Clause, one might have assumed that states would be constitutionally precluded from discriminating against programs involving religious studies. Yet, in a surprising decision, the Court upheld Washington's refusal to fund ministerial studies in *Locke v. Davey*.[81]

Locke involved a Washington state scholarship program that was designed to help academically gifted students pursue postsecondary education. Joshua Davey was awarded a scholarship and wanted to use it to train to become a church pastor. However, because that area of study was excluded from the fields of study that were permissibly funded, he was told that he could not use the scholarship for those purposes.

The Court explained that the Establishment Clause did not bar a state from awarding scholarship monies to help students pursue ministerial studies. However, the question at hand was whether the state's refusing to permit the use of monies to pursue that field of study violated Free Exercise guarantees. Thus, the state had not argued that it was precluded by the Establishment Clause from awarding the funds to the student—that issue had allegedly been resolved in *Witters*. Instead, the state argued that it was precluded by its own constitutional limitations from awarding the funds at issue, and thus the question at hand was whether the Federal Constitution precluded the state of Washington from having such a limitation in the Washington Constitution.

The Court began its analysis by noting that merely because an action is permissible under the Establishment Clause does not entail that it is required under

---

80 536 U.S. 639 (2002). For a discussion of *Zelman*, see Chapter 1, eighth section.
81 540 U.S. 712 (2004).

the Free Exercise Clause. The Court noted that training for a religious profession is different in important ways from training for a secular profession, suggesting that the former was in essence a religious endeavor. Noting that the Washington grant program permitted students to attend pervasively religious schools, the Court rejected that the state's refusal to fund ministerial studies evidenced hostility towards religion.

A number of points might be made about *Locke*. First, it is a far cry from the analysis offered in the *Tilton–Roemer* line of cases, which precludes state funding of pervasively sectarian schools. In contrast, *Locke* suggests that as long as the federal monies go through a student or parent conduit, there is no limitation on the state funds being used for religious purposes.

After *Locke*, the decision whether to permit state scholarship monies to fund ministerial studies is left up to the states—doing so is permitted by the Establishment Clause but not required by the Free Exercise Clause. The Court explained: "The State's interest in not funding the pursuit of devotional degrees is substantial and the exclusion of such funding places a relatively minor burden on Promise Scholars," concluding that if "any room exists between the two Religion Clauses, it must be here."[82]

Yet, the Court did not explain why the state had a substantial interest in not funding devotional degrees. The Court noted that "[m]ost states that sought to avoid an establishment of religion around the time of the founding placed in their constitutions formal prohibitions against using tax funds to support the ministry."[83] But the Court had already explained that this funding would not involve an establishment of religion, so it is not clear how this state policy would promote that anti-Establishment interest. As Justice Scalia pointed out in his dissent, while "a State has a compelling interest in not committing actual Establishment Clause violations," it does not follow that "a State has a constitutionally sufficient interest in discriminating against religion in whatever other context it pleases, so long as it claims some connection, however attenuated, to establishment concerns."[84] Nor did the Court explain why the exclusion of such funding placed a minor burden on Promise Scholars, given that the denial of funding might well mean that the student could not pursue these studies.

One might have expected the *Locke* Court to offer a careful exposition of *McDaniel*, so that it would be clear how *Locke* was compatible with that case. Regrettably, no such analysis was forthcoming.

The Court distinguished the case before it from what was at issue in *McDaniel* by noting that the Washington program did not deny "to ministers the right to participate in community political affairs."[85] Certainly that is true, but the claim was not that Washington had imposed a restriction identical to Tennessee's, but

---

82 *Id.* at 725.
83 *Id.* at 723.
84 *Id.* at 730 n.2 (Scalia, J., dissenting).
85 *Id.* at 713.

merely that the *McDaniel* rationale precluded the holding in *Locke*. The *McDaniel* Court had noted that "under the clergy-disqualification provision, McDaniel cannot exercise both rights simultaneously because the State has conditioned the exercise of one on the surrender of the other."[86] Here, Davey could not receive the benefit and study to become a minister.

Perhaps the Court was suggesting that there was an important difference between acting as a minister (once one had already been ordained) and studying to become one. Yet, the Court did not seem to be emphasizing that, since the *Locke* Court argued that Washington did not require "students to choose between their religious beliefs and receiving a government benefit."[87] While the Court is correct in the sense that a student who had strong religious beliefs could receive a grant as long as he was not seeking to pursue devotional studies, that should not have ended the inquiry.

At this point, it may be helpful to consider *McDaniel* again. There, too, the Court had emphasized that Tennessee had not been forcing the minister to choose between his beliefs and political participation, explaining that this was something the state simply could not do. "If the Tennessee disqualification provision were viewed as depriving the clergy of a civil right solely because of their religious beliefs, our inquiry would be at an end. The Free Exercise Clause categorically prohibits government from regulating, prohibiting, or rewarding religious beliefs as such."[88] Yet, the *McDaniel* Court did not end its analysis there. The Court noted that "to condition the availability of benefits [including access to the ballot] upon this appellant's willingness to violate a cardinal principle of [his] religious faith [by surrendering his religiously impelled ministry] effectively penalizes the free exercise of [his] constitutional liberties."[89] By the same token, however, one would expect that the state could not condition the receipt of student benefits on the student's willingness to surrender a religiously compelled calling to become a minister. As the *Locke* Court itself pointed out, "[M]ajoring in devotional theology is akin to a religious calling as well as an academic pursuit."[90]

The *Locke* Court emphasized that there had been no finding of animus. Yet, there had been no finding of animus in *McDaniel* and the Court had nonetheless eschewed examining the classification in light of the rational basis test, instead suggesting that a more searching inquiry was due because the individual's free exercise rights had been adversely affected. In contrast, the *Locke* Court implied that because there was no per se burdening of beliefs, the free exercise inquiry must end.

---

86 *McDaniel*, 435 U.S. at 626.
87 *Locke*, 540 U.S. at 713.
88 *McDaniel*, 435 U.S. at 626.
89 *Id.*
90 *Locke*, 540 U.S. at 721.

The *Locke* Court minimized the burden imposed by Washington, noting that the "State has merely chosen not to fund a distinct category of instruction."[91] Yet, one would have expected the Court to suggest that the Establishment Clause did not permit Washington to single out devotional studies for disfavored treatment.

The *Locke* Court wanted to preserve some "play in the joints"[92] between the Free Exercise and Establishment Clauses. To do so persuasively, it would have had to explain how *McDaniel's* analysis of Free Exercise was not controlling. Rather than offer a careful exposition, the Court basically announced that *Locke* did not involve some of the evils that the Religion Clauses are designed to prevent and thus was permissible. Such an analysis neither furthers an understanding of the Religion Clauses jurisprudence nor is likely to stand.

Viteritti wonders whether "the room "between the joints" of the two First Amendment clauses [is] a place that furnishes government, at any level, with grounds for discrimination on the basis of religion."[93] Yet, the difficulty is not merely that we do not have a clear analysis of the relationship between the Free Exercise Clause and the Establishment Clause, but also that the Establishment Clause jurisprudence is itself incoherent. If it were plausible to believe that the state's refusal to fund ministerial studies involved state discrimination against religion, then the Establishment Clause itself would bar such a refusal.

Conclusion

The Court's attitude toward state funding of religious studies has been anything but consistent. In the *Tilton–Roemer* line of cases, the Court made clear that the state could not fund religious studies, while the *McDaniel* Court made clear that the Constitution does not countenance the imposition of undue burdens on the ministry. The *Witters* Court upheld state funding of ministerial studies against an Establishment Clause challenge without clearly articulating what the Establishment Clause prohibits, permits, and requires. Indeed, *Witters* is compatible with any number of accounts of the Establishment Clause, especially if it is viewed as upholding what it viewed as a de minimis exception to the traditional Establishment Clause limitations.

Locke might seem to be a kind of compromise giving the states some latitude with respect to what they fund. However, the Court failed to offer a coherent account of either Free Exercise or Establishment jurisprudence, making it virtually impossible to reconcile *Locke* with the other cases or even to get a general idea of what the jurisprudence requires, permits, or prohibits. Further, too much should not be made of the compromise allegedly struck. *Locke* does not suggest that the funding of religious programs should be private. Indeed, the Court noted with

---

91 *Id.* at 713.
92 *Id.* at 719.
93 Viteritti, *supra* note 79, at 144.

approval that the program at issue would fund pervasively sectarian education, so the case can hardly be read as immunizing state refusals to fund religious activities.

Some commentators suggest that *Locke* gives states wide discretion to refuse to fund religion as long as they do not thereby evidence animus or hostility. Yet, *McDaniel* suggests that that the jurisprudence cannot be read so broadly, and *Locke* nowhere suggests that *McDaniel* was wrongly decided.

Perhaps *Locke* should be read as a narrow case about free exercise, but there are at least two reasons that such a reading is not persuasive. First, *McDaniel* was a free exercise case, and the Court was not deferential to the state merely because no animus had been established. Thus, *Locke* is not persuasively written, even if it were solely about free exercise. Second, reading *Locke* so narrowly would seem to misrepresent what Davey had argued, since he had challenged the Washington program on both free exercise and establishment grounds.

Perhaps the Court suddenly realized that striking down the Washington program would have had important implications for various state and federal programs. Yet, the Court provided no explanation of why the state's refusal to fund devotional studies did not create a perception that certain religious viewpoints were being disfavored.

Locke cannot be reconciled with the then-existing jurisprudence, and the then-existing jurisprudence could not be reconciled with the pre-*Mueller* and pre-*Witters* jurisprudence. Basically, the Court has radically altered the guarantees of the Religion Clauses, making them yield results that would have been unimaginable not so long ago, and that can only be reconciled with Establishment and Free Exercise Clauses whose dictates are anyone's guess.

Chapter 4

Religious Groups at Public Colleges and Universities

Over the past several decades, the Court has addressed some of the limitations imposed by the Establishment Clause on public higher education. The cases before the Court have involved student groups: which groups must be recognized, what conditions may be imposed on them without offending constitutional guarantees, and who must help fund them. All too often, the Court has ignored or retroactively modified the prevailing jurisprudence to reach its desired result.

The implicated issues in these cases are not easy to resolve. Individuals on all sides have sincere and deeply held convictions, and it simply is not possible to come up with a policy or reading of the Constitution that will satisfy all parties. Nonetheless, by mischaracterizing or retroactively modifying the case law, the Court appears disingenuous and undermines confidence in both the opinions' reasoning and results.

Religious Student Groups' Use of University Facilities

In the 1940s though 1970s, the Court addressed the Establishment Clause limitations on elementary and secondary schools and also addressed limitations on state funding of sectarian college and universities. However, the Court did not attempt to establish the contours of Establishment Clause limitations on public colleges and universities until the 1980s.

In *Widmar v. Vincent*,[1] the Court examined whether the University of Missouri at Kansas City could preclude the use of school facilities by a student group wishing to engage in religious discussion and worship. The Court noted that the university had set up a system whereby student groups had access to university facilities, and the question at hand was whether the university was permitted to preclude the plaintiff group from using the facilities because of their desire to engage in religious activities. Two separate issues had to be addressed: (1) does the Establishment Clause preclude the state from permitting such groups to use facilities?, and (2) if the Establishment Clause does not preclude a university from allowing its facilities to be used in this way, does the United States Constitution in addition require that a public university afford a religious student group the

---

1 454 U.S. 263 (1981).

opportunity to use the facilities in this way if indeed other student groups are allowed to do so?

To understand the Court's analysis, it is helpful to understand some of the distinctions that are used in cases involving freedom of expression more generally. Some settings such as parks and streets are viewed as traditional public fora where the state is not permitted to prohibit speech based on its content. While the state is permitted to regulate when speech takes place so that, for example, several demonstrations do not occur at the same time in the same space possibly resulting in physical harm to the public, such regulation is subject to certain restrictions. The state is not permitted to preclude speech merely because of disagreement with the viewpoint expressed. Viewpoint- and content-based regulations are subject to strict scrutiny—in order for such regulations to pass constitutional muster, they must be narrowly tailored to promote compelling state interests.

Even if a place does not qualify as a traditional public forum, it might nonetheless be designated by the state as such a forum. In that event, the state is subject to the same restrictions with respect to the limitations on speech that it may impose as would be true were the state seeking to regulate a traditional public forum.

Assuming that a particular setting does not qualify as a traditional public forum, the state (or a state entity) has the option of declaring that setting a limited purpose forum. Some topics can be excluded from the forum, because they do not fit within its purposes. However, topics that fit within the forum's designated purposes cannot be excluded unless the very demanding strict scrutiny standard is met.

Merely because property is owned by the state does not make that property even a limited purpose public forum. Some state-owned facilities are not intended to be a location where a robust exchange of ideas is to take place, and thus the fact of state ownership does not thereby confer on a location the designation of a forum (even for limited purposes). Were such a designation automatically afforded to all state property, the state might have great difficulty in fulfilling its various functions.

The *Widmar* Court suggested that the system whereby the university permitted student groups to use university facilities was a limited purpose forum that triggered protections against state regulation of speech. While recognizing that a university forum is distinguishable from other fora such as parks or streets because of the school's educational mission, the Court nonetheless suggested that the school could not prevent the group from using the forum at issue unless that limitation could withstand examination under strict scrutiny.

The university attempted to justify its exclusion by suggesting that doing otherwise would have violated its Establishment Clause obligations. The Court agreed that complying with constitutional obligations implicated a compelling interest, but denied that Establishment Clause guarantees would be violated were the state to permit the group to meet.

In its examination of whether the Establishment Clause precluded the university from recognizing this student group, the *Widmar* Court used the *Lemon* test. The Court suggested that an open-forum policy that permitted both religious and nonreligious speech would have the secular purpose of promoting the free exchange of ideas and, further, that the entanglement prong would not be offended by an open policy permitting all kinds of speech. Indeed, the Court noted that were the state to try to decide which speech counted as religious speech or worship so that such speech could be excluded, the entanglement provision would be implicated. Because an open-forum policy would not force the state to maintain surveillance or to make the difficult decisions that would thereby be required, the third *Lemon* prong would not bar a policy that refused to place the state in such an awkward position.

The remaining question was whether an open-forum policy would have the principal or primary effect of advancing religion. To some extent, the differing views on whether the *Lemon* effect prong barred the student group from having access to the forum can be attributed to differing understandings of what would be implicated were such access permitted. The university argued that its granting the religious group access would in effect mean that the university had created a religious forum, whereas the Court suggested that the proper way to characterize the issue was to examine whether the university could exclude groups from an open forum based on the religious content of their speech.

All of the parties agreed that permitting the religious group to meet on campus would afford that organization some benefit. However, the Court had already made clear that a religious organization's receipt of "incidental" benefits is not barred by the Establishment Clause. As the *Widmar* Court recognized, an important issue in dispute was whether the benefit at issue should be classified as "incidental" in light of the relevant jurisprudence.

Two reasons were offered to justify that permitting a religious organization access to an open forum in a university setting would only afford incidental benefits. First, because many different types of groups had access to the forum, the university's permitting the religious group to participate would not communicate state endorsement of that group's beliefs or practices. Second, that there was such a broad array of nonreligious and religious speakers suggested that the primary effect of the forum was secular rather than sectarian.

Certainly, one possible way of distinguishing between affording an incidental benefit to religion on the one hand and having a primary effect of promoting religion on the other would be to examine whether the state had implicitly endorsed religion or, instead, had accorded benefits to many different groups among which one or a few happened to be religious. Yet, at least one difficulty with the Court's using this approach was that this was not how the Court had determined in the past whether a benefit was incidental, and the Court was allegedly deciding whether the benefit conferred was incidental in light of the past case law.

Consider *Tilton v. Richardson*,[2] which involved a challenge to a federal act providing construction grants to private colleges and universities. The Court used the *Lemon* test in that case as well. When analyzing the effect prong, the Court noted that the important consideration was not whether a religious institution had received some benefit but, instead, whether the program's primary effect was the advancement of religion. The Court explained that the federal act at issue had been carefully drafted to assure that only secular functions of religious institutions would receive funding. Grants and loans would only be used for "defined secular purposes,"[3] and the Act expressly prohibited the use of funds for "religious instruction, training, or worship."[4] The *Tilton* Court made clear that the Establishment Clause does not bar all state programs that afford secular benefits to religious institutions, even if the state's affording secular benefits would free up funds of the religious institution for sectarian uses. That those monies were freed up was described as an incidental rather than a primary effect of the secular aid.

The same kind of analysis of incidental benefits was employed in *Hunt v. McNair*,[5] where the Court examined the constitutionality of a South Carolina law authorizing the issuance of revenue bonds for the benefit of the Baptist College of Charleston. Because these bonds would be tax-exempt, the College would be able to market the bonds at a significantly lower rate of interest than it would otherwise have to pay. The *Hunt* Court rejected the argument that no aid is permissible because "aid to one aspect of an institution frees it to spend its other resources on religious ends,"[6] thus echoing the position articulated in *Tilton* that funds expended on secular projects need not violate Establishment Clause guarantees.

After rejecting the "all aid is forbidden" view, the *Hunt* Court clarified the process by which to determine whether a program's primary effect is to advance religion, explaining that to "identify "primary effect," we narrow our focus from the statute as a whole to the only transaction presently before us."[7] Thus, the Court was not to consider all of the institutions benefited by the statute and then see whether most were religiously affiliated. Rather, the Court was to narrow its focus and examine the effect of the statute on the particular institution at issue.

When focusing on the effect on the institution in the case at hand, the Court would find the funding to have the primary effect of advancing religion when either of two conditions was true: (1) religion was so pervasive in the institution that it would be difficult to fund (what would usually be) a purely secular function without at the same time promoting sectarian interests, or (2) the funding was going to promote religious activity even if the school was predominantly secular

---

2   403 U.S. 672 (1971). For an examination of *Tilton*, see Chapter 3, first section.

3   *Tilton*, 403 U.S. at 679.

4   *Id.* at 679–80.

5   413 U.S. 734 (1973). For an examination of *Hunt*, see Chapter 3, first section.

6   *Hunt*, 413 U.S. at 743.

7   *Id.* at 742.

in nature. Basically, the *Hunt* Court suggests that as long as the funds go only to secular projects, the effect prong of the *Lemon* test will not be violated.

When examining a New York program offering state funds to sectarian schools for maintenance and repair, the *Nyquist* Court noted with disapproval that there had been no attempt to restrict funds so that they would only be used for the "upkeep of facilities used exclusively for secular purposes."[8] Thus, nothing in the way that the program was structured would have prevented a school from using the state funds to pay individuals to maintain the chapel or to renovate classrooms where religion was taught. The *Nyquist* Court struck down this direct funding of religious expression, all the while accepting the view articulated by the *Hunt* and *Tilton* Courts that state aid could be used to support secular functions in sectarian schools, even if that aid would indirectly support religion by freeing up monies for sectarian uses. Because the state would not itself be helping these institutions to engage in religious activities, the Establishment Clause would not bar that kind of funding. However, were the state aid to promote sectarian activities or were there insufficient safeguards to assure that only secular activities would be promoted, the Establishment Clause would bar the state support.

Or, consider *Roemer v. Board of Public Works of Maryland*[9] in which the Court considered a Maryland program that gave funds to private colleges, provided that the funds would not be used for sectarian purposes. Noting that the Establishment Clause does not preclude a state from providing incidental benefits to religious organizations, the Court indicated that it was following the previous jurisprudence by characterizing incidental religious benefits as those that might result when an institution's resources had been freed up by virtue of the state's having provided secular benefits. The *Roemer* Court rejected a position that the *Widmar* Court seemed to endorse, namely, that the state's supporting religious activities is permissible as long as secular activities are promoted as well.

Given the then-existing jurisprudence, it is difficult to see how the religious benefits at issue in *Widmar* could be considered incidental. While it may well have been true that students at the university would not have inferred state endorsement of the beliefs of the religious group by virtue of that group's being afforded access to the forum and it may also have been true that the benefits were being provided to a broad spectrum of groups, those same points might have been made in the previous cases to justify state funding of sectarian activities. But the Court had repeatedly made clear that the state could not fund sectarian activities without violating the effect prong of the test determining whether Establishment Clause guarantees had been violated. Further, no exception had been offered suggesting that such funding was permissible as long as many other activities were funded so that there would be no inference of endorsement. Indeed, given *Hunt's* explanation that the primary effect analysis requires the Court to focus on the challenged state

---

8   *Committee for Public Education and Religious Liberty v. Nyquist*, 413 U.S. 756, 774 (1973).

9   426 U.S. 736 (1976). For an examination of *Roemer*, see Chapter 3, first section.

action at issue, it does not matter for purposes of deciding a program's primary effect whether there is a broad rather than a narrow array of recipients. The breadth of the range of recipients might well matter if the Court were examining whether there was a secular purpose, but that is a different prong of the test.

In one sense, the *Widmar* Court was correct to reject the university's claim that its affording access to the religious group would involve its setting up a special religious forum. Rather, the university would simply be giving access to this group, just as it had to so many other groups. Yet, for purposes of the effect prong analysis where the focus is on whether the state aid will be used to promote sectarian activities, the university's action should have been treated as if the university would be setting up a separate forum for the religious group. If, indeed, the group would be engaging in sectarian activities that the state was prohibited from supporting, then the past jurisprudence suggested that the state could not open up the forum to that group, even if the forum was open to many other groups that did not engage in sectarian activity. The different kinds of funding at issue in the *Tilton–Roemer* line of cases passed muster because they did not directly support any sectarian activity rather than because they would promote a little sectarian activity and a lot of secular activity. The funding at issue in *Nyquist* did not pass muster because it might have promoted sectarian activity in addition to secular activity. Basically, the *Widmar* Court radically altered the jurisprudence while claiming merely to apply it.

Allegedly, the University of Missouri at Kansas City was engaging in content-based discrimination without an adequate justification when not affording the religious student group access to university facilities. Yet, the university had merely been following the example set by the Court in the *Tilton–Roemer* line of cases in which the Court had suggested that the state was precluded from promoting sectarian activities. Indeed, one of the lessons of that line of cases is that the state must consider content when deciding whether its affording benefits comports with Establishment Clause limitations. The funding at issue in the *Tilton–Roemer* line of cases passed muster precisely because it would not be used to construct or maintain buildings where sectarian instruction would take place, and the New York funding program at issue in *Nyquist* was struck down precisely because those funds might have been used to promote sectarian activities.

The *Widmar* Court's very brief comments about some of the problems associated with the *Lemon* entanglement prong are worthy of note. Basically, the Court recognized the difficult line-drawing problems associated with determining which speech is religious and which is not and with determining which speech constitutes prayer and which does not. The Court's point is well-taken that it is difficult if not impossible to draw a bright line in this area. However, its implicit recommendation that the state avoid this quagmire by allowing all speech was simply not compatible with the then-existing jurisprudence distinguishing between the promotion of sectarian and nonsectarian education. Basically, the Court had previously suggested that unless the state could assure that its funding would only support secular activities, the state was barred by the Establishment

Clause from affording the funding at issue. The entanglement prong was to assure that the state would not have to get overly involved when seeking to assure that Establishment Clause guarantees would be respected. The *Widmar* solution was to throw out the baby with the bathwater—avoid the entanglement problems inherent in state oversight assuring that there would be no support of sectarian activity by allowing state support of sectarian activity. But this is simply to reject the previous jurisprudence that the Court was claiming to apply.

Religious Worship versus Speech about Religion

One of the important features of the *Widmar* opinion was its refusal to distinguish between religious worship and speech about religion. The Court recognized that "speech about religion is speech entitled to the general protections of the First Amendment,"[10] and then noted that the Court in *Heffron v. International Society for Krishna Consciousness*[11] had assumed that "religious appeals to nonbelievers constituted protected speech,"[12] as if *Heffron* thereby established that speech about religion and religious worship were equivalent for constitutional purposes. Yet, citing *Heffron* as support for such a proposition was surprising for a number of reasons.

At issue in *Heffron* was a Minnesota State Fair regulation that "require[d] a religious organization desiring to distribute and sell religious literature and to solicit donations at a state fair to conduct those activities only at an assigned location within the fairgrounds even though application of the rule limits the religious practices of the organization."[13] The Krishnas were permitted to roam the fair discussing their religious views, but were only allowed to solicit donations from a booth.

The Court accepted that "oral and written dissemination of the Krishnas' religious views and doctrines is protected by the First Amendment."[14] Nonetheless, the Court upheld the restriction as a valid time, place, manner restriction. Yet, nowhere in the *Heffron* opinion was there a discussion of the difference between describing religious views and engaging in religious worship, much less the suggestion embraced by the *Widmar* Court that the two are equivalent for constitutional purposes.

The *Widmar* Court suggested that the case law "acknowledged the right of religious speakers to use public forums on equal terms with others."[15] Yet, this is to compound the confusion. The university was not denying the speakers access to

---

10 *Widmar*, 454 U.S. at 269 n.6.

11 452 U.S. 640 (1981).

12 *Widmar*, 454 U.S. at 269 n.6.

13 *Heffron*, 452 U.S. at 642.

14 *Id.* at 647.

15 *Widmar*, 454 U.S. at 272.

the forum because they were religious—rather, the forum was not being provided to those who wished to engage in sectarian activities. Religious speakers would of course have access to the forum, although the forum could not be used to engage in prayer.

Perhaps the *Widmar* Court believed that the past jurisprudence did not accurately capture the dictates of the Establishment Clause. But that is a separate claim. Rather than address what the Court had held in the past, the *Widmar* Court simply pretended that the Court had said or done something else, and then applied the hypothesized rulings to the matter at hand.

Consider the other case cited by the Court in support of the rights of religious speakers, *Saia v. New York*.[16] At issue in *Saia* was a city law forbidding "the use of sound amplification devices except with permission of the Chief of Police."[17] Saia was a minister who used sound equipment to "amplify lectures on religious subjects."[18] The statute was struck down because there were no specified standards in light of which the police chief was to decide whether to permit the sound equipment to be used. Apparently, individuals had complained because they had found the volume annoying.

There is no discussion of what this religious individual was saying and, of course, no discussion of whether religious worship and discourse on religious subjects are equivalent for constitutional purposes. Further, in *Saia*, no question was presented regarding whether the state was prohibited, permitted, or required to support his speech. Rather, at issue was whether the state could restrict his speech by giving a public official unfettered discretion with respect to the conditions under which the speech could be amplified. Neither *Saia* nor *Heffron* was helpful in determining whether the state was obligated to provide support for religious worship in the same way that it provided support for discourse on religious or nonreligious subjects.

Justice Stevens justified the *Widmar* result in the following way:

> [T]he policy under attack would allow groups of young philosophers to meet to discuss their skepticism that a Supreme Being exists, or a group of political scientists to meet to debate the accuracy of the view that religion is the "opium of the people." If school facilities may be used to discuss anticlerical doctrine, it seems to me that comparable use by a group desiring to express a belief in God must also be permitted.[19]

Yet, Justice Stevens has not captured the relevant issue. Young religious and areligious philosophers could meet to discuss whether and why they believed or did not believe in God without engaging in religious worship. Political scientists

---

16 334 U.S. 558 (1948).

17 *Id.* at 558.

18 *Id.* at 559.

19 *Widmar*, 454 U.S. at 281 (Stevens, J., concurring in the judgment).

could meet and discuss whether religion has been a curse or blessing for humankind without offering prayers. Indeed, one can assert one's belief in God without at the same time petitioning God for forgiveness or some other sort of benefit.

Perhaps prayer should simply be treated as an assertion that God exists, at least for constitutional purposes. Or, perhaps, although prayer and assertions that God exists are not the same, they both should be permitted in a public forum, as should assertions that God does not exist or that prayer is an exercise in self-delusion. The point here is merely that the kinds of justifications offered by the Court were specious, which undercuts both the persuasiveness of the holding and perceptions of the integrity of the Court.

The *Widmar* Court was wrong to suggest that no line can be or ever has been drawn between religious worship and discussions about religion, even if the line is difficult to draw in some cases. *Schempp* was predicated on the ability to make such a distinction; else, the Court would never have suggested that it was permissible to teach about religion but impermissible to conduct religious exercises in school.[20]

The claim here is not that *Schempp* was controlling with respect to how *Widmar* should have been decided. *Widmar* involved religious exercises at a public university that were conducted during a meeting of a student group, whereas *Schempp* involved religious exercises at an elementary school during the schoolday. Nonetheless, if prayer and talk about religion were the same for constitutional purposes, *Schempp* would have made no sense.

By the same token, even after *Widmar*, the Court affirmed that prayer in school might be unconstitutional. When the *Wallace* Court struck down an Alabama statute requiring schools to have a moment of silence or voluntary prayer, the Court was quite clear that prayer was not simply reducible to a discussion about religious matters. As Justice O'Connor suggested in her concurrence, prayer is inherently religious in a way that others kinds of expression are not.

State Funding of Religious Proselytizing

A university student group was again the focus of the Court in *Rosenberger v. Rector and Visitors of University of Virginia*.[21] At issue in *Rosenberger* was a refusal by the University of Virginia to pay the printing costs incurred by one of the recognized student groups, Wide Awake Productions, in publishing a magazine that offered the group's religious views about a variety of matters. The publication was construed as a religious activity, which was defined as "any activity that primarily promotes or manifests a particular belie[f] in or about a deity or an

---

20 See School District of Abington Township v. Schempp, 374 U.S. 203, 225 (1963). For a discussion of *Schempp*, see Chapter 2, second section.

21 515 U.S. 819 (1995).

ultimate reality."[22] School policy precluded paying the costs of certain student activities, including religious activities.

The *Rosenberger* Court began its analysis by noting that it is "axiomatic that the government may not regulate speech based on its substantive content or the message it conveys."[23] The Court then explained that when the "government targets not subject matter, but particular views taken by speakers on a subject, the violation of the First Amendment is all the more blatant."[24] The state must not engage in viewpoint discrimination, even if permissibly engaging in content discrimination by setting up a limited purpose forum.

At issue in the case was whether the university was engaging in content rather than viewpoint discrimination—it was at the very least engaging in the former by virtue of its having set up a limited purpose forum. There is a sense in which the state is discriminating when setting up a limited purpose forum, because all expression not falling within the purposes of the forum is excluded. However, the university having engaged in that kind of discrimination may pass constitutional muster; the *Rosenberger* Court recognized that the "necessities of confining a forum to the limited and legitimate purposes for which it was created may justify the state in reserving it for certain groups or for the discussion of certain topics."[25] Thus, a state actor's engaging in content discrimination might well be constitutionally permissible, whereas a state actor's engaging in viewpoint discrimination is presumptively impermissible. The constitutionality of the state practice at issue hinged in large part if not entirely on whether it was construed as content or, instead, viewpoint discrimination

To assess whether the content discrimination inherent in a limited purpose forum is justified, the Court will examine whether the state has respected the boundaries it has created. The state will not be permitted to exclude speech from a limited purpose forum if the distinction is not reasonable in light of the forum's purpose, although the state may be justified in limiting discussion to certain topics. Needless to say, this is a much less demanding standard than is the strict scrutiny to be employed for viewpoint discrimination.

One might have expected that after noting the restrictions on content discrimination, the *Rosenberger* Court would then have explained why or how the state was not being reasonable in how it had set up the limitations of the public forum at issue. However, the Court did not offer that kind of analysis, instead holding that the university was engaging in impermissible viewpoint discrimination.

The *Rosenberger* Court suggested that the most instructive case for handling the issues before it was *Lamb's Chapel,* which was described in the following way:

---

22 *Id.* at 825.
23 *Id.* at 829.
24 *Id.*
25 *Id.*

There, a school district had opened school facilities for use after school hours by community groups for a wide variety of social, civic, and recreational purposes. The district, however, had enacted a formal policy against opening facilities to groups for religious purposes. Invoking its policy, the district rejected a request from a group desiring to show a film series addressing various child-rearing questions from a "Christian perspective."[26]

The *Rosenberger* Court thought that the University of Virginia policy before it was analogous to the New York policy that it had struck down in *Lamb's Chapel*.

[H]ere, as in *Lamb's Chapel*, viewpoint discrimination is the proper way to interpret the University's objections to Wide Awake. By the very terms of the SAF prohibition, the University does not exclude religion as a subject matter but selects for disfavored treatment those student journalistic efforts with religious editorial viewpoints. Religion may be a vast area of inquiry, but it also provides, as it did here, a specific premise, a perspective, a standpoint from which a variety of subjects may be discussed and considered. The prohibited perspective, not the general subject matter, resulted in the refusal to make third-party payments, for the subjects discussed were otherwise within the approved category of publications.[27]

Yet, it was not as if the state was picking out a particular viewpoint, for example, a particular Christian perspective, and precluding only that viewpoint from being expressed. On the contrary, a whole class of viewpoints had been precluded, namely, those promoting a belief about the existence or nonexistence of God. This limitation would not only apply to a whole host of Christian perspectives but also to other religious perspectives, as well as to areligious and antireligious perspectives.

The Court seemed confused when responding to the point that a broad range of views was precluded. For example, the Court suggested that the "dissent's assertion that no viewpoint discrimination occurs because the guidelines discriminate against an entire class of viewpoints reflects an insupportable assumption that all debate is bipolar and that antireligious speech is the only response to religious speech."[28] But the dissent had not been suggesting that there were only two possible viewpoints—religious and antireligious. On the contrary, the dissent had suggested that a whole class of viewpoints had been precluded—religious, nonreligious and antireligious—as well as varying viewpoints within those sub-classes.

Apparently understanding that the dissent was not characterizing the debate as bipolar, the *Rosenberger* Court suggested that the "dissent's declaration that

26 *Id.* at 830. For a discussion of *Lamb's Chapel*, see Chapter 2, third section.

27 *Rosenberger*, 515 U.S. at 831.

28 *Id.*

debate is not skewed so long as multiple voices are silenced is simply wrong; the debate is skewed in multiple ways."[29] Yet, this, too, does not capture the difference at issue.

Suppose that the subject of discussion was "family issues." Certainly, if there were 15 possible views that might be articulated and if 4 of them were barred from the discussion, the Court would be correct to suggest that such a policy would have skewed the debate in multiple ways. But that would be because some views were being permitted while others were being prohibited. If no discussions of family were permitted, there would be no viewpoint discrimination. A separate question would be whether restrictions on the forum would be reasonable in light of its purpose, but that is a different matter not involving a claim about viewpoint discrimination.

The majority's response to the dissent simply will not do. Virtually any content limitation might instead be labeled as an attempt to effect multiple-viewpoint discrimination. Unless there is a way to tell which kind of discrimination is content-based (and thus possibly permissible if the case involves a limited purpose forum) and which kind of discrimination is viewpoint-based (and thus presumptively impermissible), there will be havoc within the jurisprudence.

The Court noted that "the University does not exclude religion as a subject matter but selects for disfavored treatment those student journalistic efforts with religious editorial viewpoints,"[30] implying that the university's willingness to permit religion as a subject matter but its unwillingness to permit discussions promoting belief about the existence or non-existence of God amounted to viewpoint discrimination. Yet, to say that such an approach qualifies as viewpoint discrimination is to turn the entire Establishment Clause jurisprudence on its head.

The Court was not entirely clear what it meant when suggesting that the university had not excluded religion as a subject matter but instead had disfavored religious editorial viewpoints. Perhaps it meant that the school permitted discussions about religion but did not permit religious worship. Yet, this does not capture the university policy at issue—a prohibition on promoting or manifesting a belief or lack of belief in God meant that discussions about God's existence or nonexistence were simply excluded from the forum. Religion as a subject matter was not excluded from the forum entirely, because religion addresses a range of issues including but not limited to questions concerning God's existence, although a (possibly very large) subset of the discussion of religion has been taken off the table, namely, any discussions about God. The university would not have been authorizing discussions about religion without authorizing religious worship; instead, it would have precluded the discussion of God whether in the form of debate or prayer.

The Court's view is more understandable if, when explicating the university prohibition on publications that primarily promote a belief about a deity or ultimate

---

29 *Id*. at 831–2.

30 *Id*. at 831.

reality, the Court omits the term "primarily." In that event, anything that promotes/manifests a belief in or about a deity or ultimate reality would be barred, which might be interpreted to mean that someone writing about family, for example, could not include in her discussion that her views were premised in some way on the existence or nonexistence of God. But to offer such a reading is to analyze a policy that the university did not implement.

Had the Court understood the university policy as if it had omitted the word "primarily," then one might have expected the Court to explain that the difficulty with the policy was not that it barred payment for printing costs of publications discussing the existence or nonexistence of God, but that it barred the payment of printing costs of publications that mentioned or even implied the existence or nonexistence of God. Such a policy might be viewed as so sweeping as to be unreasonable. Indeed, the Court suggested that the Virginia policy "effects a sweeping restriction on student thought and student inquiry in the context of University sponsored publications,"[31] although the Court never explained why that was so or why it was even plausible to construe the policy as having such a broad sweep.

If the problem with the policy was that it was so broad, then one might expect that a much narrower policy would not be subject to the same objections. Yet, one infers that the Court would not have been satisfied had the University of Virginia had a narrow policy, say, only precluding the funding of inherently sectarian publications. The Court noted, "If the expenditure of governmental funds is prohibited whenever those funds pay for a service that is … used by a group for sectarian purposes, then *Widmar*, *Mergens*, and *Lamb's Chapel* would have to be overruled."[32]

Yet, those cases would have to be overruled only if one defined "sectarian purposes" in a particular way and only if one read those cases as focused on those sectarian purposes. If, for example, the government was barred from funding sectarian activities such as prayer, that would not in addition bar the government from providing a venue in which a particular subject could be addressed from a religious perspective.

The *Rosenberger* Court referred to *Tilton*, *Hunt* and *Roemer* with approval, suggesting that they stood for the principle that there are "special Establishment Clause dangers where the government makes direct money payments to sectarian institution."[33] But those cases did more than that, since they suggested that the state could not support sectarian activities even if the funds were awarded to a wide array of recipients. Ironically, after suggesting that it "does not violate the Establishment Clause for a public university to grant access to its facilities on a religion-neutral basis to a wide spectrum of student groups, including groups that use meeting rooms for sectarian activities, accompanied by some devotional

31 *Id.* at 836.
32 *Id.* at 843.
33 *Id.* at 842.

exercises,"[34] and describing the benefits to religion accorded under such a program as incidental, the *Rosenberger* Court said nothing about the apparent tension between its holding and the *Tilton–Hunt* line of cases that it had just cited with approval.

In his dissent, Justice Souter argued that "[u]sing public funds for the direct subsidization of preaching the word is categorically forbidden under the Establishment Clause, and if the Clause was meant to accomplish nothing else, it was meant to bar this use of public money."[35] Here, Justice Souter was capturing the view that had prevailed through *Roemer*. However, the Court now apparently believes that such funding is not barred as long as the principle of funding is religion-neutral. Further, a majority of the Court seems to believe that religious worship is equivalent to discussion from a religious perspective. But this is a radical reformulation of the past jurisprudence. While commentators can debate whether this would be the best constitutional approach to adopt if the Court were starting with a blank slate, such an approach simply cannot be justified as a reasonable reading of the past jurisprudence.

Rosenberger involved an attempt by the University of Virginia to avoid the difficulty articulated in Justice Stevens's *Widmar* concurrence, namely, that individuals would be free to criticize but not defend religion. Because the university refused to fund any discussions primarily focused on God, students wishing to discuss God's existence or nonexistence would similarly be restricted from the forum. Nonetheless, the Court suggested that this was religious viewpoint discrimination without making clear how the university's removing a subject matter from the forum constituted viewpoint discrimination. But if the university had engaged in content discrimination and that discrimination was reasonable in light of the forum's purpose to avoid violating Establishment Clause guarantees, then one would have expected the Court to uphold the classification.

The *Rosenberger* Court seems to suggest that permitting the discussion of religion, but not the promotion of particular views about God, involves viewpoint discrimination, implicitly if not explicitly rejecting a distinction that has long underpinned Establishment Clause analysis. Perhaps the Court believes that such a distinction is too hard to draw, although the Court had not been willing to address the implications of the impossibility of drawing such a line. Suppose, for example, that the university wanted to set up a limited purpose public forum that respected the state's anti-establishment commitment. Would the limited purpose forum have passed muster if the school had in addition refused to fund anything that touched on the subject of religion? Or would such a broad limitation be viewed as unreasonable because it potentially would exclude so many categories of discussion?

After finding that the regulation at issue denied the students' free speech rights, the *Rosenberger* Court examined whether the university's action could

---

34 *Id.*
35 *Id.* at 868 (Souter, J., dissenting).

be saved by appealing to its duties under the Establishment Clause. Rejecting that the Establishment Clause barred the state's paying the printing costs of a religious publication, the Court explained instead that the neutrality required by the Constitution was respected when the government extends benefits to promote the expression of viewpoints and ideologies across a wide spectrum. The Court failed to note that this usage of neutrality was much different from the use of neutrality extolled by the *Roemer* Court, where the neutrality was with respect to the identity of the provider of secular services rather than with respect to whether sectarian services could be supported as long as secular services were supported as well.

Shifting its focus from speech to spending, the *Rosenberger* Court explained why the expenditure at issue should not be viewed as a direct payment from the state to a religious organization. First, the monies were collected as part of the student activity fee and were transferred to a third party (the Student Activity Fund). The monies would then be sent to yet another outside party (the printer) to pay the printing costs of the publication. Further, the printer provided services for a broad range of student services, and thus, the Court suggested, any benefit to a religious group might be viewed as incidental.

Once again, the *Rosenberger* analysis differs in important ways from past analyses. The *Hunt* Court explained that when analyzing whether a particular governmental allocation had the primary effect of promoting religion, the Court would not consider all of the programs benefited by the government funding but would instead only consider the program before it. Thus, the benefits to a religious group would not be considered merely incidental because nonreligious groups also received the funding. Rather, a benefit to a religious group might be viewed as incidental if, for example, the state funds promoting secular functions freed up other funds that might then be used to pursue other projects. However, state funds promoting sectarian services would not be considered incidental merely because secular services also received funding.

The *Rosenberger* rationale would seem to permit many practices that had at least been thought to violate constitutional guarantees. Suppose, for example, that a legislature were to set up a special Book Buying Committee (BBC), which would help all schools purchase books for their students. Monies from the general tax fund would go to the BBC. The BBC could only use those monies to pay for books. The BBC would send checks to designated book suppliers, so it would never be the case that checks from the BBC went to religious organizations. Suppose further that there was a nonreligious company that published Bibles among other works. Because the BBC was a step removed from the general tax fund and because this program was open to public and private schools, both secular and sectarian, it would presumably be permissible for the BBC to purchase Bibles via the book suppliers for the religious schools. Yet, this is exactly the kind of neutrality that the current jurisprudence had been thought to prohibit. For example, when the Court upheld the state's buying books and loaning them to private schools in *Board of Education v. Allen*, the Court emphasized that the "books now loaned are text-books which are designated for use in any public, elementary or secondary schools of the state or are approved by any boards of education."[36] Basically, the Court was confident that the books themselves would not have religious content and thus it was permissible for the state to provide them. Had the *Rosenberger* view obtained, there would have been no need for the Court to have worried about whether the loaned books were secular or sectarian.

In her *Rosenberger* concurrence, Justice O'Connor implied that the case before the Court was extremely difficult because it implicated conflicting constitutional principles.

> This case lies at the intersection of the principle of government neutrality and the prohibition on state funding of religious activities. It is clear that the University has established a generally applicable program to encourage the free exchange of ideas by its students, an expressive marketplace that includes some 15 student publications with predictably divergent viewpoints. It is equally clear that petitioners' viewpoint is religious and that publication of Wide Awake is a religious activity, under both the University's regulation and a fair reading of our precedents. Not to finance Wide Awake, according to petitioners, violates the principle of neutrality by sending a message of hostility toward religion. To finance Wide Awake, argues the University, violates the prohibition on direct state funding of religious activities.[37]

But this dilemma is of the Court's own making. The neutrality required by the Establishment Clause had been with respect to the identity of the recipient of the government's largesse, not to whether the state must support secular and sectarian activities. On that understanding of neutrality, there would have been no conflict between the principles cited by Justice O'Connor. While financing religious proselytizing might violate the prohibition on state funding of religious activities, the state's refusing to finance the printing of such materials would not have violated the principle of neutrality, which merely requires that the state be neutral with respect to the identity of those providing secular services. Because the student publication involved sectarian matters, the state was not violating neutrality by refusing to pay those printing costs.

The conflict arose because the Court turned Establishment Clause jurisprudence on its head to say, for example, that the state's willingness to accord secular benefits obligates it to provide sectarian ones as well. That this contradicts the past understanding should be clear when one considers the *Roemer* Court's point that the "State may not, for example, pay for what is actually a religious education,

---

36 392 U.S. 236, 239 (1968).
37 *Rosenberger*, 515 U.S. at 847 (O'Connor, J., concurring).

even though it purports to be paying for a secular one, and even though it makes its aid available to secular and religious institutions alike."[38]

Justice O'Connor offered the consolation that the "Court's decision today therefore neither trumpets the supremacy of the neutrality principle nor signals the demise of the funding prohibition in Establishment Clause jurisprudence."[39] While that may be so, the neutrality principle when construed this way would seem to require the state to promote sectarian institutions in ways that earlier Courts had never dreamed could be required. Justice O'Connor noted that the "insistence on government neutrality toward religion explains why we have held that schools may not discriminate against religious groups by denying them equal access to facilities that the schools make available to all,"[40] since withholding access might be thought to imply that the religious groups were disfavored. Yet, if that is so, then one would expect that the refusal to fund ministerial studies would violate Establishment Clause guarantees, because such a refusal would imply that those religious studies were disfavored. While the Court rejected that position in *Locke v. Davey*,[41] the Court did not offer in that case an account of how all of these cases could be squared, instead again ignoring or re-characterizing the relevant jurisprudence.[42] The Court's present method of analysis cannot help but confuse lower courts and state entities seeking to respect constitutional limitations, because the Court sends contradictory signals about what the Constitution requires, permits, or prohibits.

Greenawalt seems to have accepted the *Rosenberger* Court's analysis with respect to viewpoint discrimination on nonreligious matters, arguing, "Insofar as the guidelines covered comment on social problems, such as war or abortion, they did discriminate against religious perspectives and in favor of nonreligious ones."[43] But it is false to think that only the religious are against war and abortion or that the views of the nonreligious would somehow be promoted. Both the religious and the nonreligious may oppose abortion rights and the waging of war, just as both the religious and the nonreligious may be in favor of abortion rights and the waging of war. To claim otherwise is to misunderstand the diversity of religious and nonreligious viewpoints.

Viteritti suggests that *Rosenberger* was best understood as distinguishing between private speech endorsing religion, which the Constitution protects, and government speech endorsing religion, which the Constitution prohibits.[44] But the whole point behind the University of Virginia regulation was simply to take

---

38 *Roemer*, 426 U.S. at 747.

39 *Rosenberger*, 515 U.S. at 852 (O'Connor, J., concurring).

40 *Id.* at 846 (O'Connor, J., concurring).

41 540 U.S. 712 (2004).

42 For a discussion of *Locke*, see Chapter 3, third section.

43 Kent Greenawalt, *Does God Belong in Public Schools?* 73 (2007).

44 See Joseph P. Viteritti, *The Last Freedom: Religion from the Public School to the Public Square* 137 (2007).

certain topics off of the table, so that the university would not be in the position of promoting or undermining religious views. To suggest that limiting a forum so that particular topics are not discussed is equivalent to viewpoint discrimination because such a limitation prevents the articulation of many viewpoints is simply to reject that the state can limit the topics to be discussed in a forum without discriminating on the basis of viewpoint. While that is a possible position to take, it involves a fundamental re-characterization of the conditions under which the First Amendment permits the state to limit speech.

Funding and Students Groups

When student groups receive funding from the state, part of that funding may be based on student fees. Yet, precisely because there are so many groups with contradictory views and missions, one would expect that some students would have religious objections to funding particular groups whose goals are antithetical to those students' religious convictions. At least one issue is whether the Constitution requires that students be given a waiver so that their student fees are not used in a way that amounts to a violation of conscience.

In *Board of Regents of the University of Wisconsin System v. Southworth*,[45] the Court addressed whether the system used by the University of Wisconsin to fund student groups violated constitutional guarantees. Some of the students claimed that they could not as a matter of conscience fund some of the student organizations that received support from the mandated student activity fees.

The *Southworth* Court noted that it is "inevitable that government will adopt and pursue programs and policies within its constitutional powers but which nevertheless are contrary to the profound beliefs and sincere convictions of some of its citizens."[46] The Court explained that "objecting students may insist upon certain safeguards with respect to the expressive activities which they are required to support,"[47] notwithstanding that the student activities fund was not a traditional public forum. Those safeguards were provided by the university requirement of "viewpoint neutrality."[48]

The *Southworth* Court accepted that free speech rights are implicated when a university conditions a right to receive a college education "on an agreement to support objectionable, extracurricular expression by other students."[49] However, the implicated rights of the students can only be understood in the context of the university's mission to facilitate a broad range of speech. Noting that the "speech the University seeks to encourage in the program before us is distinguished not

---

45 529 U.S. 217 (2000),
46 *Id.* at 229.
47 *Id.*
48 See *id.* at 230.
49 *Id.* at 231.

by discernable limits but by its vast, unexplored bounds,"[50] the Court refused to second-guess the university's judgment with respect to "what is or is not germane to the ideas to be pursued in an institution of higher learning."[51]

After *Rosenberger*, it is simply unclear how to take the Court's avowed deference to universities with respect to their educational mission. The *Southworth* Court noted that the "University may determine that its mission is well served if students have the means to engage in dynamic discussions of philosophical, religious, scientific, social, and political subjects in their extracurricular campus life outside the lecture hall,"[52] and explained that a university that so decided would be permitted to require students to pay a mandatory fee to support that mission. However, a separate question involves which limitations a university may impose on a forum and still receive the deference described by the Court. The *Southworth* Court referred to *Rosenberger*, suggesting that the Court there had made the viewpoint neutrality requirement clear. But *Rosenberger* was anything but clear in that respect. One cannot tell if the viewpoint neutrality requirement really means that universities are only at risk of violating constitutional guarantees if they limit viewpoints or if, instead, they are at risk if they limit subject matters. Suppose, for example, that a university limited dynamic discussions to philosophical, religious, scientific, social and political subjects by saying that no discussion of sports would be permitted. Bracketing whether this would be a sensible limitation, one cannot tell if the limitation at issue would be treated as content-based or viewpoint-based.

For some, sports involve an essential aspect of life. Activities must be planned to accommodate important sporting events, and a host of views about issues of public concern are colored by how various kinds of sports are affected by particular policies. Sport is a central, driving force that is considered whenever various life decisions are made

For others, the focus on sports is thought not only to be counterproductive for sports enthusiasts but positively harmful to society more generally. These anti-sports people believe that societal priorities and expenditures are out of whack because of misperceptions about the inherent value of sports.

Still others have views that are not captured by either the pro- or anti-sports individuals briefly described above. Precluding a discussion of sports would prevent a whole host of viewpoints from being discussed, and the current jurisprudence makes it difficult to predict whether a school that limited a forum to discussion of non-sports-related issues would thereby have engaged in content or viewpoint discrimination.

Rosenberger and *Southworth* suggest that a university must be very careful when constructing a limited purpose forum. While the desire might be to assure that only certain subjects are discussed, there is at the very least a danger that the attempt to restrict topics will be construed as an attempt to restrict on the basis

---

50 *Id.* at 232.

51 *Id.*

52 *Id.* at 233.

of viewpoint. The Court has not offered criteria by which to determine whether the state's limiting a forum to the discussion of certain topics will be construed as content discrimination to be evaluated in light of whether the restriction might reasonably be thought to promote the forum's purposes or, instead, as viewpoint discrimination because the state will thereby have barred the articulation of multiple viewpoints on the topics that have been declared unwelcome.

Regrettably, the Court's subsequent decisions have failed to clarify this point. Consider *Christian Legal Society Chapter of the University of California, Hastings College of the Law v. Martinez*.[53] The Christian Legal Society had attempted to limit its membership to individuals who would sign a statement of faith and who believed that sexual relations should only occur in the context of a marriage between a man and a woman. However, the Hastings College of Law had a policy that any club wishing to be a Registered Student Organization was required to have an open-door policy—no student could be barred from membership or a leadership position based on her status or beliefs.

The *Martinez* opinion was noteworthy in a number of respects, including the way that it represented past opinions. For example, *Widmar* was described in the following way:

> [A] public university, in an effort to avoid state support for religion, had closed its facilities to a registered student group that sought to use university space for religious worship and discussion. ... [B]ecause the university singled out religious organizations for disadvantageous treatment, we subjected the university's regulation to strict scrutiny. ... The school's interest "in maintaining strict separation of church and State," we held, was not "sufficiently compelling to justify ... [viewpoint] discrimination against ... religious speech."[54]

The difficulty pointed to here is not in the Court's suggesting that the First Amendment precludes the state from discriminating against religious speech. Rather, the difficulty is that one would never know from such a description that there had been a long history distinguishing between religious worship on the one hand and discussion of religious matters on the other. Would the University of Missouri at Kansas City have barred the group from meeting if it had wanted to discuss religious matters but had not also said that it had wanted to engage in religious worship? One does not know, because that eventuality was not before the Court. Perhaps the university would also have precluded such a group, because the regulation prohibited both religious worship and religious teaching.[55] On the other hand, perhaps the university would have acted differently, depending upon the way that "religious teaching" was interpreted. Certainly, were that term understood to include religious study or discussion, then the First Amendment would be violated

---

53 130 S. Ct. 2971 (2010).
54 *Id*. at 2987.
55 See *Widmar*, 454 U.S. at 265 n.3.

by the regulation, although the term might have been interpreted to have much more limited scope and to be more in accord with the existing jurisprudence. For example, the past cases were compatible with a prohibition on indoctrination on matters of faith, so it would be very important to determine what the ban on religious teaching was thought to include.

Presumably, the University of Missouri at Kansas City would also have precluded a nonreligious group such as a Photography Club from using university facilities had the group said that they wanted to begin each meeting with a prayer. The university was not targeting religious groups but religious practices. Perhaps such targeting is also unconstitutional, although such a holding would seem to have much more robust ramifications than the Court has been willing to acknowledge.

The *Martinez* Court's characterization of *Rosenberger* was also enlightening:

> [I]n *Rosenberger*, we reiterated that a university generally may not withhold benefits from student groups because of their religious outlook. The officially recognized student group in *Rosenberger* was denied student-activity-fee funding to distribute a newspaper because the publication discussed issues from a Christian perspective. ... By "select[ing] for disfavored treatment those student journalistic efforts with religious editorial viewpoints," we held, the university had engaged in "viewpoint discrimination, which is presumed impermissible when directed against speech otherwise within the forum's limitations."[56]

Here, too, the *Martinez* Court announces a constitutional position that is unexceptional. The only difficulty is that the description offered by the Court makes *Rosenberger* a much different case than it actually was. The university had not set up a limited purpose forum and then precluded religious speech that would otherwise have fallen within the forum's limitations, as if the university had flouted the very conditions that it had set up when creating the forum. Rather, the university had limited the purposes of the forum to exclude all speech about God. That topic or subject matter had been totally excluded precisely because the university wanted to avoid the charge that it was permitting some viewpoints about religion but not others.

One might infer from the *Martinez* treatment of *Rosenberger* that the University of Virginia had excluded religious editorial viewpoints but would have welcomed antireligious editorial viewpoints, which is exactly the position that the university had not adopted. By claiming that *Widmar* and *Rosenberger* involved university actions that singled out student groups because of their point of view, the *Martinez* Court characterizes the cases in a way that makes them quite understandable and not particularly noteworthy. Were these characterizations accurate, the cases would represent standard applications of the then-existing jurisprudence rather than reformulations of the prevailing jurisprudence. But such a formulation does not require or even permit an analysis of how these cases may have significantly

---

56 *Martinez*, 130 S. Ct. at 2988.

modified establishment Clause jurisprudence in particular or First Amendment jurisprudence more generally.

The *Martinez* Court was much less deferential to university judgments than was the *Southworth* Court, explaining that the Supreme "Court is the final arbiter of the question whether a public university has exceeded constitutional constraints, and we owe no deference to universities when we consider that question."[57] The Court then sought to answer whether the Hastings policy violated constitutional guarantees.

As had been true in *Southworth*, the funding for student organizations at Hastings came at least in part from a mandatory student activity fee. The Court explained that a virtue of the Hastings system was that no student would be precluded from being a member of an organization whom she had helped to fund through the mandatory activity fee,[58] although it would still be true that a student might be financially supporting a group whose aims contradicted her own. Presumably, telling an individual that she could be a member or even leader of an organization whose aims she did not share would not be viewed as a particularly attractive option.[59] But this was the compromise the school reached. The Court characterized the school as having been "caught in the crossfire between a group's desire to exclude and students' demand for equal access."[60] Concluding that the school might "reasonably draw a line in the sand permitting *all* organizations to express what they wish but *no* group to discriminate in membership,"[61] the Court was not thereby suggesting that the school had to adopt this policy but nonetheless believed such a policy permitted by the Constitution.[62]

Because the Hastings policy was viewpoint neutral—it drew no distinction based on message or perspective—the policy would be upheld if it was reasonable in light of the forum's purpose. The Court noted several legitimate interests that the policy promoted, and therefore upheld the Hastings policy. The Court did not address whether such a policy would pass muster if the open door policy required of all groups ended up changing the mission of the various groups because they had been overrun with individuals who did not share the groups' goals. The Court did not believe such an eventuality to be a realistic possibility and seemed confident that the school would take appropriate steps were such message modification to occur.

It might be noted that the Christian Legal Society had been a recognized club at Hastings prior to the adoption of the exclusionary membership policy. That policy

---

57 *Id.*

58 See *id.* at 2989.

59 It seems clear that the school did not anticipate that many students would join an organization if disagreeing with their mission. See *id.* at 2993.

60 *Id.*

61 *Id.*

62 See *id.* at 2992 ("the *advisability* of Hastings' policy does not control its *permissibility*").

was adopted because the Club had decided to affiliate with a national organization requiring the exclusionary policy as a condition of membership. But no evidence was presented that the group's message or practices (other than its membership policies) had changed once they had adopted the exclusionary policies. Thus, nothing in the record suggested that the group had not been able to have weekly prayer meetings before they had required members to sign a profession of faith and there was no evidence that the group had been overrun with nonbelievers even when the group had been permitting anyone to join.

Martinez does not stand for the proposition that a school can preclude a religious organization from meeting simply by adopting a policy like the one at issue in Hastings. Indeed, the Hastings policy did not preclude recognition of religious groups—it merely required open membership, which would mean that the group could still conduct religious teaching and worship even if not all members were of the same faith. Had it been established that that policy requiring open membership was a pretextual method to disadvantage religious groups, the policy presumably would have been struck down.[63]

Conclusion

The Court's Establishment Clause jurisprudence with respect to public higher education has been disappointing because of its consistent mischaracterization of prior cases and the then-prevailing jurisprudence. The results reached by the Court in these cases might be justified in various ways, but the justifications offered tended to ignore or mischaracterize both the past jurisprudence and the facts before the Court. Further, the reasoning offered by the Court would often provide no logical stopping point and make past decisions incomprehensible.

The Court has long suggested that state funds cannot be used to promote sectarian activities. Safeguards had to be included to assure that this prohibition was not being circumvented. The *Lemon* test was designed to provide some of these safeguards.

Perhaps the student groups at issue in *Widmar* and *Rosenberger* should have received the benefits at issue as a kind of de minimis exception to Establishment Clause limitations. Perhaps not. But the Court's suggesting that prayer is basically equivalent to speech about religion has important implications for Establishment Clause jurisprudence more generally and, at this point, it is quite difficult to predict whether the reasoning in the public higher education cases will be limited in the ways suggested in *Martinez* or expanded in unforeseeable ways. The last chapter discusses two issues that have recently received some attention: the constitutionality of the Pledge of Allegiance and the conditions under which the Ten Commandments may be displayed by the state.

---

63 Cf. *id.* at 3017 (Alito, J., dissenting) (suggesting that the policy had been adopted as a pretext).

Chapter 5

The Pledge of Allegiance in the Schools

The constitutionality of the Pledge of Allegiance ("the Pledge") has recently received much attention in part because of differing views in the circuits about its constitutionality and in part because of a growing awareness that the Court's jurisprudence in this area is in great disarray. Add to this there are now new Justices on the Court and it is likely that this area of law will continue to be the focus of much debate.

Were the constitutionality of a primary school policy requiring recitation of the Pledge to come before the Court, at least two issues would be of great interest: (1) how that issue in particular would be resolved, and (2) how, if at all, Establishment Clause jurisprudence would be clarified. Predicting how the first issue would be resolved is more difficult than might initially be thought. Various Justices have suggested in dicta that the Pledge passes constitutional muster, although they often were not addressing the specific issue of whether requiring recitation of the Pledge in a primary school violates First Amendment guarantees. Arguably, such a policy fails to pass any of the tests that the Court has articulated for determining Establishment Clause violations, although Justice O'Connor has argued that a primary school Pledge policy need not violate the endorsement test and Justice Kennedy dissented in *County of Allegheny v. American Civil Liberties Union*,[1] at least in part, because he believed that the majority decision would result in the Pledge being declared unconstitutional. As a further complicating factor, the Court has been inconsistent even when applying the tests that it has announced, so it is difficult to predict with confidence what the Court would say were this issue to come before it.

The second issue of great interest is whether the Court would reaffirm the validity of any of the Establishment Clause tests already offered—the *Lemon* test, the endorsement test, or the coercion test—or instead offer either a new test or a modified version of one of the existing tests. It is a testament to the utter confusion in this area of law that it is entirely unclear what the Court would do with respect to either the narrow question involving the constitutionality of such a school policy or the broader question involving the appropriate test for determining Establishment Clause violations.

Notwithstanding that each of the tests would be violated by such a policy, however, there is no way to predict with confidence what the Court will in fact say on this issue in particular or how, if at all, the Court will modify the existing jurisprudence. The only matters about which one can be confident are that the

---

1   492 U.S. 573 (1989).

Justices will be divided, the opinion will be rancorous, and years of litigation will be required to help clarify the Court's evolving jurisprudence in this area.

The History of the Pledge

The Pledge of Allegiance case law is much more involved than is usually appreciated, both because the Pledge did not contain the words "under God" for more than half a century and because the Pledge has been the subject of litigation for several decades. The relevant cases may be divided into two groups: (1) those challenging the constitutionality of a requirement mandating recitation of the Pledge even by those whose religious or political beliefs preclude such a recitation, and (2) those challenging the recitation of the Pledge in a particular setting, notwithstanding the existence of an exception for those who cannot recite it in good faith. The Court has held that the Constitution requires an exception for those who cannot recite the Pledge in good conscience, but has not yet addressed on the merits whether policies with such an exception may nonetheless violate constitutional guarantees.

The Pledge of Allegiance was written in 1892 by Francis Bellamy and James Upham in celebration of Columbus's discovery of America, and was officially codified by the Congress in 1942. The original Pledge did not contain the words "under God"—those words did not become part of the Pledge until 1954. Several purposes were cited to justify amending the Pledge to include "under God," such as distinguishing the United States from the atheistic Soviet Union, affirming that this is a religious country, and teaching children that the nation is under God. By amending the Pledge in this way, it was thought that children might come to appreciate the spiritual values underlying this country, including the belief in an all-seeing, all-knowing, all-powerful Supreme Being. As Delafattore notes, there was an increase in crime and social unrest after World War II, and it was believed by many that religion would provide an antidote to the rise in antisocial activity. Adding the words "under God" to the Pledge was thought by many to affirm and, perhaps, strengthen America's commitment to morality.[2]

In *Minersville School District v. Gobitis*,[3] the United States Supreme Court addressed whether children could be required to salute the flag as a condition of their attending public school. The Court characterized the conflict as between "the liberty of conscience" and the "authority to safeguard the nation's fellowship," which it believed put the "judicial conscience … to its severest test."[4] The *Gobitis* Court did not deny that a flag salute might offend religious beliefs—it instead

---

2   See Joan Delfattore, *The Fourth R: Conflicts over Religion in America's Public Schools* 69 (2004).

3   310 U.S. 586 (1940), overruled by *West Virginia State Board of Education v. Barnette*, 319 U.S. 624 (1943).

4   *Id.* at 591.

suggested that the protection of religious practices is not absolute and that the importance of the implicated state interest must also be considered. The Court made clear that the state's interest in having children recite the Pledge was of the highest order, as if the fabric of the nation would be torn asunder were children with religious objections excused from reciting the Pledge.

At least one reason the *Gobitis* Court believed the interest so important was that public school children are at an especially impressionable age. Further, because "the formative period in the development of citizenship"[5] was at issue, the Court was reluctant to second-guess the judgment of the legislature "that a particular program or exercise will best promote in the minds of children who attend the common schools an attachment to the institutions of their country."[6] Ironically, the very factors that may have convinced the *Gobitis* Court to uphold the Pledge requirement may contribute to the current Court's finding a Pledge requirement unconstitutional in those same circumstances.

The children who were being expelled from school in *Gobitis* sincerely believed that reciting the Pledge would violate their religious convictions. Justice Harlan Stone in his *Gobitis* dissent argued that the Constitution precluded the legislature from forcing these children to affirm something contrary to their religious convictions, absent "a problem so momentous or pressing as to outweigh the freedom from compulsory violation of religious faith which has been thought worthy of constitutional protection."[7] Thus, both the majority and the dissent in *Gobitis* believed that individuals could not be forced to affirm something contrary to their own religious beliefs, absent some overriding state interest—the difference between the two was in whether the state in fact had a sufficiently important interest implicated.

Justice Stone's view was vindicated a mere three years later in *West Virginia State Board of Education v. Barnette*.[8] At issue in *Barnette* was a West Virginia law requiring children to participate in the Pledge ceremony, where a failure to conform could result in expulsion, and the child would not be permitted to come back until he or she would conform. A child not attending school could be treated as a delinquent, which might result in the child being sent to a reformatory. The child's parents would be liable to prosecution for contributing to the delinquency of a minor, which might result in a fine or imprisonment.

The *Barnette* Court noted that school attendance was required, that the children wishing not to participate in ceremony were quiet and orderly, and that their refraining from participating in the ceremony would not in any way interfere with or deny others' rights. Echoing Justice Stone's *Gobitis* dissent, the *Barnette* Court explained that requiring the flag salute and recitation of the Pledge forced individuals to make an affirmation that they did not believe. However,

---

5   *Id.* at 598.
6   *Id.* at 599.
7   *Id.* at 607 (Stone, J., dissenting).
8   319 U.S. 624 (1943).

censorship or suppression of expression of opinion is tolerated by our Constitution only when the expression presents a clear and present danger of action of a kind the State is empowered to prevent and punish, ... [and it] would seem that involuntary affirmation could be commanded only on even more immediate and urgent grounds than silence.[9]

The state made no showing, however, that students refraining from participating in the ceremony would create the requisite clear and present danger.

The *Barnette* Court had no quarrel with the state's end but, rather, with the means chosen to accomplish that end. Basically, the Court suggested that students cannot be compelled to recite the Pledge, notwithstanding the legislature's decision to impose such a requirement. Rather than adopt the *Gobitis* position that the legislature's decision should not be second-guessed, the *Barnette* Court explained that certain kinds of decisions should not be up to the legislature. The Court noted:

The very purpose of a Bill of Rights was to withdraw certain subjects from the vicissitudes of political controversy, to place them beyond the reach of majorities and officials and to establish them as legal principles to be applied by the courts. One's right to life, liberty, and property, to free speech, a free press, freedom of worship and assembly, and other fundamental rights may not be submitted to vote; they depend on the outcome of no elections.[10]

The Court understood that one of the reasons that the refusal to salute the flag was upsetting was that the students were refusing to salute the American flag during a time of war. However, it was not credible to believe that there would be dire consequences were the Pledge made voluntary, since such a view underestimated the American people. "To believe that patriotism will not flourish if patriotic ceremonies are voluntary and spontaneous instead of a compulsory routine is to make an unflattering estimate of the appeal of our institutions to free minds."[11] In any event, the Constitution was not merely designed to offer protection of dissenting views that are harmless, since the "freedom to differ is not limited to things that do not matter much. That would be a mere shadow of freedom. The test of its substance is the right to differ as to things that touch the heart of the existing order."[12] Indeed, the Court emphasized the primacy of the right at issue. "If there is any fixed star in our constitutional constellation, it is that no official, high or petty, can prescribe what shall be orthodox in politics, nationalism, religion, or other matters of opinion or force citizens to confess by word or act their faith therein."[13]

---

9   *Id.* at 633.
10 *Id.* at 638.
11 *Id.* at 641.
12 *Id.* at 642.
13 *Id.*

The *Barnette* majority opinion did not focus in particular on the burden imposed by the Pledge requirement on religion—the same analysis offers protection to a student who refuses to participate in the Pledge ceremony for nonreligious reasons. Justice Black's *Barnette* concurrence discussed the burden on religion more directly. He, too, suggested that sincerely held religious beliefs do not immunize the adherent from state laws. "Religious faiths, honestly held, do not free individuals from responsibility to conduct themselves obediently to laws which are either imperatively necessary to protect society as a whole from grave and pressingly imminent dangers or which, without any general prohibition, merely regulate time, place or manner of religious activity."[14] However, where a time, place, manner restriction is not at issue and when it cannot plausibly be said that "a failure, because of religious scruples, to assume a particular physical position and to repeat the words of a patriotic formula creates a grave danger to the nation,"[15] the regulation must give way to the sincerely held religious beliefs.

Justice Frankfurter dissented in *Barnette* largely because he construed the Pledge requirement as simply "promoting good citizenship and national allegiance."[16] He made clear, however, that an "act compelling profession of allegiance to a religion, no matter how subtly or tenuously promoted, is bad,"[17] that is, is unconstitutional.

The *Barnette* Court understood that some individuals have religious objections to reciting the Pledge of which the Constitution must take account, notwithstanding the patriotic nature of the Pledge. As the Court recognized in *Thomas v. Review Board of Indiana Employment Security Division*:

> Where the state conditions receipt of an important benefit upon conduct proscribed by a religious faith, or where it denies such a benefit because of conduct mandated by religious belief, thereby putting substantial pressure on an adherent to modify his behavior and to violate his beliefs, a burden upon religion exists.[18]

Once *Barnette* was issued, students could no longer be required to affirm beliefs that violated their consciences. The recognition that recitation of the Pledge implicates religious beliefs may continue to play an important role in any analysis of the current constitutional challenges to Pledge policies, even when the operating policy permits a child to refrain from participating in the ceremony.

---

14 *Id.* at 643–4 (Black, J., concurring).
15 *Id.* at 644 (Black, J., concurring).
16 *Id.* at 654 (Frankfurter, J., dissenting).
17 *Id.* (Frankfurter, J., dissenting).
18 450 U.S. 707, 717–18 (1981).

The Later Cases

Eleven years after *Barnette* was issued, Congress modified the Pledge to include the words "under God." Member of the Court would sometimes explain in dicta why they believed that the modified Pledge did not offend constitutional guarantees. For example, in writing the opinion in *Engel v. Vitale*, Justice Black referred to "officially espoused anthems which include the composer's professions of faith in a Supreme Being."[19] In his *Schempp* concurrence, Justice Brennan suggested that there had been no showing that daily recitation of the Pledge "may not adequately serve the solely secular purposes of the devotional activities without jeopardizing either the religious liberties of any members of the community or the proper degree of separation between the spheres of religion and government."[20] Thus, he believed that the daily recitation of the Pledge promoted secular interests without infringing upon individuals' religious liberties.

Yet, someone reciting the Pledge—"I pledge allegiance to the flag of the United States of America and to the Republic for which it stands, one Nation, under God, indivisible, with liberty and justice for all"—would likely not believe that she, by reciting the words "under God," was merely acknowledging the beliefs of the Pledge's composer or merely acknowledging that faith has inspired many Americans. Rather, she presumably would believe that she, herself, was making a statement involving God, for example, that the nation was under God. Just as a flag salute involves a personal statement by the person saluting that, when forced, can be a serious infringement of personal liberties, being forced to utter the words in the Pledge might involve a serious infringement of personal liberties.

The jurisprudence in this area makes little sense if the words of the Pledge are interpreted merely to reflect others' beliefs. Individuals who refused to say the Pledge were sincerely claiming that the words of the Pledge did not represent their own beliefs—these individuals were not arguing that the words of the Pledge did not represent the beliefs of others.

Even Justice Brennan's *Schempp* concurrence is not particularly persuasive for the proposition that the Pledge passes muster when one considers some of the alternative ways that the state can instill patriotism in children. For example, the state could have children recite the Pledge as it existed in 1950, that is, before the words "under God" were added. Indeed, it is not at all clear what additional patriotism would be inculcated by including the words "under God" within the Pledge. If, however, no additional patriotism would be instilled by adding those words, then the state can achieve the desired secular purposes without entering the thicket created when God and the state are linked. By choosing to incorporate a religious message when the state could have achieved the same secular end without incorporating such a message, the state violates the Establishment Clause.

---

19 *Engel*, 370 U.S. at 435 n.21.
20 *Schempp*, 374 U.S. at 281 (Brennan, J., concurring).

In *Newdow v. United States Congress*,[21] the Ninth Circuit struck down a school policy mandating recitation of the Pledge in public schools as a violation of constitutional guarantees. The court held that the policy coerced individuals into performing a religious act and thus violated the First Amendment. The United States Supreme Court reversed, holding that the plaintiff did not have standing to bring the action.[22]

In his *Newdow* concurrence, Justice Thomas suggested that "as a matter of our precedent, the Pledge policy is unconstitutional."[23] However, he would not strike down a policy requiring recitation of the Pledge because he rejects the existing jurisprudence. If Justice Thomas's understanding of the relevant jurisprudence is accurate, however, then those non-activist Justices who wish to apply rather than recreate the relevant constitutional law, and those inferior courts who wish to follow their duty and apply existing law, are required to strike policies mandating the recitation of the Pledge in primary schools. At the very least, such a surprising result suggests that the current jurisprudence in this area should be examined carefully to see whether Justice Thomas's analysis is correct.

The Existing Establishment Clause Jurisprudence

Numerous jurists and commentators have noted that the existing Establishment Clause jurisprudence is confused and in need of either clarification or, perhaps, a fundamental rethinking. The Court has offered several tests to determine whether an action by the state violates the Establishment Clause without clearly specifying the conditions under which particular tests should be ap, :ed. But this creates the possibility that a particular state action would pass one test but fail another, making that action's constitutionality indeterminate. Of course, in some cases, it will not matter which test is applied because the implicated state action violates each of them. Arguably, the recitation of the Pledge in primary schools fails all three tests.

The Lemon Test

Consider the *Lemon* test.[24] An action will not violate the purpose prong merely because one of the purposes behind it was religious—the religious purpose must have been the predominant purpose in order for a challenged action to fail to pass muster under this prong. That said, the mere existence of a secular purpose will not immunize a state action if religious purposes predominate. As the Court recently confirmed in *McCreary County v. ACLU*, "When the government acts with the ostensible and predominant purpose of advancing religion, it violates that

---

21 328 F.3d 466 (9th Cir. 2003), *rev'd* 542 U.S. 1 (2004).

22 See *Elk Grove Unified School Dist v. Newdow*, 542 U.S. 1, 5 (2004).

23 *Id.* at 49 (Thomas, J., concurring).

24 For a discussion of the *Lemon* test, see Chapter 1, third section.

central Establishment Clause value of official religious neutrality, there being no neutrality when the government's ostensible object is to take sides."[25]

So, too, an act cannot pass muster if its principal effect is to promote religion. However, it should be noted that there has been an evolving understanding with respect to what in fact violates this prong. For example, the *Meek* Court struck down a Pennsylvania law authorizing public funding of auxiliary services such as guidance counseling and testing services in religious schools. The Court feared either that these personnel would impermissibly foster religious belief or that the state would have to engage in continuing surveillance to make sure that no impermissible fostering occurred. The former would violate the effect prong, while the latter would violate the entanglement prong.

The *Ball* Court struck down a program in which classes were taught at public expense by public employees in classrooms located in and leased from religious schools. The Court again worried that public employees might be offering religious instruction. Yet, the understanding of *Lemon* that prevailed in *Meek* and *Ball* no longer reflects the current jurisprudence.

The effect prong of the *Lemon* test has been modified somewhat. The *Agostini* Court explained that while "government inculcation of religious beliefs has the impermissible effect of advancing religion," the Court has "abandoned the presumption erected in *Meek* and *Ball* that the placement of public employees on parochial school grounds inevitably results in the impermissible effect of state-sponsored indoctrination or constitutes a symbolic union between government and religion."[26] The Court further explained that it no longer subscribes to the view that "all government aid that directly aids the educational function of religious schools is invalid."[27] The Court instead seems to have adopted a kind of neutrality principle whereby funding of religious activity is permissible if a variety of secular activities are also being funded.

The entanglement prong of *Lemon* sought to prevent two evils. First, where the state would have to monitor constantly to ensure that government funds were not being used to promote religion, there was some fear that the religious institution itself would be changed. Second, there was a fear that excessive connections between the state and religion might foster the view that religion was being given a special political role or, perhaps, that political constituencies might be forged along religious lines. Both of these fears might be characterized as possible effects of excessive entanglement and, ultimately, the *Agostini* Court suggested that the *Lemon* entanglement prong is better analyzed as an element to be included in the examination of the statute's effects.

Suppose that the constitutionality of the statute mandating that the Pledge incorporate the words "under God" were to be evaluated in light of the *Lemon* test. It is quite unlikely that the statute could survive examination under the first prong,

25 545 U.S. 844, 860 (2005).
26 *Agostini*, 521 U.S. at 223.
27 *Id.* at 225.

since the historical evidence that the Pledge was intended to promote religion is very strong. First, the precipitating cause of the addition of these words to the Pledge was a sermon in which the Reverend George M. Docherty complained that the Pledge did not contain any mention of God. As a result of this sermon, several bills were introduced to amend the Pledge so that God might be included within it. When Congress was debating whether to include "under God," it was suggested that God is the source of all of the country's power and should be recognized as such. The House and Senate Reports regarding the addition of "under God" made their religious objectives clear. Even the president when signing the relevant bill into law made clear the religious nature of the addition. Thus, the officials instrumental in the addition of "under God" to the Pledge made no attempt to hide their religious purposes. Further, lest it be argued that this is not the kind of evidence that the Court is permitted to consider, one need only consider the *Doe* Court's comments: "We refuse to turn a blind eye to the context in which this policy arose, and that context quells any doubt that this policy was implemented with the purpose of endorsing school prayer."[28]

If the addition of "under God" violates the purpose prong, then it is not even necessary to consider the effect prong. As the *Aguillard* Court suggested: "A governmental intention to promote religion is clear when the State enacts a law to serve a religious purpose. This intention may be evidenced by promotion of religion in general ... or by advancement of a particular religious belief."[29] If the purpose of a law was to endorse religion, then it is not even necessary to consider the remainder of the *Lemon* test before striking down the statute.[30]

In order to determine whether the Pledge violates the first prong of the *Lemon* test, one must characterize the predominant purpose behind the Pledge. Consider the claim that the purpose behind amending the Pledge was political rather than religious, because the United States was attempting to differentiate itself from the Soviet Union in 1954 when adding the words "under God" to the Pledge.

Yet, this is a false dichotomy, because these are not mutually exclusive categories. The Pledge can be both political and religious, and it would be an important change in the jurisprudence if religious affirmations are immunized when made in the context of a patriotic activity. Such a view implies that the government can endorse a variety of religious beliefs in the guise of a patriotic exercise and potentially constitutionally immunizes a linking that can be especially worrisome.

If the goal behind amending the Pledge in 1954 had been strictly political, there would have been ways to emphasize the differences between the United States and Soviet Union without affirming theistic beliefs. For example, language might have been included in the Pledge to emphasize that the United States protects the right of all individuals to worship or not worship as they choose. Such a focus would

---

28 *Doe*, 530 U.S. at 315.
29 *Aguillard*, 482 U.S. at 585.
30 See *id.*

have emphasized the liberty upon which this country was founded rather than particular theistic beliefs.

Compare two pledge candidates competing for adoption, each of which is designed to instill and inspire patriotism. One emphasizes a respect for religious liberty while the other emphasizes a belief in God. The former is much more likely than the latter to be viewed as not favoring one religion over another and as not favoring religion over non-religion.

Some commentators suggest that the current Pledge passes constitutional muster because it merely establishes that the nation is "under God," meaning it is a limited government subject to rights and duties created by God. Yet, there are a host of reasons that this cannot be correct. Such a view commits the state to a variety of theistic beliefs, for example, that there is a God (rather than no god or many gods), that God has created or imposed human rights and duties (rather than having been concerned with other matters), and that those rights and duties are superior rather than subservient to those created or imposed by the state.

Others believe that the Pledge passes muster because it merely asserts that God is guiding the Nation, as if acknowledgments of God's existence and active role in the state's affairs do not qualify as religious beliefs. If there is no violation of the Establishment Clause when the state asserts that it is limited by God-given rights (whose contents are defined by majority view?) or that it is subject to God's authority or even that it acts with God's guidance, then the Establishment Clause protections are very weak indeed.

The Endorsement Test

The endorsement test, often associated with Justice O'Connor, has sometimes been described as an alternative to *Lemon* and sometimes as a part of *Lemon*. The test focuses on the reactions of a reasonable, knowledgeable observer to the action at issue. The relevant question is whether the action at issue would make that observer feel like a political outsider. As Justice O'Connor explains in her *Newdow* concurrence, "the endorsement test captures the essential command of the Establishment Clause, namely, that government must not make a person's religious beliefs relevant to his or her standing in the political community by conveying a message that religion or a particular religious belief is favored or preferred."[31]

Justice O'Connor specifically addresses how the reasonable observer would react to various patriotic songs and oaths containing references to God, believing that such an observer would not understand these acknowledgments as government endorsement of a particular religion or of religion over non-religion. Because such acknowledgments act to solemnify public occasions and because the Pledge is performed routinely as an act of ceremonial patriotism,[32] she suggests that the

---

31 *Newdow*, 542 U.S. at 33–4 (O'Connor, J., concurring).
32 *Id.* at 38 (O'Connor, J., concurring).

reasonable observer would simply view the ceremonial references to God as "the inevitable consequence of the religious history that gave birth to our founding principles of liberty."[33]

Justice O'Connor explains that where there has been no endorsement, the state's acknowledgment of religion can pass constitutional muster. However, where the government endorses or takes a position on questions of religious belief, it violates the Establishment Clause, at least if that endorsement "sends a message to non-adherents that they are outsiders, not full members of the political community, and an accompanying message to adherents that they are insiders, favored members of the political community."[34]

Yet, the characterization above of how the reasonable observer would view the Pledge is a little misleading, because Justice O'Connor is not concerned with whether sincere individuals would in fact feel disfavored because of their religious beliefs. She notes, "Given the dizzying religious heterogeneity of our Nation, adopting a subjective approach would reduce the test to an absurdity. Nearly any government action could be overturned as a violation of the Establishment Clause if a 'heckler's veto' sufficed to show that its message was one of endorsement."[35] She cites her own discussion in *Capitol Square Review and Advisory Board v. Pinette* to explain her point, where she noted that there "is always someone who, with a particular quantum of knowledge, reasonably might perceive a particular action as an endorsement of religion."[36]

Justice O'Connor implicitly suggests that the person with a particular quantum of knowledge may misconstrue state action as an endorsement because the quantum of knowledge possessed by that person is too small. If the person knew more, one might conclude, then that person would not misconstrue the state's action as an endorsement. Justice O'Connor explains that:

> because the "reasonable observer" must embody a community ideal of social judgment, as well as rational judgment, the test does not evaluate a practice in isolation from its origins and context. Instead, the reasonable observer must be deemed aware of the history of the conduct in question, and must understand its place in our Nation's cultural landscape.[37]

Justice O'Connor seems to be suggesting that an individual with sufficient knowledge of the Pledge's origin and context could not believe it an endorsement of religion. Yet, someone aware of the history of the amendment to the Pledge might well construe the addition of "under God" as an endorsement. Indeed, some

---

33 *Id.* at 44 (O'Connor, J., concurring).
34 *Lynch v. Donnelly*, 465 U.S. 668, 688 (1984) (O'Connor J. concurring).
35 *Newdow*, 542 U.S. at 34–5 (O'Connor, J., concurring).
36 515 U.S. 753, 780 (1995) (O'Connor, J., concurring).
37 *Newdow*, 542 U.S. at 35 (O'Connor, J., concurring).

would argue that only those with a less than full quantum of knowledge would be tempted to believe that it was *not* an endorsement.

Justice O'Connor does not explain why the reasonable observer would think that the Pledge's inclusion of "under God" an inevitable consequence of the nation's religious history, given that the Pledge did not include a reference to God for over half a century. Suppose, however, that such an explanation could be offered. Suppose further that some, but not all, observers accepted Justice O'Connor's claim that the inclusion of "under God" is an inevitable consequence of the nation's religious history. Even so, that would not be enough to save Justice O'Connor's claim that the addition of "under God" to the Pledge passes the endorsement test.

The endorsement test does not require that all knowledgeable, reasonable persons see the Pledge as an endorsement of religion in order for the Pledge to violate the Establishment Clause. On the contrary, the test merely requires that a reasonable person with a full appreciation of the Pledge's origin and context might see it that way. Given the stated purposes behind adding "under God" to the Pledge, it seems difficult to deny that some (even if not all) reasonable, knowledgeable individuals would see the addition of those words as an endorsement of religion.

Justice O'Connor has suggested that the Pledge is an example of ceremonial deism, a term which suggests that a passage incorporating a religious reference may have lost its religious significance over time and thus is not constitutionally objectionable. The term first appeared in a Supreme Court opinion in Justice Brennan's *Lynch v. Donnelly*[38] dissent. Nonetheless, it plays an important role in Justice O'Connor's endorsement theory, because it allegedly explains why a reasonable observer would not think a reference to God involves an endorsement of religion by the state.

The Court has neither explicitly embraced nor explicitly rejected the notion of ceremonial deism. In his *Lynch* dissent, Justice Brennan wrote:

> While I remain uncertain about these questions, I would suggest that such practices as the designation of "In God We Trust" as our national motto, or the references to God contained in the Pledge of Allegiance can best be understood, in Dean Rostow's apt phrase, as a form a "ceremonial deism," protected from Establishment Clause scrutiny chiefly because they have lost through rote repetition any significant religious content.[39]

The first point to note, however, is that Justice O'Connor has a somewhat different understanding of ceremonial deism than does Justice Brennan. To Justice Brennan, but not Justice O'Connor, a phrase can be understood as a form of ceremonial deism when it has been drained of significant religious content. While Justice O'Connor suggests that "the appearance of the phrase "under God" in the Pledge of

---

38 465 U.S. 668 (1984).

39 *Id.* at 716 (Brennan, J., dissenting).

Allegiance constitutes an instance of … ceremonial deism,"[40] she also recognizes that this reference involves the language of religious belief, and that this is an acknowledgment of or reference to the divine. She does not claim that the word "God" has lost its religious meaning—she instead suggests that observers would not perceive this religious reference "as signifying a government endorsement of any specific religion, or even of religion over non-religion."[41] Thus, her use of "ceremonial deism" seems to indicate that religious terms are being used in a way that does not constitute an endorsement rather than that the terms have lost all religious significance.

Justice O'Connor emphasizes that the Pledge does not attempt to single out the belief of a particular religion, for example, by referring "to a nation 'under Jesus' or 'under Vishnu,' but instead acknowledges religion in a general way: a simple reference to a generic 'God.'"[42] She understands that this reference excludes some religions, but concludes that the "phrase 'under God,' conceived and added at a time when our national religious diversity was neither as robust nor as well recognized as it is now, represents a tolerable attempt to acknowledge religion and to invoke its solemnizing power without favoring any individual religious sect or belief system."[43] Yet, this account of the purposes behind the inclusion of "under God" does not reflect the articulated purposes of those instrumental in modifying the Pledge. Nor does Justice O'Connor's account capture the function of the phrase "under God," which is not merely to acknowledge religious beliefs but to affirm them. Further, while that phrase may not favor any single belief system, it certainly favors certain belief systems over others.

According to Justice O'Connor, certain "government acknowledgments of religion serve, in the only ways reasonably possible in our culture, the legitimate secular purposes of solemnizing public occasions, expressing confidence in the future, and encouraging the recognition of what is worthy of appreciation in society."[44] Because such acknowledgments have this secular purpose and "because of their history and ubiquity, those practices are not understood as conveying government approval of particular religious beliefs."[45] O'Connor argues that the "constitutional value of ceremonial deism turns on a shared understanding of its legitimate nonreligious purposes."[46] Such an understanding develops over time and can only occur when the practice at issue is widespread.

Yet, even if Justice O'Connor is correct that government acknowledgment of religion can serve those secular purposes, a separate question is whether the "under God" phrase in the Pledge can plausibly be thought to be performing that

---

40 *Newdow*, 542 U.S. at 37 (O'Connor, J., concurring).
41 *Id.* at 36 (O'Connor, J., concurring).
42 *Id.* at 42 (O'Connor, J., concurring).
43 *Id.* (O'Connor, J., concurring).
44 *Lynch*, 465 U.S. at 693 (O'Connor J., concurring).
45 *Id.* (O'Connor J., concurring).
46 *Newdow*, 542 U.S. at 37 (O'Connor, J., concurring).

function. At issue here is a pledge made by children daily rather than, for example, a graduation which occurs but once a year. The function of the phrase within the Pledge is not to express confidence about the future or to make judgments about what is and is not worthy in society. Instead, it is to describe a belief of the person making the pledge. Precisely because of the phrase's testimonial quality, one cannot plausibly describe "under God" as merely serving the secular purposes that Justice O'Connor describes.

Justice O'Connor offers four factors to help determine whether a practice falls into the ceremonial deism category:

    a. history and ubiquity[47]
    b. absence of prayer or worship[48]
    c. absence of reference to particular religion[49]
    d. minimal religious content[50]

Consider the first factor. Basically, this suggests that a practice generally accepted may fall into the ceremonial deism category. Yet, it is not so clear that there is general acceptance of the view that the Pledge is devoid of religious content. First, there have been many challenges to the Pledge, including *Barnette*, which establishes the right not to say the Pledge. Second, while it is fair to say that there have been relatively few constitutional challenges to the Pledge since *Barnette*, that may not be because individuals have understood the Pledge to be secular. Rather, that may be because they have thought that they would be unable to successfully challenge the invocation of God's name in the Pledge where they, themselves, were not being forced to participate.

Justice O'Connor's second factor questions whether there is prayer or worship involved. Certainly, she is correct that the Pledge is not itself a prayer, although that hardly immunizes the Pledge from constitutional invalidation. As Justice Thomas notes, the "Court has squarely held that the government cannot require a person to declare his belief in God."[51]

In *Wallace v. Jaffree*, the Court discussed the "established principle that the government must pursue a course of complete neutrality toward religion."[52] The Court's comments could easily have been written in the context of discussing whether the addition to the Pledge of only two words—"under God"—is constitutionally significant. The *Wallace* Court noted:

---

    47 *Id.* (O'Connor, J., concurring).
    48 *Id.* at 39 (O'Connor, J., concurring).
    49 *Id.* at 42 (O'Connor, J., concurring).
    50 *Id.* (O'Connor, J., concurring).
    51 *Id.* at 48 (Thomas, J., concurring).
    52 472 U.S. at 60.

The importance of [the neutrality] principle does not permit us to treat this as an inconsequential case involving nothing more than a few words of symbolic speech on behalf of the political majority. For whenever the State itself speaks on a religious subject, one of the questions that we must ask is "whether the government intends to convey a message of endorsement or disapproval of religion."[53]

Where government intends to convey its approval or disapproval of religion, the First Amendment is violated. Thus, merely because the Pledge is not a prayer as such does not mean that it cannot violate constitutional guarantees.

Justice O'Connor's third factor, which examines whether there has been a reference to a particular religion, seems to understate the relevant requirement. Given that the "touchstone for [the Court's] analysis is the principle that the First Amendment mandates governmental neutrality between religion and religion, and between religion and nonreligion,"[54] one would expect that it would be impermissible to favor some religions over others. As Justice O'Connor herself notes, the Pledge does do that. But if that is so, the Establishment Clause guarantees are being ignored. It is not at all clear that the Pledge is saved because it refers to God rather than Vishnu or Jesus. Further, as Justice Kennedy points out, atheists may well not feel particularly welcome while the Pledge is said.

Justice O'Connor's fourth factor is that there has to be only a minimal reference to religion. She argues that the "reference to 'God' in the Pledge of Allegiance qualifies as a minimal reference to religion; respondent's challenge focuses on only two of the Pledge's 31 words."[55] Yet, what might seem like a minimal reference to one individual might not seem minimal to another. Many religious individuals believe the Pledge sufficiently suffused with religious content that they would be very angry were that content deleted, while many nonreligious people feel the Pledge is sufficiently suffused with religious meaning that they are angry about the reference to God being retained. For many individuals, the reference to religion in the Pledge is not merely minimal.

A brief examination of the Pledge litigation through *Barnette* helps illustrate that Justice O'Connor's claim that this is a minimal reference to religion simply is not credible. The *Gobitis* Court recognized the religious implications of the Pledge even when the words "under God" were not included. It is difficult to understand how adding the words "under God" would not make the Pledge implicate religion even more. A separate issue is whether the Pledge's constitutionality can be upheld even if its religious nature is recognized, but the religious implications of the words "under God" should not be denied.

Ceremonial deism should be distinguished from the view that some violations of the Establishment Clause are so inconsequential that they should be viewed

---

53 *Id.* at 60–61.
54 *McCreary County*, 545 U.S. at 860.
55 *Newdow*, 542 U.S. at 43 (O'Connor, J., concurring).

as de minimis and hence not constitutionally barred. While some might claim that the Pledge should be so viewed, that is not the position taken by Justice O'Connor. Further, the Court has not been sympathetic to de minimis claims in the Establishment context. As the *Schempp* Court suggested, "[I]t is no defense to urge that the religious practices here may be relatively minor encroachments on the First Amendment. The breach of neutrality that is today a trickling stream may all too soon become a raging torrent."[56]

Justice O'Connor's endorsement test is attractive, at least in part, because it takes into account the views of religious minorities, seeking to assure that state practices do not make them feel like second-class citizens. Yet, built into this test is an analysis of what a reasonable person would feel. Justice O'Connor sometimes implies that a reasonable, knowledgeable individual could only have one reaction, as if a reasonable evangelical and a reasonable atheist would react in the same way to the inclusion or exclusion of particular words such as "under God" in the Pledge. It would be much more plausible to believe that some reasonable atheists and some reasonable evangelicals, even with all of the relevant knowledge, would have opposite reactions to the deletion of the words "under God" from the Pledge, although they would agree that such language is in fact religious.

Another difficulty with the endorsement test's reliance on the reasonable person is that the state action at issue may be directed to children rather than adults. The question then becomes whether one should be discussing what the informed reasonable elementary or high school child would think. Courts have had some difficulty in applying the reasonable person standard when schoolchildren are the target audience. Yet, if a primary school policy is at issue, it is not at all clear why the relevant concern would be how a very knowledgeable adult observer would react to a practice that was being used to instill particular religious beliefs within impressionable and malleable schoolchildren.

On any plausible understanding of the endorsement test, the state policy requiring the recitation of the Pledge as currently constituted in primary and secondary schools cannot pass constitutional muster. Justice O'Connor's protestations to the contrary notwithstanding, both knowledgeable, reasonable adults and knowledgeable, reasonable children might see the current Pledge as endorsing particular religious beliefs. If that is all that is required to violate the Establishment Clause, then the Pledge does not pass constitutional muster.

Certainly, it might be argued, this argument taken to its logical conclusion would require a significant change in our practices. Given the varying religious beliefs in our country, a whole host of state practices might reasonably be construed as endorsing or undermining some religious beliefs. Indeed, Winnifred Sullivan has suggested that "legally encompassing the religious ways of people in an intensely pluralist society is most likely impossible."[57] However, before one concludes that there is no solution to the difficulties posed, it may be helpful to examine some

---

56 *Schempp*, 374 U.S. at 225.
57 Winnifred Fallers Sullivan, *The Impossibility of Religious Freedom* 138 (2005).

of the other proposed tests for establishing whether the Establishment Clause has been violated.

The Coercion Test

An alternative to the endorsement test has been proposed by Justice Kennedy, namely, the coercion test. That test would seem to permit much more than the endorsement test, which seems to be why some on the Court have embraced it and why others believe that it will greatly dilute Establishment Clause protections.

One of the criticisms sometimes made of the endorsement test is that it cannot account for all of the practices that the Court has upheld. For example, Justice Kennedy has pointed out that legislative prayer fails the endorsement test and, indeed, that many practices currently accepted would be held unconstitutional on any principled application of the endorsement test. He suggests that the coercion test coupled with another test involving aid to religion more accurately reflect the relevant jurisprudence.

Justice Kennedy explains that coercion does not only involve a direct tax in aid of religion. He notes that accommodation of religious belief or faith may violate the Establishment Clause in an extreme case, for example, a town could not erect a permanent Latin cross on the roof of city hall. However, absent coercion, there is little risk in most cases that passive or symbolic accommodation will infringe religious liberty. Thus, Justice Kennedy suggests, unless the state is somehow coercing non-adherents to do something that violates their beliefs, most cases involving the accommodation of religious beliefs will not violate Establishment Clause guarantees.

Justice O'Connor has criticized the coercion test because she does not believe that it would "adequately protect the religious liberty or respect the religious diversity of the members of our pluralistic political community."[58] Of course, figuring out whether a particular test offers adequate protection requires, first, some notion of what the coercion test protects, and second, what would count as adequate protection. An important point to appreciate is that the coercion test is much more protective in some settings than others.

While the coercion test as a general matter may offer a much less strict Establishment hurdle than either the *Lemon* test or the endorsement test, that same test is still more protective in particular contexts. Indeed, the coercion test may be as protective as the endorsement test, if not more so, in a school setting, if only because the Court treats the primary and secondary school setting as one which has the potential to be especially coercive.

At issue in *Lee* was an invocation and benediction that seemed to reflect the school policy that they be nonsectarian and composed with inclusiveness and sensitivity. The Court struck down the policy at issue, reasoning that attendance at this state-sponsored religious activity was "in a fair and real sense obligatory,

---

58 *Allegheny*, 492 U.S. at 628 (O'Connor, J., concurring).

though the school district does not require attendance as a condition for receipt of the diploma."[59] However, the Court noted that the Constitution precludes government from coercing "anyone to support or participate in religion or its exercise, or otherwise act in a way which 'establishes a [state] religion or religious faith, or tends to do so.'"[60]

The petitioners had asked the Court to recognize the existence and constitutionality of a practice of nonsectarian prayer. However, the Court rejected the invitation, instead suggesting, "The design of the Constitution is that preservation and transmission of religious beliefs and worship is a responsibility and a choice committed to the private sphere."[61] An additional worry was that these activities were taking place in primary and secondary schools creating the possibility that non-consenting students would feel coerced into giving apparent approval of a message which they did not believe.

> The ... school district's supervision and control of a high school graduation ceremony places public pressure, as well as peer pressure, on attending students to stand as a group or, at least, maintain respectful silence during the invocation and benediction. This pressure, though subtle and indirect, can be as real as any overt compulsion. ... [F]or the dissenter of high school age, who has a reasonable perception that she is being forced by the State to pray in a manner her conscience will not allow, the injury is ... real. ... It is of little comfort to a dissenter, then, to be told that for her the act of standing or remaining in silence signifies mere respect, rather than participation. What matters is that, given our social conventions, a reasonable dissenter in this milieu could believe that the group exercise signified her own participation or approval of it.[62]

It might be argued that students voluntarily attend graduation and thus are not being coerced into doing anything—if religious invocations or benedictions offend them, they can simply choose not to attend. However, the Court suggested that "to say a teenage student has a real choice not to attend her high school graduation is formalistic in the extreme."[63] Indeed, the Court contrasted this setting to a session of a state legislature, where adults might leave freely,[64] thereby suggesting that upholding the legislative prayer in *Marsh v. Chambers*[65] was perfectly compatible with striking the benediction and invocation at issue in *Lee*. By the same token, the Court can strike down a policy mandating recitation of the Pledge in primary and secondary schools without needing to revisit the issue of legislative prayer.

---

59 *Lee*, 505 U.S. at 586.
60 *Id.* at 587.
61 *Id.* at 589.
62 *Id.* at 593.
63 *Id.* at 595.
64 *Id.* at 597.
65 463 U.S. 783 (1983).

It is precisely because of the importance of the context in which the action was occurring, namely, in school, that the Court could strike down a Pledge policy without being forced to revisit a whole host of practices that the Court has already suggested are constitutionally permissible.

The fact that *Lee* might have implications for the Pledge of Allegiance did not go unnoticed by members of the Court. In his *Lee* dissent, Justice Scalia noted:

> [S]ince the Pledge of Allegiance has been revised since *Barnette* to include the phrase "under God," recital of the Pledge would appear to raise the same Establishment Clause issue as the invocation and benediction. If students were psychologically coerced to remain standing during the invocation, they must also have been psychologically coerced, moments before, to stand for (and thereby, in the Court's view, take part in or appear to take part in) the Pledge. Must the Pledge therefore be barred from the public schools (both from graduation ceremonies and from the classroom)? ... Logically, that ought to be the next project for the Court's bulldozer.[66]

Of course, *Lee* left some questions unanswered. For example, it might be argued that it was crucial in *Lee* that the benediction and invocation were delivered by a member of the clergy. Yet, the *Doe* Court subsequently made clear that this would be a misunderstanding of the jurisprudence. In *Doe*, the Court struck down a policy whereby a student elected by the student body would deliver a statement or invocation prior to home football games, the purposes of which were to solemnize the event and promote good sportsmanship and student safety. But the Court explained that a religious message was the most obvious way to solemnize and inferred that a student attending the game would perceive such a prayer as having received the state's endorsement.

The *Doe* Court focused on the religious messages that would be delivered at home football games—the Court was not limiting its decision to a case involving religious prayers. The Court was concerned that various individuals do not attend these games voluntarily, such as cheerleaders, band members and team members. Yet, even if attendance were purely voluntary, that would not have saved the practice at issue, because those attending would have been coerced into participating in a religious exercise.

Lee and *Doe* together have important implications for a school policy mandating that the Pledge of Allegiance be recited in school, because children are especially vulnerable in that setting. Indeed, the *Gobitis* Court recognized that children are especially impressionable, which was one of the reasons that it upheld the Pledge requirement in school, although it bears repeating that the Pledge at issue in *Gobitis* did not contain the words "under God." The *Aguillard* Court suggested that the school setting requires special vigilance because the state exerts

---

66 *Lee,* 505 U.S. at 639 (Scalia, J., dissenting).

great power through its mandatory attendance laws and because of children's susceptibility to pressure from peers and others.

The kind of coercion at issue in *Lee* and *Doe* cannot be understood as legal coercion—rather, what is at issue is a form of psychological coercion, which covers much more than would legal coercion. Further, that students were permitted to remain respectfully silent rather than participate did not cure the constitutional difficulty in *Lee*. Indeed, there are a variety of respects in which it would seem easier to uphold what was at issue in *Lee* than what would be at issue in a Pledge case, since the former occurs but once a year while the latter involves a daily event. As Justice Thomas explained in his *Newdow* concurrence:

> Adherence to *Lee* would require us to strike down the Pledge policy, which, in most respects, poses more serious difficulties than the prayer at issue in *Lee*. A prayer at graduation is a one-time event, the graduating students are almost (if not already) adults, and their parents are usually present. By contrast, very young students, removed from the protection of their parents, are exposed to the Pledge each and every day.[67]

By the same token, the hypothesized Pledge scenario would seem at least as coercive as what was at issue in *Doe*, if only because of the relative frequency of the occurrences. Further, it would not be surprising were students subjected to a variety of pressures were they to consistently refuse to make the Pledge.

The Court's special solicitude for protecting students in the school context helps explain why requiring the Pledge in that context cannot pass muster under the coercion test, even if such a requirement could pass muster in a different context. But this means that someone, such as Justice Kennedy, who believes that the Pledge passes muster as a general matter, might nonetheless not believe that it passes muster when required in the primary school setting, even if there is an exception built in for those who object to saying it on political or religious grounds. The kind of coercion at issue in *Lee* and *Doe*, which made those practices unconstitutional, would be as strong if not stronger in a Pledge case, and thus a Pledge requirement in a primary or secondary school would not pass the coercion test.

Historically, it was understood that exposing children in schools to particular religious views might create a conflict if those views did not coincide with the views taught at home. However, as Delfattore notes, to some proponents of such teaching, "the fact that such observances would conflict with the religious practices taught in some families was not a disadvantage but a benefit, since one of their goals was to "Americanize" children from backgrounds they considered alien."[68] Thus far, however, no member of the current Court has suggested that the Establishment Clause permits the public schools to instruct children about which

---

67 *Newdow*, 542 U.S. at 36 (Thomas, J., concurring).
68 Delfattore, *supra* note 2, at 121.

religious beliefs and practices they should accept, possible training at home to the contrary notwithstanding.

Requiring recitation of the Pledge in primary or secondary schools violates the three Establishment Clause tests articulated by the Court—the *Lemon* test, the endorsement test, and the coercion test. However, before concluding that the issue therefore is resolved, another case must be considered.

The Marsh Exception?

In *Marsh v. Chambers*, the Court upheld the constitutionality of opening legislative sessions with prayer. The Court noted the unbroken history the practice for more than 200 years and reasoned that beginning a legislative session with a prayer was now a societally accepted practice. The Court reconciled its position with the Establishment Clause jurisprudence by saying, "To invoke Divine guidance on a public body entrusted with making the laws is not, in these circumstances, an 'establishment' of religion or a step toward establishment; it is simply a tolerable acknowledgment of beliefs widely held among the people of this country."[69]

Marsh has been open to a variety of interpretations. Some read it as grandfathering long-established customs. Others suggest that it provides an illustration of how repetition can secularize what might otherwise be considered religious. Still others have suggested that it provides a standard for what the Establishment Clause must be thought to allow. For example, Justice Kennedy suggests in his *Allegheny* concurrence and dissent that:

> *Marsh* stands for the proposition, not that specific practices common in 1791 are an exception to the otherwise broad sweep of the Establishment Clause, but rather that the meaning of the Clause is to be determined by reference to historical practices and understandings. Whatever test we choose to apply must permit not only legitimate practices two centuries old but also any other practices with no greater potential for an establishment of religion.[70]

Indeed, Justice Kennedy worries that unless the Court adopts this broad interpretation of *Marsh*, the Pledge of Allegiance may be in constitutional jeopardy. With respect to the endorsement test in particular, he notes that:

> by statute, the Pledge of Allegiance to the Flag describes the United States as "one Nation under God." … [I] t borders on sophistry to suggest that the "reasonable" atheist would not feel less than a "full membe[r] of the political community" every time his fellow Americans recited, as part of their expression of patriotism and love for country, a phrase he believed to be false.[71]

---

69 *Marsh*, 463 U.S. at 792.
70 *Allegheny*, 492 U.S. at 669 (Kennedy, J., concurring in part and dissenting in part).
71 *Id.* at 672–3 (Kennedy, J., concurring in part and dissenting in part).

If Justice Kennedy is correct that practices with no greater potential for establishing religion than legislative prayer do not violate the Establishment Clause, then that Clause would not seem to do much work. Indeed, as other members of the Court have pointed out, Justice Kennedy's *Marsh* gloss on the Establishment Clause would basically nullify that clause. Indeed, if historical practice were the only limitation set by the Establishment Clause, then the state not only could favor religion over non-religion but could also favor one religion over another.

Justice Scalia suggests that "with respect to public acknowledgment of religious belief, it is entirely clear from our Nation's historical practices that the Establishment Clause permits this disregard of polytheists and believers in unconcerned deities, just as it permits the disregard of devout atheists."[72] However, as Justice Stevens points out, "[T]he original understanding of the type of 'religion' that qualified for constitutional protection under the Establishment Clause likely did not include those followers of Judaism and Islam who are among the preferred 'monotheistic' religions Justice Scalia has embraced."[73] Lest it be thought that the Constitution therefore privileges Christianity, the *McCreary County* Court explained that "history shows that the religion of concern to the Framers was not that of the monotheistic faiths generally, but Christianity in particular, a fact that no Member of this Court takes as a premise for construing the Religion Clauses."[74]

By the same token, we presumably would not use historical practice to determine what is permissibly included in the school curriculum, given what Delfattore has described as the former "all-but-universal assumption that the public schools should promote Christianity over any other belief system."[75] Some of our historical practices simply cannot determine our current Establishment Clause protections if those protections are to do any work at all.

Marsh makes Establishment Clause jurisprudence even more difficult to understand, because it does not offer a principle upon which members of the Court can agree. Perhaps it can be limited to grandfathering those religious practices countenanced by the Framers on the theory that the Framers would not have engaged in practices that they knew violated the very Establishment Clause principle that they themselves had written into the Constitution. Perhaps it does not even stand for that. In any event, it adds a wild card to Establishment Clause jurisprudence. Precisely because the *Marsh* Court did not analyze the action before it in terms of the existing Establishment Clause tests and did not offer a new test but nonetheless upheld a practice that appeared to fail the existing tests, *Marsh* may be viewed by some as an exception to Establishment Clause jurisprudence and by others as setting a new and very forgiving standard by which to determine whether the Establishment Clause has been violated.

---

72 *McCreary County*, 545 U.S. at 893 (Scalia, J., dissenting).
73 *Van Orden v. Perry*, 545 U.S. 677, 728–9 (2005) (Stevens, J., dissenting).
74 *McCreary County,* 545 U.S. at 880.
75 Delfattore, *supra* note 2, at 15.

Perhaps it would be better to say, following Ravtich, that *Marsh* was simply wrongly decided, because it both privileged religion over non-religion and, in practice, privileged one religion over others.[76] However, the Court's overruling *Marsh* is quite unlikely, which means that some other way will have to be devised to account for it within Establishment Clause jurisprudence.

Conclusion

Arguably, a policy requiring recitation of the Pledge of Allegiance in primary and secondary schools is unconstitutional according to each of the Establishment Clause tests articulated by the Court. However, as the *Lynch* Court noted, "the Court consistently has declined to take a rigid, absolutist view of the Establishment Clause," explaining that the Court has "refused 'to construe the Religion Clauses with a literalness that would undermine the ultimate constitutional objective as illuminated by history.'"[77] Ironically, the *Lynch* Court justified its approach by claiming that an absolutist approach is unworkable in our modern, complex, pluralistic society. Yet, the diversity of religious viewpoints in America would seem to support deleting "under God" from the Pledge so as not to alienate those with minority viewpoints on religious matters.

It is one thing to point out that there is no one test that will explain the relevant jurisprudence. It is quite another when the Court fails to follow all of the tests that it has thus far articulated. Yet, ever since *Everson*, the Court's Establishment Clause jurisprudence has been far from consistent.

The *Everson* Court suggested, "The First Amendment has erected a wall between church and state. That wall must be kept high and impregnable. We could not approve the slightest breach."[78] Yet, the Court itself has admitted that it has not consistently followed *Everson*. Indeed, the *Lynch* Court noted:

> The metaphor [of a wall between church and state] has served as a reminder that the Establishment Clause forbids an established church or anything approaching it. But the metaphor itself is not a wholly accurate description of the practical aspects of the relationship that in fact exists between church and state.[79]

Thus, the *Lynch* Court suggests that *Everson* is not to be taken literally but instead is merely a reminder about what the Establishment Clause precludes. Yet, at other times, the Court has taken *Everson* quite seriously. Further, members of the Court have occasionally wished that the *Everson* doctrine would be reinstated. For

---

76 *See* Frank Ravitch, *Masters of Illusion: The Supreme Court and the Religion Clauses* 181 (2007).

77 *Lynch*, 465 U.S. at 678.

78 *Everson*, 330 U.S. at 18.

79 *Lynch*, 465 U.S. at 673.

example, Justice Stevens worried that *Lemon* was too malleable and longed for the days of *Everson*—"Rather than continuing with the sisyphean task of trying to patch together the 'blurred, indistinct, and variable barrier' described in *Lemon v. Kurtzman*, I would resurrect the 'high and impregnable' wall between church and state constructed by the Framers of the First Amendment."[80]

One difficulty in predicting whether a particular policy will pass muster under the Establishment Clause is that the Court has articulated various tests and has never been clear about which to apply in particular situations. Yet another difficulty is that the Court has signaled that the Religion Clause Jurisprudence itself has to be understood in a particular way, so that argumentation that in other areas of law might be persuasive or dispositive would nonetheless not win the day in this area of law.

What will the Court do if a case comes before it in which the constitutionality of a primary school policy requiring daily recitation of the Pledge of Allegiance is at issue? One possibility would be for the Court to require that the Pledge be returned to its pre-1954 version. Justice O'Connor noted that "the presence of those words [under God] is not absolutely essential to the Pledge, as demonstrated by the fact that it existed without them for over 50 years."[81] Her point was that even those objecting to the inclusion of those words "still can consider themselves meaningful participants in the exercise if they join in reciting the remainder of the Pledge."[82] Yet, *Doe* and *Lee* counsel that the state is not permitted to endorse religious beliefs merely because it is willing to permit those who disagree to remain respectfully silent. Thus, Justice O'Connor's point that the Pledge existed without "under God" for 50 years at least suggests that the Pledge could serve useful purposes even without "under God" included, and that a reinstatement of the pre-1954 version might merit serious consideration.

It might be argued that the pre-1954 Pledge puts students who believe that the nation is under God at a disadvantage. However, in his *Lee* concurrence, Justice Souter suggests:

> Religious students cannot complain that omitting prayers from their graduation ceremony would, in any realistic sense, "burden" their spiritual callings ... Because they ... have no need for the machinery of the State to affirm their beliefs, the government's sponsorship of prayer at the graduation ceremony is most reasonably understood as an official endorsement of religion and, in this instance, of theistic religion.[83]

---

80 *Committee for Public Education and Religious Liberty v. Regan*, 444 U.S. 646, 671 (1980) (Stevens, J., dissenting).

81 *Newdow*, 542 U.S. at 43 (O'Connor, J., concurring).

82 *Id.* (O'Connor, J., concurring).

83 *Lee*, 505 U.S. at 629–30 (Souter, J., concurring).

By the same token, Justice Souter might suggest that students do not need the state to affirm their belief that the country is subordinate to God. Arguably, where the Pledge would neither affirm nor deny God's existence, the state would simply be remaining neutral on that question.

To some extent, the question is whether by omitting "under God" the state is offering a neutral position or, instead, one which is hostile to religion, where no one is being forced to say the Pledge in any event. However, were the Pledge modified to say, "I pledge allegiance to the flag of the United States of America and to the Republic for which it stands, one Nation, indivisible, with liberty and justice for all," it still would not be saying "I pledge allegiance to the flag of the United States of America and to the Republic for which it stands, one Nation, under no God, indivisible, with liberty and justice for all." To hold that the deletion of "under God" is the equivalent of saying "under no God" would mean that the Pledge could not help but either promote or undermine religion, which might mean that the Establishment Clause would bar its being said in public schools whether or not it included a reference to God.

One possibility would be for the Court to offer a hybrid Establishment Clause Test, for example, by combining the endorsement and coercion tests. But a much more likely possibility is that the Court will adopt a standard that is much more lax with respect to the kinds of religious messages that might be endorsed by the state without offending constitutional guarantees. Yet another possibility is that the Court will continue to eschew an approach using one or even a few principles, instead opting for a case-by-case approach that requires "the exercise of legal judgment."[84]

It is very difficult to predict whether the Court would uphold the constitutionality of a primary school Pledge requirement, much less whether it would modify the existing jurisprudence. However, one can predict with some confidence that should the Court actually reach the merits, one or more Justices will invoke the *Lemon* test (if only because the purpose behind amending the Pledge was so clearly religious), one or more will invoke the endorsement test, and justices will disagree among themselves as to whether it is coercive to recite the Pledge even when students can opt of participating. Further, one or more justices will play the *Marsh* wild card, wondering how legislative prayer can be upheld if something as innocuous as including "under God" in the Pledge could somehow be viewed as unconstitutional even in the primary school setting. The Court will be divided, and either the majority or the dissent will accuse one or more justices of being hostile to religion. Those charges will be denied, perhaps accompanied by the suggestion that those making such an accusation assume either that a respect for pluralism is somehow hostility to religion or that a refusal to support religion must be equated with hostility to religion. The Court will be divided with respect to the correct test to use and whether the relevant test establishes the constitutionality or unconstitutionality of the policy at issue. Perhaps the only matters about which

---

84 See *Van Orden*, 545 U.S. at 700 (Breyer, J., concurring).

one can be very confident are that the separate opinions will manifest hostility to one or more views expressed in the opinion and that the time when the Court can present a coherent test for determining whether the Establishment Clause has been violated will have to wait for another day.

Chapter 6

The Ten Commandments in the Schools

Recently, the United States Supreme Court decided two cases respecting the constitutionality of Ten Commandments displays, upholding the constitutionality of one but striking down the other as a violation of Establishment Clause guarantees. That the Court might reach a compromise about such a contentious matter should not be surprising. What is surprising, however, is that the Court could not decide the appropriate test to apply in this kind of case, making a jurisprudence that was already confusing even more convoluted and increasing the likelihood that there will be inconsistency in the lower courts regarding similar cases implicating Establishment Clause guarantees. Indeed, some of the reasoning offered by the Court suggests a reworking of the jurisprudence with respect to the conditions under which posting the Ten Commandments in the schools would not violate the Establishment Clause.

There are three main cases involving Ten Commandments displays, one decided in 1980 and the other two decided in 2005. Those cases can only be understood in light of the twists and turns that the Court's jurisprudence has taken. Regrettably, some of the content and tone in recent opinions can only weaken respect for the diversity of religious belief in this country and promote divisiveness along religious lines, results which are neither in accord with the intentions of the Framers nor with good public policy.

The Ten Commandments Cases

The Court has issued three decisions on the merits during the past few decades regarding displays of the Ten Commandments, two of which were handed down in 2005. Each of those decisions is discussed below. Ironically, by differentiating the factual scenarios in each case, the Court might have used one principled method of decision-making to strike down the displays in *Stone* and *McCreary County* and uphold the display in *Van Orden*. The results in the cases would then have mirrored the results that were in fact reached and, in addition, there would have been a clear method by which to decide Ten Commandments cases in particular or, perhaps, Establishment Clause cases more generally. Regrettably, the recent decisions give the states and lower courts contradictory signals regarding which test to apply and how to apply it, increasing the likelihood that relevantly similar cases will be decided dissimilarly. The Court has wasted an excellent opportunity to clarify Establishment Clause jurisprudence, almost guaranteeing confusion in this area of law for years to come.

Stone v. Graham

Before 2005, the major Ten Commandments case decided by the Supreme Court was *Stone v. Graham*,[1] in which a Kentucky law requiring the posting of a copy of the Ten Commandments on the walls of all pubic classrooms was at issue. The copies were to be purchased with private contributions, but that did not immunize the postings from constitutional challenge, because state-run schools were being used to convey the message at issue. After noting the sacred role played by the Ten Commandments within Judaism and Christianity and finding that the primary purpose for posting the Ten Commandments in schools was religious, the Court held that the statute was unconstitutional.

In addition to mentioning the Ten Commandments' sacred role, the *Stone* Court analyzed the contents of the posted Commandments, themselves. The Commandments did not only address secular concerns such as honoring one's parents, refraining from stealing, and refraining from committing adultery or murder, but also addressed religious matters. By focusing on the contents, the Court implicitly suggested that a partial posting of the Ten Commandments, for example, the latter five which concern more secular matters, might not violate constitutional guarantees, whereas a display that includes or perhaps emphasizes the first five Commandments would be more likely to offend the Constitution because they include matters of a more religious nature such as observing the Sabbath and avoiding the worship of idols.

The *Stone* Court made clear that the Ten Commandments could be "integrated" into a public school curriculum where the document is treated as a historical text in a broader context of secular study. However, the posting at issue did not serve that kind of educational function. Instead, this posting might "induce the schoolchildren to read, meditate upon, perhaps to venerate and obey, the Commandments ... [which] is not a permissible state objective under the Establishment Clause."[2]

After admitting in his dissent that the Ten Commandments are sacred within some religious traditions, then-Justice Rehnquist noted that the Commandments have had a significant impact on the development of legal codes in the Western world. Because the Kentucky Legislature had required that each display of the Commandments include a notation about their secular application, Justice Rehnquist argued that Kentucky had not violated the Constitution by placing a document with such secular importance before its students. An issue that continues to complicate and confuse constitutional analyses of state displays of the Ten Commandments is whether and under what conditions an articulated secular purpose can make such a display pass constitutional muster.

In 2005, the Court was handed a golden opportunity to clear up Establishment Clause jurisprudence more generally or, at least, clarify the conditions under which the state can display the Ten Commandments in particular. In that year, the

---

1   449 U.S. 39 (1980).
2   *Id.* at 42.

Court issued two Ten Commandments decisions, *McCreary County v. ACLU*[3] and *Van Orden v. Perry*.[4] While not creating a clear change in Establishment Clause jurisprudence, the decisions were striking in some of the ways in which they were at odds, for example, in whether the *Lemon* test should be used in this kind of case. Instead of clarifying an area which is notoriously obscure and confusing, the Court made matters worse, making what seemed to be a hopelessly confusing area even murkier.

McCreary County v. ACLU

At issue in *McCreary County* was a posting of the Ten Commandments on the walls of two counties' courthouses. In both counties, the following textual version of the Ten Commandments was posted:

> Thou shalt have no other gods before me. Thou shalt not make unto thee any graven images. Thou shalt not take the name of the Lord thy God in vain. Remember the sabbath day, to keep it holy. Honor thy father and thy mother. Thou shalt not kill. Thou shalt not commit adultery. Thou shalt not steal. Thou shalt not bear false witness. Thou shalt not covet. Exodus 20:3–17[5]

The Ten Commandments were accompanied by other displays including copies of the Magna Carta, the Declaration of Independence, the Bill of Rights, the Mayflower Compact, and the Preamble to the Kentucky Constitution. The Court did not analyze the effect of including the Ten Commandments with all of these other exhibits, for example, by discussing whether the inclusion of these additional documents made the display as a whole secular, but focused instead on the purpose behind the inclusion of the Ten Commandments, striking down the display as a violation of the purpose prong of *Lemon*.

The *McCreary County* Court explained that the touchstone of Establishment Clause jurisprudence is state neutrality among religions and between religion and non-religion, noting that when the "government acts with the ostensible and predominant purpose of advancing religion, it violates that central Establishment Clause value of official religious neutrality, there being no neutrality when the government's ostensible object is to take sides."[6] The Court considered the history behind the display when attempting to discern the state's purpose, noting that at first the Ten Commandments had been displayed alone, unaccompanied by other documents. It was only after a suit had been filed challenging the displays that the exhibits were modified. Further, the Court made clear that it should look at the evolution of the display when seeking to determine whether the motivation behind

---

3   545 U.S. 844 (2005).
4   545 U.S. 677 (2005).
5   *McCreary County*, 545 U.S. at 851–2.
6   *Id*. at 860.

the final display was constitutionally permissible. That is not to say that once a state has manifested a religious motivation it will forever have that motivation imputed to it for purposes of figuring out whether a particular display violates the Establishment Clause. Instead, the reviewing court will have to discern when there had been a genuine, constitutionally relevant change in motivation.

Analysis of legislative purpose is often a difficult task. In many cases, there will be no dispositive statements establishing the state's purpose, although a statute's wording itself may provide a basis for ascertaining the intent, especially in light of comments made by those promoting the measure. Sometimes, it will be too difficult to establish improper motivation even when such a motivation was indeed behind the action at issue. The *McCreary County* Court admits that under the jurisprudence an Establishment Clause challenge may fail if the existing religious purpose has been well-disguised and the "objective" observer cannot discern it, although the Court offers the consolation that non-adherents will not feel like outsiders if the religious purpose is extremely well-hidden. Thus, the *McCreary County* Court was willing to countenance the following anomaly. There might be two courthouses with identical displays including the Ten Commandments among other works. The display in one town would be declared unconstitutional, because the history behind the display made clear that the town was trying to promote religion. However, the other display in the other town might be upheld, because the history behind that display was quite different and it was not at all clear that the latter town was trying to promote religion in the same way that the former town had attempted.

For some observers, such a result would not be anomalous. For those who knew the history behind the former town's display and who understood that the Constitution precluded the town from promoting religion, the Court's decision would make sense. The former town could be shown to have violated the purpose prong while the latter town could not be shown to have done so.

In his *McCreary County* dissent, Justice Scalia does not worry about instances in which state action was secretly motivated by a desire to promote religion but, instead, about instances in which the reasonably informed observer would wrongly believe that a particular action was motivated by religion. He writes:

> Because in the Court's view the true danger to be guarded against is that the objective observer would feel like an "outside[r]" or "not [a] full membe[r] of the political community," its inquiry focuses not on the actual purpose of government action, but the "purpose apparent from government action." Under this approach, even if a government could show that its actual purpose was not to advance religion, it would presumably violate the Constitution as long as the Court's objective observer would think otherwise.[7]

---

7   *Id.* at 900–901 (Scalia, J., dissenting).

Thus, Justice Scalia suggests, the constitutionality of a government action with wholly secular effects might depend on whether some "imaginary" observer misperceived that the action had been intended to promote religion.

Justice Scalia's points are not persuasive. First, he fails to explain why the informed observer would misunderstand the state's purposes, notwithstanding the state's ability to establish its secular purposes. Second, Justice Scalia fails to show how the allegedly new standard changes anything, since it has always been true that the trier-of-fact might misperceive the "true" purposes of the state. The traditional *Lemon* test requires that the state meet each prong. If, for example, a state action was found by a court to have been motivated by a desire to promote religion, then it would not matter whether that in fact was the state's purpose. Given the difficulty in discerning motivation and the likelihood that individuals might wish to mask illicit motivation, it would hardly be surprising to find that there would be mistakes about a state actor's true motivation—sometimes, it would be inferred that the state did not have a motivation to promote or undermine religion when in fact the state did have such a motivation and at other times the state would be inferred to have such a motivation when in fact the state did not.

The *McCreary County* Court began its analysis by citing *Stone*, which suggests that a display of the Ten Commandments should presumptively be viewed as intended to promote religion. The *McCreary County* Court noted that the display at issue before it (prior to the First Amendment challenge) was relevantly similar to the *Stone* display in two important ways: (1) each set out the text of the Ten Commandments rather than a symbolic representation of that text; and (2) each stood alone and was not part of a secular display. The Court explained that *Stone* had emphasized the importance of integrating the Commandments into a secular display. Otherwise, the message would clearly be religious by declaring the existence of one God or by specifying religious obligations such as observing the Sabbath or not worshipping idols. Indeed, even the secular prohibitions against stealing and murder might be thought to derive their force from having been prohibited by God.

The *McCreary County* Court suggested that the way the amendments themselves were depicted was important—a display of the text itself suggests a religious message, whereas a symbolic representation such as 10 Roman numerals might be seen as representing a general notion of law. The Court was not denying the influence of the Ten Commandments on secular law, but was merely noting that the original text is an unmistakably religious statement, and that the purpose behind the state's publicly displaying such a religious statement without any other accompanying displays is unmistakable.

Two very different points might be made about the Court's suggestion that Roman numerals rather than actual text be used. When symbols rather than particular text are used, there is no commitment to one version of the Ten Commandments over another, whereas when particular text is used, a choice must be made among the differing versions. Thus, by using Roman numerals, no choice would have to be made between, for example, "Do Not Murder" and "Do Not Kill." Further, as

Delafattore points out, "Thou Shalt Not Steal" is the Seventh Commandment in the Catholic version and the Eighth Commandment in the Protestant version of the Ten Commandments.[8] Were Roman numerals used, one would not have to choose between the versions.

The *Stone* Court noted that certain amendments are more readily viewed as secular than others. Thus, a representation of amendments 6 through 10, as is represented in the Supreme Court frieze containing the amendments, is farther removed from the Commandments concerning obligations to the Deity than are the first few amendments. Indeed, the *McCreary County* Court mentions the Court's own courtroom frieze which includes Moses holding tablets exhibiting the secularly phrased Commandments, and, further, which puts Moses with 17 other lawgivers, most of whom are secular figures. There was no risk that this image of Moses would suggest that the Government was somehow violating its obligation to remain neutral. By mentioning all of these points, the Court offered several ways to differentiate the image in its frieze from the depiction at issue in *McCreary County*.

The *McCreary County* Court reiterated that the key to Establishment Clause jurisprudence is state neutrality among religions and between religion and non-religion, although not all members of the Court agree that this is the correct understanding of Establishment Clause jurisprudence. In his *McCreary County* dissent, Justice Scalia writes, "Nothing stands behind the Court's assertion that governmental affirmation of the society's belief in God is unconstitutional except the Court's own say-so, citing as support only the unsubstantiated say-so of earlier Courts going back no farther than the mid twentieth century."[9] However, Justice Scalia is not only suggesting that the state may prefer religion over non-religion; he is also suggesting that the state can prefer some religions over others. He writes:

> If religion in the public forum had to be entirely nondenominational, there could be no religion in the public forum at all. One cannot say the word "God," or "the Almighty," one cannot offer public supplication or thanksgiving, without contradicting the beliefs of some people that there are many gods, or that God or the gods pay no attention to human affairs. With respect to public acknowledgment of religious belief, it is entirely clear from our Nation's historical practices that the Establishment Clause permits this disregard of polytheists and believers in unconcerned deities, just as it permits the disregard of devout atheists.[10]

The *McCreary County* Court responded to Justice Scalia's challenge in two ways. First, the Court noted that there is a historical basis for its position, since there is "evidence supporting the proposition that the Framers intended the

---

8   *See* Joan Delfattore, *The Fourth R: Conflicts over Religion in America's Public Schools* 47 (2004).

9   *McCreary County*, 545 U.S. at 889 (Scalia, J., dissenting).

10   *Id.* at 892 (Scalia, J., dissenting).

Establishment Clause to require governmental neutrality in matters of religion, including neutrality in statements acknowledging religion."[11] The Court did not claim that the evidence supporting its position was conclusive, but merely that the "fair inference is that there was no common understanding about the limits of the establishment prohibition."[12]

Second, the Court noted that if historical practice is to be the guide, then Justice Scalia is misleading when suggesting that the Constitution permits the state to privilege monotheism, since historical practice suggests that the state is permitted to privilege Christianity over the other religions. "[H]istory shows that the religion of concern to the Framers was not that of the monotheistic faiths generally, but Christianity in particular, a fact that no member of this Court takes as a premise for construing the Religion Clauses."[13] Indeed, the Court quotes Justice Story's suggestion that "the purpose of the Clause was 'not to countenance, much less to advance, Mahometanism, or Judaism, or infidelity, by prostrating Christianity; but to exclude all rivalry among Christian sects,'"[14] When mentioning Justice Story's interpretation, the Court was not trying to lend credence to that view, but to suggest that Justice Scalia has not accurately represented the views of the Framers and, further, that there is good reason not to let the views of the Framers determine the meaning of the Establishment Clause in contemporary society.

Needless to say, there is no agreement among the Justices with respect to what the Framers intended. For example, Justice O'Connor discusses the Founders' plan to protect religious liberty to the greatest extent possible. She, too, suggests that the Establishment Clause requires state neutrality among religions and between religion and non-religion, although, as Justice Scalia points out, the Court has certainly upheld practices that had the effect of benefiting religion.

Justice O'Connor worries about the potential divisiveness that might be caused by government's taking a particular side in religious disputes.

> When the government associates one set of religious beliefs with the state and identifies non-adherents as outsiders, it encroaches upon the individual's decision about whether and how to worship. In the marketplace of ideas, the government has vast resources and special status. Government religious expression therefore risks crowding out private observance and distorting the natural interplay between competing beliefs. Allowing government to be a potential mouthpiece for competing religious ideas risks the sort of division that might easily spill over into suppression of rival beliefs. Tying secular and religious authority together poses risks to both.[15]

---

11 *Id.* at 878.
12 *Id.* at 879.
13 *Id.* at 880.
14 *Id.*
15 *Id.* at 883 (O'Connor, J., concurring).

Were *McCreary County* the only post-*Stone* Supreme Court decision dealing with the Ten Commandments, there still would be many questions left unanswered. For example, the Court addresses the constitutionality of posting the Ten Commandments alone, because the decision to include other elements in the display was in response to the legal challenge to the Ten Commandments being posted without any other accompanying displays. The evolution of the display occurred over a relatively short period, so it is unclear whether *McCreary County* analysis would have any implications for a display that evolved over a longer period or, perhaps, whose evolution was not in response to a court challenge. Further, because *McCreary County's* focus was on the *Lemon* purpose prong, there is no helpful discussion regarding the effects of displaying the Ten Commandments with other nonreligious symbols. It would be helpful to know when combining religious and nonreligious displays dilutes the religious message sufficiently to avoid Establishment Clause difficulties and when, instead, such a combination aggravates such difficulties because church and state are viewed as intertwined.

Yet, the lessons of *McCreary County* are utterly unfathomable in light of *Van Orden*, leaving lower courts without direction or, perhaps, with contradictory directions so that they can do whatever they have an inclination to do. Thus, the claim here is not, for example, that it would have been impossible for the Court to have offered an internally consistent position in which it struck down the display at issue in *McCreary County* and upheld the display at issue in *Van Orden*. On the contrary, the Court could have done so but did not, which suggests that the Establishment Clause jurisprudence offered over the next several years may well continue to be the antithesis of clarity and consistency.

Van Orden v. Perry

In *Van Orden v. Perry*, the Court addressed whether the Ten Commandments could be displayed on the Texas State Capitol grounds without violating Establishment Clause guarantees. The Court upheld the display, noting that the 22 acres surrounding the Texas State Capitol contained 17 monuments and 21 historical markers commemorating the "people, ideals, and events that compose Texan identity."[16] The Court tried to account for the existing jurisprudence by suggesting that the cases are "Januslike,"[17] one face looking toward the role played by religion in the Nation's history and the other looking toward the principle that "governmental intervention in religious matters can itself endanger religious freedom."[18] The *Van Orden* plurality explained:

> One face looks to the past in acknowledgment of our Nation's heritage, while the other looks to the present in demanding a separation between church and state.

---

16 *Van Orden*, 545 U.S. at 681.
17 *Id*. at 683.
18 *Id*.

> Reconciling these two faces requires that we neither abdicate our responsibility
> to maintain a division between church and state nor evince a hostility to religion
> by disabling the government from in some ways recognizing our religious
> heritage.[19]

While one might quibble with this characterization unless, for example, religious freedom is meant to include the freedom to believe in many gods or in no god, this understanding nonetheless might be consistent with any of the traditional tests used to determine whether the Establishment Clause has been violated. Yet, the *Van Orden* plurality is not simply finessing the difficulty posed by the Court having articulated several Establishment Clause tests without ever having specified which was appropriate in which circumstances. On the contrary, the plurality wrote, "Whatever may be the fate of the *Lemon* test in the larger scheme of Establishment Clause jurisprudence, we think it not useful in dealing with the sort of passive monument that Texas has erected on its Capitol grounds."[20]

The difficulty posed by the plurality's statement is not in limiting the conditions under which *Lemon* will be used, for example, saying that it is the test in cases involving state aid but not in cases in which the posting of a display with a religious message is at issue. Rather, the difficulty is that *Van Orden* suggests that in a case involving a passive display of the Ten Commandments *Lemon* should not be used, while *McCreary County* suggests that in a case involving the passive display of the Ten Commandments *Lemon* should be used.

It is at best regrettable that the *Van Orden* plurality describes *Marsh v. Chambers*—in which the Court held that a state can open its daily session with a prayer by a state-paid chaplain—as merely implicating the recognition of the role that belief in God has played in this nation's heritage. If the paradigmatically religious exercise—prayer—is merely a recognition that the belief in God has played an important role in the nation's development or even that many people believe in God, then it is difficult to imagine what the Establishment Clause prohibits.

While recognizing that the Ten Commandments are religious, the *Van Orden* plurality noted that they also have an historical meaning. Because the Ten Commandments have both meanings, there are contexts in which they might be permissibly displayed. For example, as the *Stone* Court noted, the Ten Commandments can be integrated into a school curriculum. Yet, given that there are contexts in which the Ten Commandments may not be displayed and other contexts in which they may be displayed, one might have expected the *Van Orden* plurality to have offered a careful analysis explaining why this display was permissible. Regrettably, no such analysis was offered.

The *Van Orden* Court differentiated what was before it from what had been at issue in *Stone*, suggesting that the placement at issue before it was "far more

---

19 *Id.*
20 *Id.* at 685.

passive" than was the *Stone* display.[21] Yet, it is not as if the Ten Commandments "did" anything in *Stone* other than remain passively on the wall. Nor is it clear that the Ten Commandments in *Van Orden* were any more passive than the Ten Commandments in *McCreary County*.

The *Van Orden* plurality might not have been trying to distinguish what was at issue in *McCreary County* from what was at issue in *Van Orden*, because the *Van Orden* plurality disagreed with the holding in *McCreary County*. Of course, it is also true that then-Justice Rehnquist dissented in *Stone*, so he might not have been expected to try to distinguish *Stone* either.

The discussion of passive displays in *Van Orden* raised more questions than it answered. However, it may well not have been designed to explicate the notion of what counts as passive for Establishment Clause purposes but instead merely to secure Justice Kennedy's vote.

In *County of Allegheny v. ACLU*, Justice Kennedy suggested in his dissent that "where the government's act of recognition or accommodation is passive and symbolic ... any intangible benefit to religion is unlikely to present a realistic risk of establishment. Absent coercion, the risk of infringement of religious liberty by passive or symbolic accommodation is minimal."[22] Of course, even Justice Kennedy believes that some passive displays might violate constitutional guarantees, for example, the permanent placement of a large Latin cross on a city hall roof, although he does not make clear why such a display would be unconstitutional. While he suggests that such a display would place the government behind an obvious attempt to proselytize for a particular religion, one does not know which features would make such a display unconstitutional. Would it matter, for example, if a large Latin cross and a Star of David were permanently erected on the roof of city hall, since it would then not be the case that the state was trying to proselytize on behalf of a particular religion? Would it matter if year after year the city erected a large Latin cross on the city hall roof for six months of the year? Would it matter if the cross were in a park rather than on top of a city hall?

While Justices Scalia and Thomas signed onto Chief Justice Rehnquist's plurality opinion in *Van Orden*, their concurrences made clear that they were not exactly endorsing Rehnquist's analysis. Justice Scalia writes, "I join the opinion of The Chief Justice because I think it accurately reflects our current Establishment Clause jurisprudence—or at least the Establishment Clause jurisprudence we currently apply some of the time."[23] Of course, given the variation in the Court's Establishment Clause jurisprudence, it is not a ringing endorsement to say that a decision captures how the Establishment Clause is sometimes applied. In any event, Justice Scalia's view is that the Establishment Clause is rather forgiving. He suggests that "there is nothing unconstitutional in a State's favoring religion generally, honoring God through public prayer and acknowledgment, or, in a

21 *Id.* at 691.

22 *Allegheny*, 492 U.S. at 662 (Kennedy, J., dissenting).

23 *Van Orden*, 545 U.S. at 692 (Scalia, J., concurring).

non-proselytizing manner, venerating the Ten Commandments."[24] While he does not specify what would count as venerating the Ten Commandments in a non-proselytizing manner, one infers that Ten Commandments that do not represent the views of one sect in particular but, instead, represent an amalgam of beliefs would not count as proselytizing. Ironically, this is exactly the kind of position rejected in *Lynch* in which the Court denied that there could be a kind of civil religious language that could somehow bypass Establishment Clause guarantees.

At this point, it is helpful to distinguish between a nonsectarian version of the Ten Commandments, for example, one which incorporates Jewish, Catholic and Protestant views, and a secularized version of the Ten Commandments. While the Ten Commandments in *Van Orden* might be viewed as nonsectarian, they certainly should not be viewed as secular, since they did concern the nature of God and human relations with God. The Establishment Clause requires more than mere neutrality among several religious faiths—nonsectarian should not be thought the equivalent of secular.

Justice Thomas joined the opinion because Chief Justice Rehnquist recognized the role of religion in this Nation's history and the permissibility of government displays that acknowledge that history. However, Justice Thomas's view of the Establishment Clause is even more forgiving than that of Justice Scalia in that Justice Thomas does not believe that the Establishment Clause restrains state (as opposed to federal) action. Further, Justice Thomas believes that the only coercion prohibited by the Establishment Clause is actual legal coercion. Justice Thomas notes:

> In no sense does Texas compel petitioner Van Orden to do anything. The only injury to him is that he takes offense at seeing the monument as he passes it on his way to the Texas Supreme Court Library. He need not stop to read it or even to look at it, let alone to express support for it or adopt the Commandments as guides for his life. The mere presence of the monument along his path involves no coercion and thus does not violate the Establishment Clause.[25]

Thus, on Justice Thomas's view, even Justice Kennedy's example of the Latin Cross permanently erected on city hall would not violate Establishment Clause guarantees.

Justice Stephen Breyer's *Van Orden* concurrence in the judgment is perhaps the most difficult to read insofar as one wishes prospective guidance. He mentions the basic purposes of the Religion Clauses, which he suggests include assuring the greatest possible religious liberty and tolerance for all,[26] avoiding divisiveness that

---

24 *Id.* at 692 (Scalia, J., concurring).
25 *Id.* at 694 (Thomas, J., concurring).
26 *Id.* at 698 (Breyer, J., concurring in the judgment).

is based upon religion,[27] and maintaining separation of church and state.[28] While noting that the government must avoid excessively interfering with or promoting religion, he also suggests that "the Establishment Clause does not compel the government to purge from the public sphere all that in any way partakes of the religious."[29] Yet, no one suggests that everything remotely religious must be kept out of the public sphere, and it is unclear why a discussion of matters that partake of the religious only slightly is relevant in a discussion of something paradigmatically religious like the Ten Commandments, especially because the real question before the Court is when rather than if something paradigmatically religious such as the Ten Commandments can be in the public sphere.

Justice Breyer suggests that in borderline cases there is no substitute for the exercise of "legal judgment."[30] The case before the Court was allegedly borderline because, on the one hand, the text of the Ten Commandments is undeniably religious, whereas, on the other hand, such a display can convey a secular message about morality. Justice Breyer noted that in the instant case the tablets were part of a display communicating both a religious and a secular message, and that the group that had donated the monument had sought to highlight the role of the Ten Commandments in shaping public morality in an effort to combat juvenile delinquency. As evidence of their *nonreligious* motivation, he noted the group had consulted with members of several faiths to find a nonsectarian text.

Justice Breyer seems to conflate a nonsectarian motivation with a nonreligious one. It may be that the group wanted to reach (or at least not offend) a broad base of religious groups, but that hardly speaks to whether the group's motivation was religious rather than nonreligious. Further, even were the Ten Commandments viewed as broadly nonsectarian (rather than as favoring some religions over others), the state's displaying the Commandments might well violate an obligation to remain neutral between religion and non-religion.

As further evidence of the secular nature of the message, Justice Breyer noted that 40 years had gone by without a legal challenge to the display. Indeed, he found that silence extremely important, apparently believing that "[t]hose 40 years suggest that the public visiting the capitol grounds has considered the religious aspect of the tablets' message as part of what is a broader moral and historical message reflective of a cultural heritage."[31] Yet, there might be a variety of reasons that such a display would not be challenged. As Justice Souter notes, "Suing a State over religion puts nothing in a plaintiff's pocket and can take a great deal out, and even with volunteer litigators to supply time and energy, the risk of social ostracism can be powerfully deterrent."[32] Thus, it is hardly safe to infer that no

---

27 *Id.* (Breyer, J., concurring in the judgment).

28 *Id.* (Breyer, J., concurring in the judgment).

29 *Id.* (Breyer, J., concurring in the judgment).

30 *Id.* at 742 (Breyer, J., concurring in the judgment).

31 *Id.* at 702 (Breyer, J., concurring in the judgment).

32 *Id.* at 747 (Souter, J., dissenting).

one was religiously offended by the Ten Commandments merely because no one was willing to spend dollars, time, energy, and social standing to challenge them in court.

Numerous concerns might have motivated Justice Breyer's concurrence. For example, he noted that the Ten Commandments are displayed in many of the nation's courthouses, including the United States Supreme Court, and perhaps feared that any other decision would result in challenges to those displays as well as to a number of displays in other public buildings, thereby creating the kind of divisiveness based on religion that the Establishment Clause is designed to prevent. Viteritti notes, "One can imagine miles of scaffolding raised throughout the land to remove the offensive images, ringed by political protesters, if the Court had decided *Van Orden* differently."[33] However, it may well be that Justice Breyer's concurrence in the judgment will not reduce the amount of litigation, divisiveness, and protest, but will simply result in a modification of the kinds of cases that will come before the courts. Public entities may well feel emboldened by *Van Orden* to erect more religious displays if only to test the limits of the relevant jurisprudence, which may produce the very evils Justice Breyer seeks to prevent.

Whether or not there is an increase in the number and type of religious displays erected by public entities, Justice Breyer's suggested mode of analysis is itself likely to bring about an increase in litigation. There are a great many factors to be taken into account when one exercises "legal judgment," and a difference in any one of them might be reason to bring a challenge to a particular display. Suppose, for example, that a display of the Ten Commandments was not surrounded by other secular displays. Would that be enough to make it unconstitutional? Suppose that a new display rather than a longstanding one was at issue, although this time the display did not involve the Ten Commandments but, instead, the motto "With God All Things Are Possible." Would that pass constitutional muster?

In his dissent, Justice Stevens argued that the "sole function of the monument on the grounds of Texas' State Capitol is to display the full text of one version of the Ten Commandments."[34] Noting that the monument did not refer to any particular event in the state's history, he explained:

> Viewed on its face, Texas' display has no purported connection to God's role in the formation of Texas or the founding of our Nation; nor does it provide the reasonable observer with any basis to guess that it was erected to honor any individual or organization. The message transmitted by Texas' chosen display is quite plain: This State endorses the divine code of the "Judeo-Christian" God.[35]

---

33 Joseph P. Viteritti, *The Last Freedom: Religion from the Public School to the Public Square* xii (2007).

34 *Van Orden*, 545 U.S. at 707 (Stevens, J., dissenting).

35 *Id.* (Stevens, J., dissenting).

One of the factors dividing the Court is in how to explain the "religious neutrality" demanded by the First Amendment. Under one understanding of the view that "government may not exercise a preference for one religious faith over another,"[36] First Amendment guarantees are not violated as long as no particular religion is privileged. When the Fraternal Order of Eagles consulted with a committee composed of individuals of different religions to come up with a nonsectarian version of the Ten Commandments, they were not seeking to privilege one religious view, although they would nonetheless privilege some religious views over others. For example, those religions that do not have a tenet that there is one and only one God would seem to have their views undermined by the Ten Commandments display.

Consider the analysis offered by Justice Blackmun as to why the government is precluded from favoring one religion. "When the government puts its imprimatur on a particular religion, it conveys a message of exclusion to all those who do not adhere to the favored beliefs. A government cannot be premised on the belief that all persons are created equal when it asserts that God prefers some."[37] Yet, by the same token, if the government were to favor two or three religions, the same difficulty arises, namely, that the government cannot be premised on the belief that all are equal when it asserts that God favors the views of some religions over others.

Like the majority, Justice Stevens argued that the "wall that separates the church from the state does not prohibit the government from acknowledging the religious beliefs and practices of the American people, nor does it require governments to hide works of art or historic memorabilia from public view just because they also have religious significance."[38] Yet, the question at hand is what must be done to make sure that a paradigmatically religious display such as the Ten Commandments does not offend constitutional guarantees.

Part of the analysis involves whether the Ten Commandments are being displayed for a secular purpose. In *Van Orden*, the donors were motivated by a desire to inspire youth and curb juvenile delinquency, goals which are certainly secular in nature. However, having secular goals does not somehow immunize the method by which one seeks to achieve those goals. As Justice Stevens suggests, "But achieving that goal through biblical teachings injects a religious purpose into an otherwise secular endeavor."[39] Otherwise, missionary work would seem immune from constitutional challenge, since "missionaries expect to enlighten their converts, enhance their satisfaction with life, and improve their behavior."[40]

In *Schempp*, Justice Brennan wrote that the Framers meant to foreclose "those involvements of religious with secular institutions which ... use essentially

---

36 *Id.* at 709 (Stevens, J., dissenting).

37 *Lee*, 505 U.S. at 606–7 (Blackmun, J., concurring).

38 *Van Orden*, 545 U.S. at 711 (Stevens, J., dissenting).

39 *Id.* at 714 (Stevens, J., dissenting).

40 *Id.* (Stevens, J., dissenting).

religious means to serve governmental ends, where secular means would suffice."[41] Justice Stevens is making a similar suggestion in *Van Orden* when writing, "Though the State of Texas may genuinely wish to combat juvenile delinquency, and may rightly want to honor the Eagles for their efforts, it cannot effectuate these admirable purposes through an explicitly religious medium."[42]

The dissenting Justices in *Van Orden* were not arguing that the Ten Commandments can never be displayed by the state; instead, they wanted the state to take steps so that it would not be viewed as sending a religious message. Thus, Justice Souter suggests that a "governmental display of an obviously religious text cannot be squared with neutrality, except in a setting that plausibly indicates that the statement is not placed in view with a predominant purpose on the part of government either to adopt the religious message or to urge its acceptance by others."[43] For example, suppose that a state wants to call attention to the influence of the Ten Commandments on current secular law. Justice Souter writes:

> Government may, of course, constitutionally call attention to this influence, and may post displays or erect monuments recounting this aspect of our history no less than any other, so long as there is a context and that context is historical. Hence, a display of the Commandments accompanied by an exposition of how they have influenced modern law would most likely be constitutionally unobjectionable.[44]

One issue that divides courts is what steps must be taken to make a religious display such as the Ten Commandments less religious. Given that a state's purpose in displaying the Ten Commandments might have been secular rather than religious, a separate question is whether in a given instance the state's purpose was in fact to promote religion. It is not at all clear that merely including different types of displays would make clear that the purpose behind their being displayed was secular without some kind of writing which explains how the displays are related.

One example of such a writing would be the explanation described by Justice Souter, although the Court should not require particular talismanic language to secularize religious displays, both because such wording might be included to mask a secret purpose to promote religion and because other wording might nonetheless provide the requisite secularizing context. Nonetheless, the *Van Orden* plurality could have been helpful in at least pointing to examples of how to secularize rather than in simply implying that because it is possible to include a religious display for nonreligious purposes the state should therefore be assumed to have included the religious display for nonreligious purposes.

---

41 *Schempp*, 374 U.S. at 295.
42 *Van Orden*, 545 U.S. at 715 (Stevens, J., dissenting).
43 *Id.* at 737 (Souter, J., dissenting).
44 *Id.* at 740–41 (Souter, J., dissenting).

A separate issue is which version of the Ten Commandments to include. One cannot create a neutral version of the Ten Commandments in the sense that it would accord with the beliefs of all those for whom the Commandments play an important religious role, although that difficulty might be skirted by refraining from using particular text and instead using symbols to stand for the differing amendments. Of course, that modification might detract from a display if, for example, the point was to include a copy of the Ten Commandments that was thought to have influenced particular Framers. In any event, even a display of a nonspecific version of the Ten Commandments would disfavor those religions not having an analog within their belief system unless the secular purpose for including that version was made very clear.

Conclusion

Some commentators suggest that the Ten Commandments have not played a role in the development of our law, and should not be displayed for that reason. Yet, such a claim would of course depend upon the criteria used to determine which works have played a role in the law's development. For example, to argue that the Ten Commandments have played no role because the Court has never cited them as legal authority is to impose an unfair burden on those wishing to establish that the Ten Commandments have played such a role. As a general matter, when members of the Court mention or discuss the Ten Commandments, they tend to downplay their role in our law if only to avoid Establishment Clause difficulties. Thus, Justices would be more likely to discuss the state's purposes as coinciding or harmonizing with religious purposes as a way of demonstrating that the Ten Commandments did not have undue influence on the development of the law. Yet, their downplaying the influence is more a testament to their believing that the Commandments have had a great influence than that they have had no influence.

It is a matter of some dispute among members of the Court as to how foundational the Ten Commandments are, but it simply is not credible to believe that the Establishment Clause would preclude the exhibition of the Ten Commandments solely because of some implicit requirement regarding the degree to which they must be foundational for them to be displayed publicly. Any plausible standard would be extremely difficult to articulate and even more difficult to justify in light of the relevant history, case law, or even good public policy.

Suppose that one could get past the difficulties involved in spelling out this foundationalism requirement. Further, suppose that the Ten Commandments met the relevant test. Their being displayed might nonetheless violate Establishment Clause guarantees, at least in light of the *Lemon* test, the endorsement test, or the coercion test. Basically, the relevant question is not whether the Framers or others were influenced by religious texts. Rather, the important questions would involve what the state was trying to do when posting the display and what effects the posting of the display would have.

The Court's recent Ten Commandments decisions are not only disappointing because they do not apply the same principle to determine a display's constitutionality, but because they made it so obvious that the current Establishment Clause jurisprudence does too little. When the Court employs a particular constitutional test to determine the outcome in one case but in a relevantly similar case suggests that the constitutional test is irrelevant, state actors and courts wishing to understand the constitutional limitations in the area are simply offered no guidance.

When members of the Court continue to engage in conclusory name-calling merely because others disagree with them, instantiating the kind of religious discord that the Establishment Clause seeks to avoid, one cannot help but be disappointed. Not only do Chief Justice Rehnquist and Justice Scalia suggest that those disagreeing with them are hostile to religion, but even Justice Breyer suggests that the dissenters in *Van Orden* interpret "the law to exhibit a hostility toward religion that has no place in our Establishment Clause traditions."[45] Yet, one would expect that in a "borderline" case requiring "legal judgment," even reasonable Justices open to religion might nonetheless disagree about the disposition of a close case.

Under the best of circumstances, it is very difficult to offer a plausible interpretation of the Establishment Clauses that gives due respect to the Framers' intentions, our history, the developing case law, and the widely differing faith traditions represented in this country. But these are not the best of circumstances. When the Court refuses to apply the tests it claims applicable or applies the applicable tests in ways belied by its own jurisprudence, the Court, conscientious belief and society itself are all losers.

Suppose that a school wanted to post a copy of the Ten Commandments in the library. *Stone* and *McCreary County* suggest that such a display would be impermissible if the purpose behind it was to promote religion, whereas *Van Orden* suggests that the constitutionality of a passive display should not be judged in light of a purpose prong analysis. Would a copy of the Ten Commandments be less passive in a school library than on state grounds? One does not know, because members of the *Van Orden* plurality were unwilling to discuss how to identify passive displays other than to suggest that the display at issue in *Stone* was not as passive as the display at issue in *Van Orden*.

Stone, *McCreary County* and *Van Orden* are compatible in that they all suggest that the Constitution does not ban the Ten Commandments from the schools in all circumstances. However, they are utterly unhelpful for anyone seeking to know prospectively what the Constitution requires, permits or prohibits in this area.

---

45 *Id.* at 704 (Breyer, J., concurring in the judgment).

Final Thoughts

Everson v. Board of Education is the seminal case in modern Establishment Clause jurisprudence. It sets a particular tone both by talking about the importance of a wall of separation between church and state and by explaining that the Constitution does not require the state to refuse to have anything to do with religion, making clear that police and fire personnel could of course permissibly aid a religious establishment in need. The *Everson* Court thereby suggested that some sort of balance had to be struck. Ever since then, the Court has tried to work out the proper way to characterize the limitations imposed by the Establishment Clause in the context of education.

One factor that has played a role in the analysis involves the age of the students. Elementary students are thought especially susceptible to influence by teachers and peers, and the Court sometimes suggests that special care must be taken when young minds are being exposed to differing doctrines. Sectarian teaching would be more likely to indoctrinate a student of 7 rather than 19 years of age, and for this reason the state must be very careful not to fund sectarian education of young and impressionable children.

A different consideration sometimes mentioned by the Court is whether a public school student would be likely to take offense if subjected to unwelcome religious activities. But when the fear involves causing offense by virtue of an unwelcome exposure to religious teaching, it is much less clear that the special solicitude for younger children is warranted, since older individuals would seem as likely to be offended by such exposure as younger individuals.

Some of the Establishment Clause jurisprudence is focused on the state being precluded from offering financial support for sectarian activities. The *Everson* Court distinguished between state support of religious teaching on the one hand and state support of health and safety on the other, reasoning that support of the latter was so far removed from sectarian teaching that it could not sensibly be thought to be precluded by the Establishment Clause. The Court subsequently drew a different line, reasoning that support of secular teaching was sufficiently far removed from the support of sectarian teaching that the Establishment Clause would not bar the former as long as there was good reason to believe that the state was not also supporting the latter. This meant that both religious and nonreligious entities could receive support for providing secular services, and in this sense the Establishment Clause required neutrality between religion and non-religion. Regrettably, the Court subsequently modified the type of neutrality required by the Establishment Clause from the identity of the provider to the content of the service, as if the Establishment Clause requires the state to fund sectarian activities if it is funding secular activities. But such an interpretation makes no sense if the jurisprudence is supposed to spell out the ways in which church and state must be separate, and certainly cannot be thought a good faith attempt to account for the relevant jurisprudence.

The Court has offered different tests to help determine when Establishment Clause guarantees are violated: the *Lemon* test, the endorsement test, and the coercion test. Regrettably, the Court not only has not specified the condition under which one rather than the other test should be used, but seems to use different tests even in relevantly similar cases. To make matters worse, the Court has consistently mischaracterized the holdings and facts of previous cases when modifying the jurisprudence. This not only results in the absence of a coherent or consistent jurisprudence but it undercuts confidence in the Court's integrity and good faith in dealing with what is admittedly a vexing issue.

Parents and society more generally have a vested stake in the education of their children, especially with respect to the kinds of religious views to which the children might be exposed. Yet, there is no consensus even among the religious or even among the nonreligious about where lines should be drawn with respect to those educational areas in which church and state must remain separate. Members of the Court mirror that lack of consensus.

Establishment Clause guarantees are by no means easy to discern in the best of circumstances. There are numerous factors to consider, and it is not at all clear how these different factors should be weighed. That said, the Court's jurisprudence in this area has been especially disappointing. When the Court consistently rejects previous analyses and results while claiming to follow them, it is difficult for courts or state actors to know what to do. When the justifications offered by the Court often provide no logical stopping point and, further, make past decisions incomprehensible, the Court merely undermines its own integrity and increases the likelihood of religious divisiveness. One can only hope that the Court in the not-too-distant future will start pursuing the goals of the Establishment Clause rather than promoting the evils that the Clause was designed to avoid.

Bibliography

Supreme Court Cases

Agostini v. Felton, 521 U.S. 203 (1997).
Aguilar v. Felton, 473 U.S. 402 (1985), overruled by *Agostini v. Felton*, 521 U.S. 203 (1997).
Board of Education v. Allen, 392 U.S. 236 (1968).
Board of Education of Westside Community Schools v. Mergens, 496 U.S. 226 (1990).
Board of Regents of the University of Wisconsin System v. Southworth, 529 U.S. 217 (2000).
Capitol Square Review and Advisory Board v. Pinette, 515 U.S. 753 (1995).
Christian Legal Society Chapter of the University of California, Hastings College of the Law v. Martinez, 130 S. Ct. 2971 (2010).
Committee for Public Education and Religious Liberty v. Nyquist, 413 U.S. 756 (1973).
Committee for Public Education and Religious Liberty v. Regan, 444 U.S. 646 (1980).
County of Allegheny v. ACLU Greater Pittsburgh Chapter, 492 U.S. 573 (1989).
Elk Grove Unified School District v. Newdow, 542 U.S. 1 (2004).
Engel v. Vitale, 370 U.S. 421 (1962).
Everson v. Board of Education, 330 U.S. 1 (1947).
Good News Club v. Milford Central School, 533 U.S. 98 (2001).
Heffron v. International Society for Krishna Consciousness, 452 U.S. 640 (1981).
Hunt v. McNair, 413 U.S. 734 (1973).
Lamb's Chapel v. Center Moriches Union Free School District, 508 U.S. 384 (1993).
Lawrence v. Texas, 539 U.S. 558 (2003).
Lee v. Weisman, 505 U.S. 577 (1992).
Lemon v. Kurtzman, 403 U.S. 602 (1971).
Locke v. Davey, 540 U.S. 712 (2004).
Lynch v. Donnelly, 465 U.S. 668 (1984).
Marsh v. Chambers, 463 U.S. 783 (1983).
McCollum v. Board of Education, 333 U.S. 203 (1948).
McCreary County v. ACLU, 545 U.S. 844 (2005).
McDaniel v. Paty, 435 U.S. 618 (1978).
McGowan v. Maryland, 366 U.S. 420 (1961).

Meek v. Pittenger, 421 U.S. 349 (1975), overruled by *Mitchell v. Helms*, 530 U.S. 793 (2000).

Minersville School District v. Gobitis, 310 U.S. 586 (1940), overruled by *West Virginia State Board of Education v. Barnette*, 319 U.S. 624 (1943).

Mitchell v. Helms, 530 U.S. 793 (2000).

Mueller v. Allen, 463 U.S. 388 (1983).

Roemer v. Board of Public Works, 426 U.S. 736 (1976).

Rosenberger v. Rector and Visitors of University of Virginia, 515 U.S. 819 (1995).

Santa Fe School District v. Doe, 530 U.S. 290 (2000).

School District of Abington Township v. Schempp, 374 U.S. 203 (1963).

School District of Grand Rapids v. Ball, 473 U.S. 373 (1985), overruled by *Agostini v. Felton*, 521 U.S. 203 (1997).

Stone v. Graham, 449 U.S. 39 (1980).

Thomas v. Review Board of Indiana Employment Security Division, 450 U.S. 707 (1981).

Tilton v. Richardson, 403 U.S. 672 (1971).

Van Orden v. Perry, 545 U.S. 677 (2005).

Wallace v. Jaffree, 472 U.S. 38 (1985).

Walz v. Tax Commission of the City of New York, 397 U.S. 664 (1970).

Witters v. Washington Department of Services for the Blind, 474 U.S. 481 (1986).

West Virginia State Board of Education v. Barnette, 319 U.S. 624 (1943).

Widmar v. Vincent, 454 U.S. 263 (1981).

Wolman v. Walter, 433 U.S. 229 (1977), overruled by *Mitchell v. Helms*, 530 U.S. 793 (2000).

Zelman v. Simmons-Harris, 536 U.S. 639 (2002).

Zobrest v. Catalina Foothills School District, 509 U.S. 1 (1993).

Zorach v. Clauson, 343 U.S. 306 (1952).

Secondary Literature

Abbott, Greg, Upholding the Unbroken Tradition: Constitutional Acknowledgment of the Ten Commandments in the Public Square, 14 *William and Mary Bill of Rights Journal* 51 (2005).

Aden, Steven H., Who Speaks for the State?: Religious Speakers on Government Platforms and the Role of Disclaiming Endorsement, 9 *William and Mary Bill of Rights Journal* 419 (2001).

Adler, Matthew D., Expressive Theories of Law: A Skeptical Overview, 148 *University of Pennsylvania Law Review* 1363 (2000).

Albert, Richard, Popular Will and the Establishment Clause: Rethinking Public Funding to Religious Schools, 35 *University of Memphis Law Review* 199 (2005).

Alexander, F. King and Klinton W. Alexander, The Reassertion of Church Doctrine in American Higher Education: The Legal and Fiscal Implications of the Ex

Corde Ecclesiae for Catholic Colleges and Universities in the United States, 29 *Journal of Law and Education* 149 (2000).

Alexander, Klint, The Road to Vouchers: The Supreme Court's Compliance and the Crumbling of the Wall of Separation between Church and State in American Education, 92 *Kentucky Law Journal* 439 (2004).

Alito, Samuel, Note, "The Released Time" Cases Revisited: A Study of Group Decision Making by the Supreme Court, 83 *Yale Law Journal* 1202 (1974).

Amar, Akhil Reed, 2000 Daniel J. Meador Lecture: Hugo Black and the Hall of Fame, 53 *Alabama Law Review* 1221 (2002).

American Association of University Professors (AAUP), 1940 Statement of Principles on Academic Freedom and Tenure with 1970 Interpretive Comments (1990).

Anderson, Maya, Note, The Constitutionality of Faith-Based Prison Programs: A Real World Analysis Based in New Mexico, 37 *New Mexico Law Review* 487 (2007).

Arnold, Julie M., Note, "Divine" Justice and the Lack of Secular Intervention: Abrogating the Clergy-Communicant Privilege in Mandatory Reporting Statutes to Combat Child Sexual Abuse, 42 *Valparaiso University Law Review* 849 (2008).

Astle, Matthew J., An Ounce of Prevention: Marital Counseling Laws as an Anti-Divorce Measure, 38 *Family Law Quarterly* 733 (2004).

Axtell, Katie, Note, Public Funding for Theological Training under the Free Exercise Clause: Pragmatic Implications and Theoretical Questions Posed to the Supreme Court in Locke v. Davey, 27 *Seattle University Law Review* 585 (2003).

Barker, Melinda, Comment, From Everson to Zelman: The Advent of "True Private Choice" and the Erosion of the Wall between Church and State, 44 *Santa Clara Law Review* 529 (2004).

Beattie, Jr., James R., Taking Liberalism and Religious Liberty Seriously: Shifting Our Notion of Toleration from Locke to Mill, 43 *Catholic Lawyer* 367 (2004).

Beckwith, Francis J., Public Education, Religious Establishment, and the Challenge of Intelligent Design, 17 *Notre Dame Journal of Law, Ethics and Public Policy* 461 (2003).

Beglin, Tara P., Note, "One Nation under God," Indeed: The Ninth Circuit's Problematic Decision to Change Our Pledge of Allegiance, 20 *Saint John's Journal of Legal Commentary* 129 (2005).

Belknap, Michal R., God and the Warren Court: The Quest for "A Wholesome Neutrality," 9 *Seton Hall Constitutional Law Journal* 401 (1999).

Berg, Thomas C., Church-State Relations and the Social Ethics of Reinhold Niebuhr, 73 *North Carolina Law Review* 1567 (1995).

Berg, Thomas C., Anti-Catholicism and Modern Church-State Relations, 33 *Loyola University of Chicago Law Journal* 121 (2001).

Berg, Thomas C., The Pledge of Allegiance and the Limited State, 8 *Texas Review of Law and Politics* 41 (2003).

Berg, Thomas C. and Douglas Laycock, The Mistakes in Locke v. Davey and the Future of State Payments for Services Provided by Religious Institutions, 40 *Tulsa Law Review* 227 (2004).

Beutler, Mark J., Public Funding of Sectarian Education: Establishment and Free Exercise Clause Implications, 2 *George Mason Independent Law Review* 7 (1993).

Bizzano, Allison C., Recent Development, Are We Headed for a New Era in Religious Discrimination?: A Closer Look at Locke v. Davey, 9 *Lewis and Clark Law Review* 469 (2005).

Boden, Martha A., Compassion Inaction: Why President Bush's Faith-Based Initiatives Violate the Establishment Clause, 29 *Seattle University Law Review* 991 (2006).

Boland, James M., Constitutional Legitimacy and the Culture Wars: Rule of Law or Dictatorship of a Shifting Supreme Court Majority? 36 *Cumberland Law Review* 245 (2005–2006).

Bowman, Kristi L., Seeing Government Purpose through the Objective Observer's Eyes: The Evolution-Intelligent Design Debates, 29 *Harvard Journal of Law and Public Policy* 417 (2006).

Bowman, Kristi L., An Empirical Study of Evolution, Creationism, and Intelligent Design Instruction in Public Schools, 36 *Journal of Law and Education* 301 (2007).

Brady, Kathleen A., The Push to Private Religious Expression: Are We Missing Something?, 70 *Fordham Law Review* 1147 (2002).

Budd, Jordan C., Cross Purposes: Remedying the Endorsement of Symbolic Religious Speech, 82 *Denver University Law Review* 183 (2004).

Cates, Patrick B., Faith-Based Prisons and the Establishment Clause: The Constitutionality of Employing Religion as an Engine of Correctional Policy, 41 *Willamette Law Review* 777 (2005).

Chadsey, Mark J., State Aid to Religious Schools: From Everson to Zelman a Critical Review, 44 *Santa Clara Law Review* 699 (2004).

Chadsey, Mark J., Thomas Jefferson and the Establishment Clause, 40 *Akron Law Review* 623 (2007).

Chemerinsky, Erwin, Why Justice Breyer Was Wrong in Van Orden v. Perry, 14 *William and Mary Bill of Rights. Journal* 1 (2005).

Chemerinsky, Erwin, The Future of Constitutional Law, 34 *Capital University Law Review* 647 (2006).

Choper, Jesse H., Religion in the Public Schools: A Proposed Constitutional Standard, 47 *Minnesota Law Review* 329 (1963).

Choper, Jesse H., The Endorsement Test: Its Status and Desirability, 18 *Journal of Law and Politics* 499 (2002).

Claeys, Eric R., Justice Scalia and the Religion Clauses: A Comment on Professor Epps, 21 *Washington University Journal of Law and Policy* 349 (2006).

Collier, Trent, Note, Revenue Bonds and Religious Education: The Constitutionality of Conduit Financing Involving Pervasively Sectarian Institutions, 100 *Michigan Law Review* 1108 (2002).

Concannon III, John J., The Pledge of Allegiance and the First Amendment, 23 *Suffolk University Law Review* 1019 (1989).

Conkle, Daniel O., The Path of American Religious Liberty: From the Original Theology to Formal Neutrality and an Uncertain Future, 75 *Indiana Law Journal* 1 (2000).

Conkle, Daniel O., The Establishment Clause and Religious Expression in Governmental Settings: Four Variables in Search of a Standard, 110 *West Virginia Law Review* 315 (2007).

Cox, Jr., William F., The Original Meaning of the Establishment Clause and Its Application to Education, 13 *Regent University Law Review* 111 (2000).

Delfattore, Joan, *The Fourth R: Conflicts over Religion in America's Public Schools* (New Haven: Yale University Press, 2004).

Detroy, Kevin M., A Coherent Standard, If You Please: The Supreme Court's Failure to Adhere to a Consistent Standard in Establishment Clause Cases and Why a Revision of Justice O'Connor's Endorsement Test May Be Just What Is Needed, 33 *Northern Kentucky Law Review* 571 (2006).

Deverich, Carolyn A., Comment, Establishment Clause Jurisprudence and the Free Exercise Dilemma: A Structural Unitary-Accommodationist Argument for the Constitutionality of God in the Public Square, 2006 *Brigham Young University Law Review* 211 (2006).

Diamond, Shari Seidman and Andrew Koppelman, Measured Endorsement, 60 *Maryland Law Review* 713 (2001).

Dokupil, Susanna, Function Follows Form: Locke v. Davey's Unnecessary Parsing, 2004 *Cato Supreme Court Review* 327 (2004).

Dokupil, Susanna, "Thou Shalt Not Bear False Witness": "Sham" Secular Purposes in Ten Commandments Displays, 28 *Harvard Journal of Law and Public Policy* 609 (2005).

Dolan, Mary Jean, Government-Sponsored Chaplains and Crisis: Walking the Fine Line in Disaster Response and Daily Life, 35 *Hastings Constitutional Law Quarterly* 505 (2008).

Duncan, Richard F., Locked Out: Locke v. Davey and the Broken Promise of Equal Access, 8 *University of Pennsylvania Journal of Constitutional Law* 699 (2006).

Eberle, Edward J., Religion in the Classroom in Germany and the United States, 81 *Tulane Law Review* 67 (2006).

Eisgruber, Christopher L., Constitutional Self-Government and Judicial Review: A Reply to Five Critics, 37 *University of San Francisco Law Review* 115 (2002).

Epstein, Steven B., Rethinking the Constitutionality of Ceremonial Deism, 96 *Columbia Law Review* 2083 (1996).

Esbeck, Carl H., The 60th Anniversary of the Everson Decision and America's Church-State Proposition, 23 *Journal of Law and Religion* 15 (2007).

Feigenson, Neal R., Political Standing and Governmental Endorsement of Religion: An Alternative to Current Establishment Clause Doctrine, 40 *DePaul Law Review* 53 (1990).

Feldman, Noah, From Liberty to Equality: The Transformation of the Establishment Clause, 90 *California Law Review* 673 (2002).

Fields, Richard R.W., Comment, Perks for Prisoners Who Pray: Using the Coercion Test to Decide Establishment Clause Challenges to Faith-Based Prison Units, 2005 *University of Chicago Legal Forum* 541 (2005).

Finkelman, Paul, The Ten Commandments on the Courthouse Lawn and Elsewhere, 73 *Fordham Law Review* 1477 (2005).

Fitzgerald, John J., Note, Today's Catholic Law Schools in Theory and Practice: Are We Preserving Our Identity?, 15 *Notre Dame Journal of Law, Ethics and Public Policy* 245 (2001).

Forman, Jr., James, The Rise and Fall of School Vouchers: A Story of Religion, Race and Politics, 54 *UCLA Law Review* 547 (2007).

Frey, William G. and Virginia Lynn Hogben, Vouchers, Tuition Tax Credits, and Scholarship-Donation Tax Credits: A Constitutional and Practical Analysis, 31 *Stetson Law Review* 165 (2002).

Gaffney, Jr., Edward M., Tales of Two Cities: Canon Law and Constitutional Law at the Crossroads, 25 *Journal of College and University Law* 801 (1999).

Garfield, Alan E., What Should We Celebrate on Constitution Day? 41 *Georgia Law Review* 453 (2007).

Garry, Patrick M., Religious Freedom Deserves More than Neutrality: The Constitutional Argument for Nonpreferential Favoritism of Religion, 57 *Florida Law Review* 1 (2005).

Gey, Steven G., Why Is Religion Special?: Reconsidering the Accommodation of Religion under the Religion Clauses of the First Amendment, 52 *University of Pittsburgh Law Review* 75 (1990).

Gey, Steven G., Religious Coercion and the Establishment Clause, 1994 *University of Illinois Law Review* 463 (1994).

Gey, Steven G., "Under God," the Pledge of Allegiance, and Other Constitutional Trivia, 81 *North Carolina Law Review* 1865 (2003).

Gey, Steven G., Reconciling the Supreme Court's Four Establishment Clauses, 8 *University of Pennsylvania Journal of Constitutional Law* 725 (2006).

Gey, Steven G., Vestiges of the Establishment Clause, 5 *First Amendment Law Review* 1 (2006).

Giannella, Donald A., Lemon and Tilton: The Bitter and the Sweet of Church-State Entanglement, 1971 *Supreme Court Review* 147 (1971).

Green, Steven K., Locke v. Davey and the Limits to Neutrality Theory, 77 *Temple Law Review* 913 (2004).

Greenawalt, Kent, *Does God Belong in Public Schools?* (Princeton, NJ: Princeton University Press, 2005).

Greenawalt, Kent, Religiously Based Judgments and Discourse in Political Life, 22 *Saint John's Journal of Legal Commentary* 445 (2007).

Greene, Abner S., The Pledge of Allegiance Problem, 64 *Fordham Law Review* 451 (1995).

Gregory, David L., Where to Pray? A Survey Regarding Prayer Rooms in A.B.A. Accredited, Religiously Affiliated Law Schools, 1993 *Brigham Young University Law Review* 1287 (1993).

Griffin, Leslie, "We Do Not Preach. We Teach.": Religion Professors and the First Amendment, 19 *Quinnipiac Law Review* 1 (2000).

Griffin, Leslie C., Their Own Prepossessions: The Establishment Clause, 1999–2000, 33 *Loyola University of Chicago Law Journal* 237 (2001).

Guggenheim, Martin, Stealth Indoctrination: Forced Speech in the Classroom, 2004 *University of Chicago Legal Forum* 57 (2004).

Hall, Timothy L., Sacred Solemnity: Civic Prayer, Civil Communion, and the Establishment Clause, 79 *Iowa Law Review* 35 (1993).

Hamilton, Marci A., Power, the Establishment Clause, and Vouchers, 31 *Connecticut Law Review* 807 (1999).

Hamilton, Marci A., *God vs. the Gavel: Religion and the Rule of Law* (New York. Cambridge University Press, 2005).

Hamilton, Vivian E., Religious v. Secular Ideologies and Sex Education: A Response to Professors Cahn and Carbone, 110 *West Virginia Law Review* 501 (2007).

Hancock, Kevin P., Comment, Closing the Endorsement Test Escape-Hatch in the Pledge of Allegiance Debate, 35 *Seton Hall Law Review* 739 (2005).

Hawkins, Richard J., Comment, Dysfunctional Equivalence: The New Approach to Defining "Postal Channels" under the Hague Service Convention, 55 *UCLA Law Review* 205 (2007).

Hill, B. Jessie, Putting Religious Symbolism in Context: A Linguistic Critique of the Endorsement Test, 104 *Michigan Law Review* 491 (2005).

Holland, Robert A., A Theory of Establishment Clause Adjudication: Individualism, Social Contract, and the Significance of Coercion in Identifying Threats to Religious Liberty, 80 *California Law Review* 1595 (1992).

Jacobs, Joel S., Endorsement as "Adoptive Action:" A Suggested Definition of, and an Argument for, Justice O'Connor's Establishment Clause Test, 22 *Hastings Constitutional Law Quarterly* 29 (1994).

Jeffries, Jr., John C. and James E. Ryan, A Political History of the Establishment Clause, 100 *Michigan Law Review* 279 (2001).

Kahle, Lisa M., Comment, Making "Lemon-Aid" from the Supreme Court's Lemon: Why Current Establishment Clause Jurisprudence Should Be Replaced by a Modified Coercion Test, 42 *San Diego Law Review* 349 (2005).

Kang, John M., Deliberating the Divine: On Extending the Justification from Truth to Religious Expression, 73 *Brooklyn Law Review* 1 (2007).

Karst, Kenneth L., The First Amendment, the Politics of Religion and the Symbols of Government, 27 *Harvard Civil Rights-Civil Liberties Law Review* 503 (1992).

Kemp, Megan A., Comment, Blessed Are the Born Again: An Analysis of Christian Fundamentalists, the Faith-Based Initiative, and the Establishment Clause, 43 *Houston Law Review* 1523 (2007).

Kolenc, Anthony Barone, "Mr. Scalia's Neighborhood": A Home for Minority Religions?, 81 *Saint John's Law Review* 819 (2007).

Komp, Kathryn Elizabeth, Note, Unincorporated, Unprotected: Religion in an Established State, 58 *Vanderbilt Law Review* 301 (2005).

Lahav, Pnina, The Republic of Choice, the Pledge of Allegiance, the American Taliban, 40 *Tulsa Law Review* 599 (2005).

Laycock, Douglas, Theology Scholarships, the Pledge of Allegiance, and Religious Liberty: Avoiding the Extremes But Missing the Liberty, 118 *Harvard Law Review* 155 (2004).

Lewis, James M. and Michael L. Vid, A Controversial Twist of Lemon: The Endorsement Test as the New Establishment Clause Standard, 65 *Notre Dame Law Review* 671 (1990).

Lupu, Ira C., Government Messages and Government Money: Santa Fe, Mitchell v. Helms and the Arc of the Establishment Clause, 42 *William and Mary Law Review* 771 (2001).

Lupu, Ira C. and Robert W. Tuttle, Federalism and Faith, 56 *Emory Law Journal* 19 (2006).

Lynch, Walter, Comment, "Under God" Does Not Need to Be Placed under Wraps: The Phrase "Under God" Used in the Pledge of Allegiance Is Not an Impermissible Recognition of Religion, 41 *Houston Law Review* 647 (2004).

Magarian, Gregory P., The Jurisprudence of Colliding First Amendment Interests: From the Dead End of Neutrality to the Open Road of Participation-Enhancing Review, 83 *Notre Dame Law Review* 185 (2007).

Maguire, Marjorie Reiley, Comment, Having One's Cake and Eating It Too: Government Funding and Religious Exemptions for Religiously Affiliated Colleges and Universities, 1989 *Wisconsin Law Review* 1061 (1989).

Marques, Jason, Note, To Bear a Cross: The Establishment Clause, Historic Preservation, and Eminent Domain Intersect at the Mt. Soledad Veterans Memorial, 59 *Florida Law Review* 829 (2007).

Marshall, William P., "We Know It When We See It" The Supreme Court and Establishment, 59 *Southern California Law Review* 495 (1986).

Massey, Calvin, The Political Marketplace of Religion, 57 *Hastings Law Journal* 1 (2005).

Mawdsley, Ralph D., Access to Tax Exempt Bonds by Religious Higher Education Institutions, 65 *Education Law Reporter* 289 (1991).

McConnell, Michael W., Neutrality under the Religion Clauses, 81 *Northwestern University Law Review* 146 (1986).

McConnell, Michael W., Free Exercise Revisionism and the Smith Decision, 57 *University of Chicago Law Review* 1109 (1990).

McConnell, Michael W., Religious Freedom at a Crossroads, 59 *University of Chicago Law Review* 115 (1992).

McConnell, Michael W., State Action and the Supreme Court's Emerging Consensus on the Line between Establishment and Private Religious Expression, 28 *Pepperdine Law Review* 681 (2001).

McKenzie, Linda P., Note, The Pledge of Allegiance: One Nation Under God?, 46 *Arizona Law Review* 379 (2004).

McMillan, Joseph M., Zobrest v. Catalina Foothills School District: Lowering the Establishment Clause Barrier in School-Aid Controversies, 39 *Saint Louis University Law Journal* 337 (1994).

Mead, Julie F., Preston C. Green and Joseph O. Oluwole, Re-Examining the Constitutionality of Prayer in School in Light of the Resignation of Justice O'Connor, 36 *Journal of Law and Education* 381 (2007).

Meares, Tracey L. and Kelsi Brown Corkran, When 2 or 3 Come Together, 48 *William and Mary Law Review* 1315 (2007).

Merriam, Jesse R., Finding a Ceiling in a Circular Room: Locke v. Davey, Federalism, and Religious Neutrality, 16 *Temple Political and Civil Rights Law Review* 103 (2006).

Modak-Truran, Mark C., Beyond Theocracy and Secularism (Part I): Toward A New Paradigm for Law and Religion, 27 *Mississippi College Law Review* 159 (2007).

Montoya, Carlos S., Constitutional Developments, Locke v. Davey and the "Play in the Joints" between the Religion Clauses, 6 *University of Pennsylvania Journal of Constitutional Law* 1159 (2004).

Muehlhoff, Inke, Freedom of Religion in Public Schools in Germany and in the United States, 28 *Georgia Journal of International and Comparative Law* 405 (2000).

Murphy, Bruce Allen, *Wild Bill: The Legend and Life of William O. Douglas* (New York: Random House, 2003).

Newhouse, Emily D., Comment, I Pledge Allegiance to the Flag of the United States of America: One Nation under No God, 35 *Texas Tech Law Review* 383 (2004).

O'Connell, Tyson Radley, Note, How Did the Ten Commandments End on Both Sides of the Wall of Separation between Church and State? The Contradicting Opinions of Van Orden v. Perry and McCreary v. ACLU, 69 *Montana Law Review* 263 (2008).

Paulsen, Michael A., Religion, Equality, and the Constitution: An Equal Protection Approach to Establishment Clause Adjudication, 61 *Notre Dame Law Review* 311 (1986).

Peters, Keith T., Note, Small Town Establishment of Religion in ACLU of Nebraska Foundation v. City of Plattsmouth, 419 F.3d 772 (8th Cir. 2005); Eagles Soaring in the Eighth Circuit, 84 *Nebraska Law Review* 997 (2006).

Pierre, Christopher, Note, "With God All Things Are Possible," Including Finding Ohio's State Motto Constitutional under the Establishment Clause of the First Amendment, 49 *Cleveland. State Law Review* 749 (2001).

Pybas, Kevin, Two Concepts of Liberalism in Establishment Clause Jurisprudence, 36 *Cumberland Law Review* 205 (2005–2006).

Rabe, Lee Ann, A Rose by Any Other Name: School Prayer Redefined as a Moment of Silence Is Still Unconstitutional, 82 *Denver University Law Review* 57 (2004).

Raskin, Jamin B., Polling Establishment: Judicial Review, Democracy, and the Endorsement Theory of the Establishment Clause—Commentary on Measured Endorsement, 60 *Maryland Law Review* 761 (2001).

Ravitch, Frank S., *School Prayer and Discrimination: The Civil Rights of Religious Minorities and Dissenters* (Boston: Northeastern University Press, 1999).

Ravitch, Frank S., Religious Objects as Legal Subjects, 40 *Wake Forest Law Review* 1011 (2005).

Ravitch, Frank S., *Masters of Illusion: The Supreme Court and the Religion Clauses* (New York: New York University Press, 2007).

Redlich, Norman, Separation of Church and State: The Burger Court's Tortuous Journey, 60 *Notre Dame Law Review* 1094 (1985).

Rezai, Shahin, Note, County of Allegheny v. ACLU: Evolution of Chaos in Establishment Clause Analysis, 40 *American University Law Review* 503 (1990).

Rotstein, Andrew, Good Faith? Religious-Secular Parallelism and the Establishment Clause, 93 *Columbia Law Review* 1763 (1993).

Russo, Charles J. and Ralph D. Mawdsley, Commentary, Trumped Again: The Supreme Court Reverses the Ninth Circuit and Upholds the Pledge of Allegiance, 192 *Education Law Reporter* 287 (2004).

Sachs, Benjamin I., Whose Reasonableness Counts?, 107 *Yale Law Journal* 1523 (1998).

Sakaria, Anjali, Worshipping Substantive Equality over Formal Neutrality: Applying the Endorsement Test to Sect-Specific Legislative Accommodations, 37 *Harvard Civil Rights-Civil Liberties Law Review* 483 (2002).

Salamanca, Paul E., The Role of Religion in Public Life and Official Pressure to Participate in Alcoholics Anonymous, 65 *University of Cincinnati Law Review* 1093 (1997).

Samaha, Adam M., Endorsement Retires: From Religious Symbols to Anti-Sorting Principles, 2005 *Supreme Court Review* 135 (2005).

Schultz, Nina S., Note, Davey's Deviant Discretion: An Incorporated Establishment Clause Should Require the State to Maintain Funding Neutrality, 81 *Indiana Law Journal* 785 (2006).

Schuneman, Nicholas A., One Nation, Under ... the Watchmaker?: Intelligent Design and the Establishment Clause, 22 *Brigham Young University Journal of Public Law* 179 (2007).

Sedler, Robert A., The Settled Nature of American Constitutional Law, 48 *Wayne Law Review* 173 (2002).

Seidman, Steven A., County of Allegheny v. American Civil Liberties Union: Embracing the Endorsement Test, 9 *Journal of Law and Religion* 211 (1991).

Sekulow, Jay A. and Francis J. Manion, The Supreme Court and the Ten Commandments: Compounding the Establishment Clause Confusion, 14 *William and Mary Bill of Rights Journal* 33 (2005).

Shaffer, Thomas L., Erastian and Sectarian Arguments in Religiously Affiliated American Law Schools, 45 *Stanford Law Review* 1859 (1993).

Shatz, Naomi Rivkind, Comment, Unconstitutional Entanglements: The Religious Right, the Federal Government and Abstinence Education in the Schools, 19 *Yale Journal of Law and Feminism* 495 (2008).

Shiffrin, Steven H., The Pluralistic Foundations of the Religion Clauses, 90 *Cornell Law Review* 9 (2004).

Schultz, Nina S., Note, Davey's Deviant Discretion: An Incorporated Establishment Clause Should Require the State to Maintain Funding Neutrality, 81 *Indiana Law Journal* 785 (2006).

Silverstein, Helena and Kathryn Lundwall Alessi, Religious Establishment in Hearings to Waive Parental Consent for Abortion, 7 *University of Pennsylvania Journal of Constitutional Law* 473 (2004).

Sisk, Gregory C., Michael Heise and Andrew P. Morriss, Searching for the Soul of Judicial Decisionmaking: An Empirical Study of Religious Freedom Decisions, 65 *Ohio State. Law Journal* 491 (2004).

Smith, Douglas G., The Establishment Clause: Corollary of Eighteenth-Century Corporate Law?, 98 *Northwestern University Law Review* 239 (2003).

Smith, Douglas G., The Constitutionality of Religious Symbolism after McCreary and Van Orden, 12 *Texas Review of Law and Politics* 93 (2007).

Smith, Steven D., Symbols, Perceptions, and Doctrinal Illusions: Establishment Neutrality and the 'No Endorsement' Test, 86 *Michigan Law Review* 266 (1987).

Smith, L. Scott, From Typology to Synthesis: Recasting the Jurisprudence of Religion, 34 *Capital University Law Review* 51 (2005).

Strasser, Mark, Thou Shalt Not?, 6 *University of Maryland Law Journal of Race, Religion, Gender & Class* 439 (2006).

Strasser, Mark, Establishing the Pledge: On Coercion, Endorsement and the Marsh Wild Card, 40 *Indiana Law Review* 529 (2007).

Strasser, Mark, The Protection and Alienation of Religious Minorities: On the Evolution of the Endorsement Test, 2008 *Michigan State Law Review* 667 (2008).

Strasser, Mark, Death by a Thousand Cuts: The Illusory Safeguards against Funding Pervasively Sectarian Institutions of Higher Learning, 56 *Buffalo Law Review* 353 (2008).

Strasser, Mark, State Funding of Devotional Studies: A Failed Jurisprudence that Has Lost Its Moorings, 11 *Journal of Law and Family Studies* 1 (2008).

Strasser, Mark, The Coercion Test: On Prayer, Offense, and Doctrinal Inculcation, 53 *Saint Louis University Law Journal* 417 (2009).

Strasser, Mark, Religion in the Schools: On Prayer, Neutrality, and Sectarian Perspectives, 42 *Akron Law Review* 185 (2009).

Strasser, Mark, Repudiating Everson: On Buses, Books, and Teaching Articles of Faith, 78 *Mississippi Law Journal* 567–36 (2009).

Strasser, Mark, Passive Observers, Passive Displays, and the Establishment Clause, 14 *Lewis and Clark Law Review* 1123 (2010).

Sullivan, Kathleen M., Religion and Liberal Democracy, 59 *University of Chicago Law Review* 195 (1992).

Sullivan, Winnifred Fallers, *The Impossibility of Religious Freedom* (Princeton NJ: Princeton University Press, 2005).

Thaxton Larry R., Comment, Silence Begets Religion: Bown v. Gwinnett County School District and the Unconstitutionality of Moments of Silence in Public Schools, 57 *Ohio State Law Journal* 1399 (1996).

Thompson, John E., Note, What's The Big Deal? The Unconstitutionality of God in the Pledge of Allegiance, 38 *Harvard Civil Rights-Civil Liberties Law Review* 563 (2003).

Tomlinson, Christopher D., Changing the Rules of Establishment Clause Litigation: An Alternative to the Public Expression of Religion Act, 61 *Vanderbilt Law Review* 261 (2008).

Toy, David A., The Pledge: The Constitutionality of an American Icon, 34 *Journal of Law and Education* 25 (2005).

Trammell, Alan, Note, The Cabining of Rosenberger: Locke v. Davey and the Broad Nondiscrimination Principle that Never Was, 92 *Virginia Law Review* 1957 (2006).

Trunk, William, The Scourge of Contextualism: Ceremonial Deism and the Establishment Clause, 49 *Boston College Law Review* 571 (2008).

Tupi, Bradley S., Religious Freedom and the First Amendment, 45 *Duquesne Law Review* 195 (2007).

Underkuffler, Laura S., Davey and the Limits of Equality, 40 *Tulsa Law Review* 267 (2004).

Underwood, Julie K., Changing Establishment Analysis within and outside the Context of Education, 33 *Howard Law Journal* 53 (1990).

Vaccari, Michael A., Public Purpose and the Public Funding of Sectarian Educational Institutions: A More Rational Approach after Rosenberger and Agostini, 82 *Marquette Law Review* 1 (1998).

Van Alstyne, William, Ten Commandments, Nine Judges, and Five Versions of One Amendment—The First. ("Now What?"), 14 *William and Mary Bill of Rights Journal* 17 (2005).

Van Groningen, Julie, Note, Thou Shalt Reasonably Focus on Its Context: Analyzing Public Displays of the Ten Commandments, 39 *Valparaiso University Law Review* 219 (2004).

Viteritti, Joseph P., Davey's Plea: Blaine, Blair, Witters, and the Protection of Religious Freedom, 27 *Harvard Journal of Law and Public Policy* 299 (2003).

Viteritti, Joseph P., *The Last Freedom: Religion from the Public School to the Public Square* (Princeton, NJ: Princeton University Press, 2007).

Ward, Cynthia V., Coercion and Choice under the Establishment Clause, 39 *University of California at Davis Law Review* 1621 (2006).

Wexler, Jay D., The Endorsement Court, 21 *Washington University Journal of Law and Policy* 263 (2006).

Wheeler, Brian, Note, The Pledge of Allegiance in the Classroom and the Court: An Epic Struggle over the Meaning of the Establishment Clause of the First Amendment, 2008 *Brigham Young University Education and Law Journal* 281 (2008).

Wilson, Justin T., Note, Preservationism, or the Elephant in the Room: How Opponents of Same-Sex Marriage Deceive Us into Establishing Religion, 14 *Duke Journal of Gender Law and Policy* 561 (2007).

Winders, Richard D., Casenote, Building on the Establishment Clause: Government Conduit Financing of Construction Projects at Religiously Affiliated Schools in Johnson v. Economic Development Corp., 35 *Creighton Law Review* 1151 (2002).

Yannella, Philip N., Stuck in the Web of Formalism: Why Reversing the Ninth Circuit's Ruling on the Pledge of Allegiance Won't Be So Easy, 12 *Temple Political and Civil Rights Law Review* 79 (2002).

Zucker, James E., Note, Better a Catholic than a Communist: Reexamining McCollum v. Board of Education and Zorach v. Clauson, 93 *Virginia Law Review* 2069 (2007).

Index